Penguin Books

Brain Games

David Pritchard is currently the editor of *The Gamer* magazine. He is an authority on indoor games but allows he has neither the time nor the talent to be expert at any. He believes that games demand both social and emotional involvement and should not be treated as abstractions – not even the abstract games.

David Pritchard's work has taken him all over the world and he has had the opportunity to study traditional games in their countries of origin. He is married to Elaine Saunders who, as a child prodigy, won the British Ladies Chess Championship at the age of thirteen. They have one daughter, Wanda, who he concedes is the family's real games enthusiast. He has written and edited a number of books on games, including the best-selling *Begin Chess*.

• BRAIN GAMES •

The World's Best Games for Two

David Pritchard

Penguin Books

Penguin Books Ltd, Harmondsworth,
Middlesex, England
Penguin Books, 625 Madison Avenue,
New York, New York 10022, U.S.A.
Penguin Books Australia Ltd, Ringwood,
Victoria, Australia
Penguin Books Canada Ltd, 2801 John Street,
Markham, Ontario, Canada L3R 1B4
Penguin Books (N.Z.) Ltd, 182–190 Wairau Road,
Auckland 10, New Zealand

First published 1982

The acknowledgements to the copyright holders
of the proprietary games given on pages 7–8
constitute an extension of this copyright page.

Made and printed in Great Britain by
Richard Clay (The Chaucer Press) Ltd,
Bungay, Suffolk
Set in Monotype Bembo

• CONTENTS •

• ACKNOWLEDGEMENTS •

It is not possible to mention everyone who has assisted, consciously or unconsciously, in the preparation of this book. In many years as editor of *Games & Puzzles* magazine I have gathered material from discussions and correspondence with experts and enthusiasts round the world. These I must ask to accept a collective acknowledgement.

This does not preclude me from expressing appreciation to those who went out of their way to be helpful: Edward de Bono, Wladyslaw Glinski, Wataru Ikawa, Dr Nicholas Jacobs, Derek Oldbury, Nicky Palmer and Alex Randolph and my exacting editor, Matthew Reisz of Penguin Books. Any errors are not theirs.

The author is indebted to the copyright holders of the following proprietary games for permission to review the games here:

Black Box. Black Box is manufactured by Waddingtons House of Games, Leeds, England, who reserve all copyrights.

Hexagonal Chess. The game is the copyright of Hexgames Ltd.

L Game. Copyright Edward de Bono 1968 and protected under the laws of Copyright in all Berne Convention countries. U.K. Patent No. 1,148,172; U.S. Patent No. 3,455,555; Canadian Patent No. 787,261. Patent applications in other countries pending.

Master Mind. Copyright of Invicta Plastics Ltd, Oadby, Leicester, England, and subject to many patents and design registrations throughout the world.

Napoleon at Waterloo. Copyright 1979 Simulations Publications Inc. (SPI), New York, N.Y. 10010.

Scrabble. Scrabble (R) is the registered trademark owned in the

• INTRODUCTION •

This selection of brain games for two has no limits. It extends across traditional games, proprietary games, card games, pencil-and-paper games; games of strategy, of logic, of calculation and others which do not lend themselves easily to classification. Selection was not easy. Different games please different people and different occasions call for different games. For these reasons I have included a few games which are arguably not amongst the best in order to keep some balance between the different types of games, while a few more, notably the two wargames, have been chosen as representatives of groups rather than on individual superiority.

You can play many of the games without preparation; for others you will easily be able to make or assemble the necessary components. Some games you will have to buy if you wish to play them, but in terms of return on investment a good game is the best bargain you will ever get. Sources of equipment and recommended books are listed at the back.

This book is designed to fulfil two purposes: to introduce the world's best games, many of them little known outside the countries in which they flourish and whose societies they often reflect, and to indicate the attractions of each. Strategy and tactics have accordingly been emphasized. Sample games where given are mostly illustrations rather than models of play – only masters can truly comprehend master games.

We play games for a variety of reasons but mainly because they satisfy a number of human needs, conscious and unconscious, anti-social as well as social. This is no place for a discourse on psychology, but it is worth remarking that games of strategy, which call for a succession of judgements and decisions, are becoming increasingly popular as a means of self-assertion in an age where the machine is gradually taking over as decision-maker.

It is generally true that the better one understands a game, the more satisfaction one derives from it. One learns to plan ahead rather than simply reacting to the opponent's moves. The game becomes a mental challenge rather than a casual time-filler, and of course one's play improves. We like to excel at our chosen games, but the qualities required to make a good player are not easy to identify. Commitment and concentration would seem to be essential for serious play, yet some people succeed with very little effort. Although there are all-round games-players, different games generally call for different talents. Curiously, there are many experts who display no aptitudes outside their chosen games. At the top level, games demand constant study and practice, which probably explains why very few people, notable in other fields, have ever achieved success at games. Napoleon was a keen chess-player but he found Europe easier to control than a handful of chessmen.

While it is hard to agree on what makes a good games-player, there is consensus on the qualities of a good game. It should have balance, variety in the sense of a range of strategic options and be sufficiently amenable to analysis to permit forward planning yet profound enough to place it beyond the control of the human mind. If a game is totally analysable, like Noughts and Crosses or Nim, it becomes trivial; if it is too complex, on the other hand, it loses appeal. Consider two examples: the well-known children's game of Boxes and the ancient Japanese boardgame of Tai-Shogi.

Boxes would, on the face of it, seem open to complete analysis. In theory it is, but no satisfactory opening strategy has been discovered, so that in practice chance often determines the outcome.

Tai-Shogi is played on a 25 by 25 cell board with 354 pieces. Like Boxes, it is a 'perfect information' game; that is, a game in which both players have access at all times to the situation in its totality. It is also, like Boxes, a game of pure skill. Unlike Boxes, however, it has many plausible strategies but resists sensible analysis because of its complexity.

A game that few people tire of is Chess. Chess is the world's most widely played game, yet at least two other traditional games can claim a parallel excellence: Go (Weiqi) and Shogi. Probably one of the reasons why Shogi has made little impact in the West is because the pieces are not easy to distinguish. Instant recognition of the physical elements of a game is essential if concentration is not to be disturbed. Ideally, pieces and board should harmonize and be of simple and unambiguous design: no serious chess-player would consider playing with any of the outrageously decorative sets now on the market.

The origins of traditional games like Backgammon, Chess and Go are clouded in attractive but implausible legends. Facts are emphatically absent: the best the historians can do is to credit a country or region as the birthplace, and a century or two as the time. Pastimes were unfortunately beneath the attention of most early chroniclers. Many games, like Chess, have been much modified across the centuries, whilst others, like Go, have changed little from their earliest known forms. It is curious that mankind, despite the massive intellectual and technological advances of the last hundred years or so, has yet to devise a game that can seriously challenge the ancient favourites.

The great traditional games flourish because they are eternally fresh. They have stood the test of centuries of unremitting scrutiny by unnumbered experts; analysis is continually advanced by an increasing number of dedicated, often professional researchers and in practice by players who are immeasurably stronger than those of the past. As Tennyson observed:

> As we surpass our father's skill
> Our sons shall shame our own:
> A thousand things are hidden still
> And not a hundred known.

Yet, surprisingly, some traditional games have been little investigated – Tablut and Fanorona are two – and these offer a small niche in history for anyone with the energy and time to research them.

A few words must be said about proprietary games. These as a group have been with us for some while (the Game of Goose goes back to the seventeenth century) but the sophisticated adult game can be said to date from after World War II. Of those included here, one or two, like Black Box and the L game, are strikingly original, whilst others have incorporated play concepts of earlier games.

Special mention must be made of wargames, which hardly existed a generation ago. Wargaming is now established as a hobby in its own right. It is immensely popular in America and is quickly advancing in Britain and elsewhere and already supports a small industry and a thriving press. Wargames are usually played on maps overlaid with an hexagonal grid on which military units, represented by small pieces of treated card, engage in combat. Strictly, this is known as Board Wargaming and should not be confused with Miniature Wargaming, which uses table-top models and was popularized by H. G. Wells in *Little Wars*.

It is now possible to buy a board wargame for almost every major conflict in history from Marathon to the present day. A popular engagement (from the wargamer's viewpoint!) like the Battle of the Bulge may be the subject of several games produced by different manufacturers. A range of tactical wargames is also available, from a Wild-West shoot-out to an urban guerrilla street-fight.

Wargames are really simulations. A wargame is designed to recreate, in proper balance, all those factors that influenced, or could have influenced, the actual battle: not just the men and weapons engaged but considerations such as mobility, supply, leadership, morale, the weather. Because of their historical origin, wargames set the players different objectives; thus the player of the weaker force may only be required to hold a defence line or a few strong points for a specified number of game turns to 'win'.

A new era of games-playing is being unlocked by the electronics explosion. Pocket calculators offer certain functions useful to the games-enthusiast – e.g., random number generation – but they do not introduce new play elements. I have yet to see a good game designed around a pocket calculator although there are many books devoted to calculator games.

The computer versions of traditional games (Backgammon, Chess, Draughts, Reversi) do not concern us, but the future holds out good prospects for new games based on micro-computers. One of the first games in this field is Star Chess, included here as a forerunner of what we can expect tomorrow.

The other groups of games represented need little comment. Card games seem to be suffering a slight and perhaps permanent decline, but this could be due to purely social factors, such as the gradual dissolution of the family circle. Pencil-and-paper games retain their popularity because they require no preparation and are suitable to odd places and moments.

Two classes of game have codified rules: proprietary games and those traditional games that are governed, like Chess, by a national or international authority. In nearly all other games one can find different rules in force in different places. Mancala, for example, is played in so many different forms that it is really a group of games, though probably with a single origin.

The rules given here of what might be called the unadopted games are those known to be in common use and amongst the best; there are no 'correct' rules for these games, only accepted rules.

In card games in particular, but also with proprietary games, it is quite common to find 'house rules' in force. Most games are open to improvement and experience will often recommend a minor modification or two: house rules can stimulate a waning interest. It is common for an inventor or manufacturer to make changes in a proprietary game based on the suggestions of an enthusiast. Even the rules of traditional games, honed by centuries of experience, undergo occasional change. A splendid example of the contribution a house rule can make to a game is the introduction of the doubling die into Backgammon, a relatively recent innovation that rescued this old game from near-oblivion.

It is hoped to expand this book in future editions and to this end I would welcome research and suggestions from readers. Particularly required is analysis of those games on which source material is scarce. All material used will be properly acknowledged.

Meanwhile I hope you will enjoy the games here and seek out more information on those that appeal to you.

• BACKGAMMON •

- Boardgame
- Backgammon board and men
- Twenty minutes
- A race game of skill and chance

Background

Backgammon is a race game which blends chance with skill. Extravagant claims have been made for its age, as for many other games. It probably derives from the Roman *Ludos Duodecim Scriptorum*, which in turn owed much to older games we know about from tomb paintings, board fragments and the like but whose rules are unrecorded. It has always been popular in Mediterranean lands, where it is known as *Trictrac* and where many versions are practised.

Backgammon became popular in Europe in the 17th and 18th centuries, but it was played much earlier; Chaucer refers to it, among others. The game has enjoyed surges of modish support, most recently in the 1970s when its image suffered from its adoption as a parlour game by the well-to-do. Backgammon, however, is essentially a gambling game, much improved by the introduction of the doubling die in the 1920s. Technique also has greatly improved in recent years. Today's experts are mathematicians, alert to the subtleties of probability. Mastery is hard earned, but the dice give the modest player a chance against the experienced.

Play

The game is played on a backgammon board, usually in the form of a hinged box. Each half has a raised perimeter so that when the box is opened and laid flat, the board, as well as being enclosed, is divided into two by a central partition known as the *bar*. The board is marked regularly with twenty-four tapered triangles, known as *points*, in two parallel lines, the triangles being in two alternating and contrasting colours. The backgammon board is notionally divided into four *tables*. (See Figure 1, where the points are numbered for reference.)

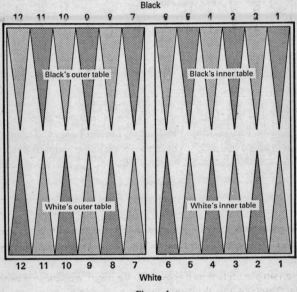

Figure 1

Each player has fifteen men, the two sides being in contrasting colours, here black and white. The players are identified accordingly.

To start the game the men are placed on the board in the arrangement shown in Figure 2. A pair of dice is used to determine the moves. The object is to transfer all your men into your inner table and then to *bear them off* the board. The first player to do so wins the game. A double game or *gammon* is won by a player who succeeds in removing all his men before his opponent has removed any; while a triple game

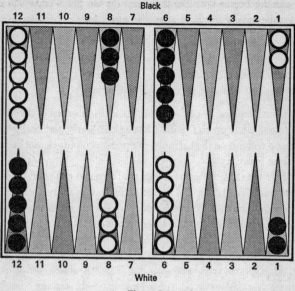

Figure 2

or *backgammon* is scored where the loser has not removed any men and still has one or more men on the bar or in the winner's inner table.

The two players face each other with the board lengthwise between them. Traditionally, the home (inner) tables are those nearest the light source, but this can be determined by agreement. Both players roll a die. The highest score wins (if equal, roll again); the winner then moves the sum of the two dice thrown. Play alternates thereafter, the players casting both dice and moving accordingly. Movement is from the opponent's inner table to one's own inner table; thus the opposing men always travel in opposite directions.

The player moves the number of points there are spots showing on the dice. He may move two separate men, or one man the total of the two dice. If the dice are cocked he must cast *both* again. The dice are always rolled in the inner tables.

Counting begins with the point next to the point on which the man to be moved stands. A man may move to:

(1) Any vacant point
(2) Any point occupied by his own men (there is no limit on the number of men on a point)
(3) Any point occupied by a single enemy man.

A point occupied by one man is called a *blot*. If a man of the opposite colour lands on this point ('hitting the blot'), the occupant is taken up and put on the bar; men of opposite colours cannot occupy the same point.

Where the total of the two dice is used to move one man, the man must 'touch down' on one of the points indicated by the dice. In other words, he must be capable of two legal moves. A player must move if he is able to do so; if he can move to either but not both of two points indicated by the dice, he must move to the higher number.

A double, often called a doublet, (e.g. 1:1, 4:4) entitles the thrower to twice the numbers on both dice. He may use these in any combination he pleases: he can move one man the total number of points or he can elect to split the points between two, three or four men.

A man sent to the bar must re-enter on the opponent's inner table at the next turn. If it cannot do so (because the dice indicate points occupied by enemy men), then that turn cannot be used to move any other man.

It is as well now to look at these rules with the help of an example or two. Moves will be shown by giving the number of the point on which the man stands and the number to which it moves. Thus W11–B5 means a move from point 11 in White's outer table to point 5 in Black's inner table. The direction of play shows that this man is black.

In Figure 3 we see the early stage of a game in progress. Let us now consider various dice throws for White, who, of course, is moving anti-clockwise. A 6:3 would allow him to move the man B1 to B10, notionally touching down at B4 on the way. If instead a 5:4 had been

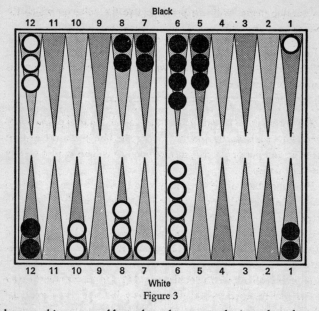

Black
12 11 10 9 8 7 6 5 4 · 3 2 1

12 11 10 9 8 7 6 5 4 3 2 1
White

Figure 3

thrown, this man could not have been moved, since the relevant points are closed to him.

A 1:1 doublet would allow him to cover his blot by W8–W7. He could then move two men W6–W5 to secure W5 (this is known as 'making a point') and he would still have a single 1 to play. The men on B12 cannot be moved as W12 is in Black's hands. White will not wish to leave a blot which Black might hit so would probably choose to play a third man to W5. B1–B2 is less good since it would reduce this man's chances of passing the black group.

Suppose in the diagram position the white man W7 was on the bar and White cast a 4:3. This man could be brought on at either B4 or B3 but could not then move again. No matter: B4 is a good play since the man B1 could be moved up to make the point. If instead of throwing 4:3, however, White had cast any combination of 5s and 6s, he could not bring on the man from the bar and would have to pass up his turn.

When a player has all his men on his inner table he may start to bear off. Figure 4 shows an end position where White can begin bearing off, but Black cannot, as he has two men on White's inner table and three on his own outer table. We will follow a few plays.

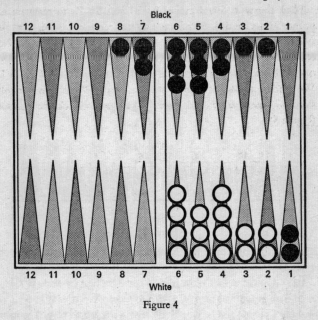

Figure 4

White throws 6:6, a fortunate throw that allows him to bear off all his men on W6 (the men are simply removed from the table).

Black throws 6:2. He could move out one of his *runners* (the term given to men on the opponent's first point), but if he did so it is odds-on that the other would be sent to the bar on White's next turn. Instead he plays B8 –B2 and B5–B3, securing both points and creating a *prime*. A prime is where one side holds six consecutive points. It is very strong since it presents an impassable wall – and Black is hoping to send a white man to the bar with one of his runners. At this point White is clearly winning – he could finish with a gammon or even

20

a backgammon – but much will depend on the dice. If he loses a man to the bar, Black could still bear off first.

White casts 4:2. To take a man off W2 would give Black a chance to hit a blot, so White bears off from W4 and plays W4–W2.

Black throws 6:5 and moves B7–B1 and B6–B1 to maintain his prime. White has 6:4. He has no man that can move 6 points, so the rule is that he must play a 5 if he can, failing that a 4, and so on. Accordingly, he bears off one man each from W5 and W4 – he has no option. Black now hits lucky with a 6:4. He plays W1–W7 and W1–W4 sending the white man to the bar. Now White does not roll, since he cannot enter, and Black plays again. Check the position (Figure 5).

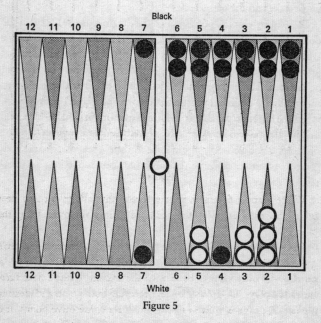

Figure 5

It is White's turn to hope that Black will expose a blot on his inner table. Notice that until the white man re-enters and moves round into his inner table, no more white men can be borne off.

Black rolls 6:6 and moves W4–B9 and W7–B6. Again White cannot play and Black throws 5:3. This allows him to bring the two men in his outer table into his inner table and to start bearing off. Notice the impact of the prime, which has already cost White three turns and has changed the game round. We must leave it here: Black has the better chances.

Now you can play Backgammon, but there remains the doubling die. This is a small cube showing on its six faces the numbers 2, 4, 8, 16, 32, 64. The die is initially placed between the players with the 64 uppermost. Either player may, after his turn, pick up the die and place it with the 2 uppermost beside his opponent. This doubles the stakes for the game if accepted; if not accepted, the opponent must pay the single stake and the game ends.

The player who has possession of the die (because he accepted the double) may, after any future turn, place it in front of his opponent with the 4 uppermost, signifying that the stakes are again doubled (quadruple the original stake); again the challenge may be accepted or declined. The highest possible win, therefore, is with a backgammon and the doubling die beside one of the players showing 64, when the amount payable is 192 times the original stake. The skill in using the die is to know exactly when to double and when to refuse or accept a double – a lot more difficult than it sounds. The die adds greatly to the excitement of the game, but there is of course no compulsion to gamble at all.

Strategy

Books have been written on this, so we will not go into details here.

Strategies in Backgammon can be reduced to two: the running game and the back game. In the running game a player strives to get all his men into his home table as soon as possible; little attention is paid to the opposition. The back game is the reverse of this. The player deliberately holds back two men (often the runners) or more, with the intention of hitting the opponent's blots as he is forced to abandon points, and only at the end, when the rest of his men are safely waiting in the home table, does he move out his defence in an effort to bear off first. In the end-game position above, White's position probably arose from a running game, Black's from a back game.

This division of strategies is inevitably simplistic. In practice, play between experts is much more subtle, with the laws of probability being invoked at every turn.

It is wise to build up points in your own home table and just outside it; the bar point (W7/B7) is particularly valuable. A strong home table discourages venturesome play by the opponent since, if he suffers a hit, the man on the bar may have difficulty getting back into circulation. However, it is not wise to occupy the first three points of your inner table early in the game because an opponent's man re-entering will be able to by-pass them. You should strive to get all your men contributing actively to the position: do not stack men on one or two points – they are far more effective distributed round the board, even though this probably means leaving the odd man at risk. In the early stages of a game a man sent to the bar can usually be brought back into play fairly quickly, though as the game progresses and your opponent builds up points in his home table you will need to be more cautious about your 'widowers'.

Probabilities are easy to calculate. The chance of a desired number coming up on at least one of the two dice is rather less than 1 in 3, a combination of two numbers 1 in 18, a doublet 1 in 6 and a specific doublet 1 in 36. No games-player has to be advised not to flout the sacred laws of numbers except as a considered gamble.

The probability of a blot being hit will obviously depend on the number of points from which it is attacked and its distance from these points. If a blot is under attack from a single point, the area of extreme danger is between three and six points away. Above six the threat recedes rapidly since a hit will require the right total of both dice. Of course, there are other factors: if you are in your own home table it is more serious to be hit than if you are in your opponent's home table since you will need to spend more dice throws recovering your position.

Again, although your blot may theoretically be in danger, hitting it may not be a good move for your opponent (it may, for example, cause him to leave a blot). As you get into the game, you will find there is much more to think about than is at first apparent.

To play first is a slight advantage. There are three opening rolls that allow you to make useful points (remember that you are debarred from starting with a double): 6:1; the best of all, since this allows you to secure the important bar point 3:1 and 4:2, both of which permit you to make good points in your inner table. Throws of 6:4 and 5:3 also win you points on your inner table, but, as explained above, it is not wise to occupy these early in the game.

Whilst the best opening plays and responses to them are generally agreed, one or two are disputed by the experts, so even at the start of the game we have no agreement on the right path to choose – and that must be a healthy symptom!

A list of suggested opening moves for all possible dice combinations is given in the following table. Equally good alternatives are available in two or three cases.

6:5	B1–B7	B7–B12
6:4	B1–B7	B7–B11
6:3	B1–B7	B12–W10
6:2	B1–B7	B12–W11
6:1	B12–W7	W8–W7
5:4	B12–W8	B12–W9
5:3	B12–W8	B12–W10
5:2	B12–W8	B12–W11
5:1	B12–W8	W6–W5
4:3	B12–W9	B12–W10
4:2	W8–W4	W6–W4
4:1	B12–W9	B1–B2
3:2	B12–W10	B12–W11
3:1	W8–W5	W6–W5
2:1	B12–W11	B1–B2

Variants

One aberration – it can hardly be called a variant – allows the first player to roll both dice again, so that an opening doublet is possible; in another, the stakes are automatically doubled every time the initial throws to determine who plays first are equal.

A simple variant has all the men off the board to start with. They are brought on in the usual way except that a player is not compelled to bring a man on unless no other move is available; otherwise rules are as in Backgammon.

A Turkish version, Moultezim, has the players' first points at opposite corners of the board. The white points are numbered identically to those in Backgammon, but the black points are in reverse order; thus Black's 1 point is at B12 (Figure 1) and his 12 point at B1. All 15 men of each player start on the opponent's 12 point. There are no blots: a single man controls a point, but you are not permitted to control more than four points in your outer table (otherwise primes would be too easy to establish). Each player must get one man into his outer or inner table before moving another. Directions of play are as in Backgammon.

In Plakato, a Greek game, the men start facing each other stacked on the opponent's 1 point. When a blot is hit, the man is not removed to the bar but may not move again so long as his opponent (who may bring other men to it if he wishes) stays on the point. In short, the single man is 'pinned'. Otherwise the rules are those of Backgammon.

Finally, there is a variant, common in the Middle East, called Gioul. Men start as in Plakato and there are no blots, as in Moultezim. The difference is that a player takes any doublet he rolls, as in Backgammon, and all the doubles above it. Thus a 3:3 confers the plays 3:3, 4:4, 5:5, 6:6 (i.e. four 3s, four 4s, four 5s and four 6s). The player works his way up the plays but if he reaches a stage (say, the second 4:4) when he cannot execute a move, then the second player takes over and continues upwards until he in turn is unable to play. A doublet can clearly be a double-edged throw in Gioul!

• BÉZIQUE •

- Card game
- Two Piquet packs
- One hour
- A game of marriages and families

Background

The genesis of Bézique, like that of so many card games, is obscure, but it is probably of French origin and is closely related to Pinochle, which is widely played in the U.S.A. Bézique is the better game, and, although not now popular, has a dedicated if declining following.

Play

Cards rank Ace high down to Seven (the cards below the Seven are not used) but with the Ten standing between the Ace and King. Cut for dealer; higher ranking deals. Dealer distributes eight cards to each player in batches of 3–2–3, turns the next card over as trumps and places the stock face-down beside it. Points are scored for card combinations and certain bonuses. The game is up to1, 000 points or as agreed.

Bézique is a trick-taking game played in two stages. There are twenty-four tricks in the first stage, players replenishing their hands, winner first, from the stock after each trick, with Elder Hand (non-dealer) taking the turn-up card at the end. Normal trick-taking rules apply (e.g. winner of trick leads to next) except that there is no obligation to follow suit. The second player may thus, if able, choose to follow suit, trump or discard – curious options for a trick-taking game! If cards are of equal rank, first player takes the trick. The winner of a trick may declare one combination (see below) by placing the cards face up in front of him and scoring appropriately. Face-up cards may be played to any subsequent tricks.

When the stock is exhausted, players take back into hand any cards still on the table in front of them and the second stage – the play of the final eight tricks – begins.

Now the rules are different: a player *must* follow suit (if he can); he is also obliged to take a trick if he can, either by playing a higher card of the same suit or by trumping. No combinations may be declared during the play of the last eight tricks.

Scoring. If the turn-up card is a Seven, dealer scores 10 points. Every Ace or Ten (known as *brisques*) taken in play counts 10, and the winner of the last trick also scores 10 points. Other tricks have no value except that the winner of a trick has the privilege of declaring a combination. The holder of a Seven of trumps may score 10 points by exchanging it with the face-up card, by simply declaring it or by playing it to a trick.

The point-scoring combinations are:

Bézique (♠ Q and ♦ J)	40
Double Bézique (both ♠ Qs and ♦ Js)	500
Sequence (A, 10, K, Q, J of trumps)	250
Quartet (any four Aces)	100
Quartet (any four Kings)	80
Quartet (any four Queens)	60
Quartet (any four Jacks)	40
Royal Marriage (K and Q of trumps)	40
Common Marriage (K and Q of another suit)	20

Points are scored when combinations are declared; *brisques* are normally totalled at the end of play. A Bézique score card, which has dials similar to those on a domestic power meter, is commonly used but is a luxury.

The rules governing combinations are a little complex. A card declared in a combination may later be used in a different combination, but not in one of the same type. A card cannot be part of two combinations simultaneously. For example, if a Sequence is declared the Royal Marriage contained within it does not score.

A combination may not be broken and then built again. For example, if a Quartet of Jacks is declared and one is later played to a trick, another Jack cannot be added to the three on the table to score a second quartet. However, since it is a different combination, a Jack of Diamonds on the table could be paired with a Queen of Spades from hand to score Bézique and could also be used subsequently in a Sequence. A Double Bézique (rare indeed!) is only scored if put down together or if, when the second Bézique is claimed, the first Bézique is intact on the table.

Strategy

Don't be in a hurry to declare combinations – they give information. On the other hand, if you hold back too long you may fail to make another trick and find yourself left with some good points. If you have a sequence, put down the Royal Marriage first for 40 – provided you are confident of winning another trick; but remember that you will only have three cards at most to play with as the other five (two on table, three in hand) form the declaration.

Kings and Queens are useful because 'engagements' are frequent and marriages are a fruitful source of points. So are *brisques* – sixteen of them to be won in every game. Trick-taking requires skill, though there is no point in taking a trick unless you want to declare a combination or it contains a *brisque*. Look for good trumps and a void suit for the play-off. Between three and five hands should decide a game.

Variants

It is quite common to vary the Bézique pair: ♠Q and ♥J when Clubs or Diamonds are trumps; ♣Q and ♦J when Hearts or Spades are trumps. In Rubicon Bézique, four Piquet packs are used and the deal is nine cards each, singly or in threes. There is no turn-up and the game is played in no trumps until a marriage is declared; thereafter trumps are of that suit and the declaration is scored as a Royal Marriage. The Seven of trumps has no special privilege.

In many variants, including Rubicon Bézique, *carte blanche* is incorporated. If a player picks up a hand without a court card, he may expose his cards and claim 10 (sometimes 50) points. He may subsequently score 10 (sometimes 50) after each trick by exposing the card he draws from stock until he picks up a court card. Another variant requires a quartet to be made up of the four different suits. Experiment and suit your taste.

• BLACK BOX •

- Code-breaking game
- Boxed proprietary game (Waddingtons)
- Fifteen minutes (twin game)
- A most original game in a contemporary setting

Background

Dr Eric Solomon is a thoughtful inventor whose games are marked by originality. Black Box, as unusual as any game you're likely to see, has had considerable success in America, but elsewhere sales have been only moderate. I doubt if most people have heard of it.

The theme is modern: atoms, rays and black boxes, but basically it is a sort of code-breaking game in which one player sets the other a problem that has to be solved by deduction. The players then change roles and there is a scoring system to determine who has won.

In science, a black box describes a device whose inner workings are unknown but whose behaviour, observed only from the outside, can be described by an observer.

The game calls for a Challenger, who secretes a molecule of four atoms within a box; and an Experimenter, who projects rays into the box, is informed by the Challenger of their external behaviour, and has to deduce the location of the atoms within the box.

Play

The black box is divided into a regular array of 8 by 8 cells. Each line of cells, horizontal and vertical, is assumed to have an entry/exit point at both ends through which a ray can pass. These points are numbered for reference (Figure 6).

One player (the Challenger) now marks four atoms, one in each of

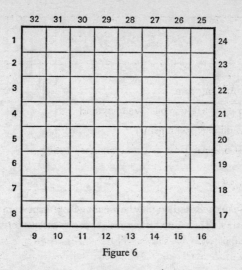

Figure 6

four squares of the grid, on a marker board diagram which he keeps hidden. His object is to place the atoms so that they will be hard to find.

The Experimenter's task is to locate the molecule (arrangement of atoms). He informs the Challenger that he is shooting a ray through a certain line – say, 14. The Challenger will then tell him at what point, if at all, the ray will emerge. False information, intentional or otherwise, is penalized. By shooting further rays the Experimenter will gather information which will allow him to place correctly the four atoms.

The Experimenter will use the black box, which is equipped with atoms and ray markers, both to register his shots and their results and to experiment with placing the atoms.

There are six basic ways in which a ray can be affected by an atom:
(1) A ray hits an atom, when it is absorbed. The Challenger announces: 'Absorbed' (Figure 7).
(2) A ray which enters a square orthogonally adjacent to any atom is deflected ninety degrees away from it. In fact the ray 'overshoots'

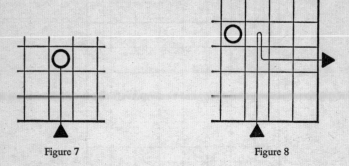

Figure 7   Figure 8

(Figure 8) but the deflection may be visualized as a simple right-angled turn (Figure 9). The reason for the overshoot is to resolve certain other situations (below).

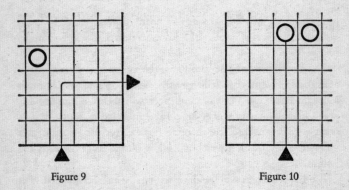

Figure 9   Figure 10

(3) A ray may be absorbed by an overshoot. In Figure 10 the ray is influenced by the right-hand atom but is absorbed by the atom in its path on the overshoot.

(4) A ray may be reflected back through its entry point by an atom in an edge square. Again, this effect is created by the overshoot (Figure 11).

(5) A ray is reflected when there is a double deflection as shown in

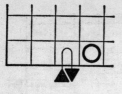

Figure 11   Figure 12

Figure 12. This is because the sideways element of each deflection cancels out whereas the reversal element does not.

(6) A ray is not influenced by any atom and passes out at the end of the line which it entered (Figure 13).

A ray may be influenced by several atoms. Figure 14, from which the overshoots have been omitted for simplicity, illustrates one example. The Challenger would simply announce 'Absorbed' and the

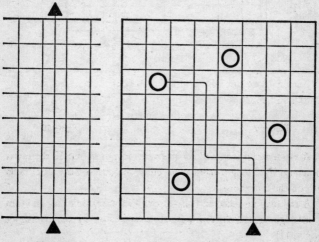

Figure 13   Figure 14

Experimenter could not, from this single attempt, have any idea where the hit atom lies – it could be in almost any of the 64 cells.

Another example of a ray suffering multiple effects is shown in Figure 15. The Experimenter could wrongly conclude that the ray had not been affected by any atom when in fact its path had been changed by all of them!

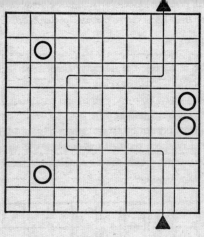

Figure 15

The Experimenter scores one penalty point for each marker used. Thus, a ray which is absorbed or reflected will count only one point, but a ray which emerges other than at its input point will require two markers and so counts two. At any time he may try to guess the position of the four atoms. Any atom incorrectly positioned exacts a five-point penalty. The winner is the player who, after an agreed even number of turns, has the lower number of penalty points or whose opponent first reaches 50.

Strategy

There are two types of atom that pose special problems to the Experimenter and which offer the Challenger scope for deceit: hidden atoms and ambiguous atoms.

A hidden atom is one which no ray can reach because of the arrangement of the other atoms. Such an atom can only occupy one point and its presence can be deduced from the configuration of the others. The marked atom in Figure 16 is hidden. On discovering the position of the other three, the Experimenter may decide to 'guess' that the fourth is in the hidden position, for a possible penalty of five points, rather than hunt elsewhere and perhaps run up a lot more points.

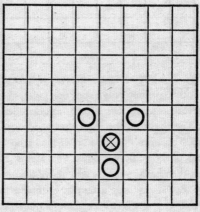

Figure 16

An ambiguous atom may occupy either one of two different points, but, because of the configuration of the other atoms, the outputs are identical. In Figure 17 the fourth atom could be at *A* or *B* with identical ray outputs. Assuming that the Experimenter is satisfied that the fourth atom is ambiguous, he obviously has one chance in two of guessing right.

The inventor's researches have shown that hidden or ambiguous atoms are likely to help the Experimenter slightly. As a guide, the average number of penalty points per game is 13.

The strategy for the Challenger must include complexity, deceit

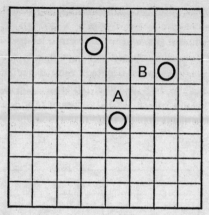

Figure 17

and psychology. The Experimenter must try to use each ray to maximum effect. Although they only count one point, absorbed and reflected rays reveal, as a rule, less information than deflected and unaffected rays. The Experimenter must always calculate when it may pay him to guess an atom's position rather than shoot more rays. He can at the start of the game put down four atoms. His most likely penalty would then be 20 points – well above the average, so not a good strategy. But at any stage it may be profitable for him, on the laws of probability, to guess the remaining atom(s), and he may on occasion plan his game with this possibility in mind.

The longer the path a ray follows, the more intelligence it is likely to gather. For this reason it is often a good idea to deflect a ray off an atom whose position is known. If you wish to test a suspicion by entering a certain cell, consider the different possible ways of getting there (alternative ray inputs). There is no point in taking a path that you know to be barren if another could reveal further information.

Variants

The scoring system in the original rules awards a 10-point penalty for any atom that is incorrectly placed. This seems harsh and in my view reduces the element of skill. An Experimenter, unsure of the location of an atom, will have little hesitation in shooting further rays rather than risking the loss of 10 points.

Players may agree to bar hidden and ambiguous atoms, but since these enrich strategy the ban would result in some simplification.

A harder game uses five atoms. Larger boxes with more atoms would complicate the game but would not add anything to it. The marketed version of Black Box probably cannot be improved on.

• CHESS •

- Board wargame
- Chess set and board
- One hour upwards
- The world's most popular boardgame

Background

Chess is the most popular of all boardgames and has the largest literature. It is played everywhere to standard rules approved by the
Fédération Internationale des Échecs (F.I.D.E.), the governing international body.

Chess is an offspring of the Indian Chaturanga that dates from
about the 7th century. It reached Europe some eight centuries later
and for a long time thereafter remained a pastime of the privileged.
Literacy and a cheap press extended its popularity and today's player
has the benefit of a rich inheritance of recorded wisdom.

For some years the U.S.S.R. has dominated world events, but its
supremacy is now under strong challenge. Most countries run rating
systems for players who compete regularly in organized matches and
tournaments, and also award titles. There is also an international
grading system and F.I.D.E. confers *inter alia* the titles of International
Master and Grandmaster. Grandmasters are few: Britain had none
until recently but now has five.

Chess computers are energetically marketed, but their playing
strength is often overrated. Popular models are all in the beginner
class.

The appeal of Chess lies in its abundance of elegant strategical and
tactical possibilities and its endless variety. It can be enjoyed by
novices as a game offering a succession of simple yet exciting ideas or
by experts who are taxed to the highest reaches of complexity. Per-

fection at Chess is beyond the limits of the human mind but near enough to be in part perceived. Chess challenges and beckons, mastery always just out of reach. It is no wonder it has enslaved so many.

Play

The game is played on the familiar chess or chequer board. Each side has sixteen men, a King, a Queen, two Rooks, two Bishops, two Knights and eight Pawns (Figure 18). Players move alternately and the object is to capture (checkmate) the opponent's King. Games between experienced players are usually won by one side resigning.

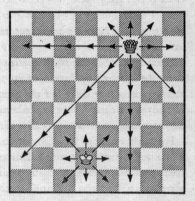

♔	♚	King
♕	♛	Queen
♖	♜	Rook
♗	♝	Bishop
♘	♞	Knight
♙	♟	Pawn

Figure 18   Figure 19

Each type of man moves differently but all the men of like type move in the same way. The *King* moves one square in any direction, the *Queen* any number of vacant squares in a straight line – i.e. the King's move extended to the board edges (see Figure 19). The *Rook* (sometimes and wrongly called a castle) moves any number of vacant squares orthogonally, the *Bishop* the same but diagonally. The *Knight* has a curious move which can be described as a jump to the far corner of a 3 × 2 rectangle. (Figure 20 shows the moves of these

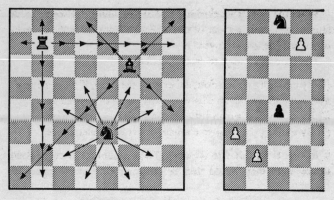

Figure 20   Figure 21

three pieces.) The *Pawn* moves one square straight forward but every Pawn has the option of advancing two squares on its first move.

Capturing is by displacement and is optional. All men capture in the manner in which they move except the Pawn, which attacks the adjacent squares diagonally in front of it. Also, a Pawn making the initial two-square move may be captured by an opposing Pawn as if it had moved only one square. This is the *en passant* capture and must be taken on the next move or forfeited.

Only the Pawn cannot retreat. However, it is the only man that can be promoted. When it reaches the end rank it is at once exchanged for a piece of the player's choice, other than a King, and regardless of what pieces remain on the board. A Queen is the obvious and almost invariable choice.

The behaviour of the Pawn is demonstrated in Figure 21. The white Pawn on the left can move one square forward (White moves up the board in most diagrams). The white Pawn on its initial square can move either one or two squares forward. In both cases it will be under attack from the black Pawn, in the second case under the *en passant* rule. The advanced white Pawn may move one square ahead or capture the black Knight; in either case it must be promoted at once.

When the King is attacked it is said to be in *check*. A King in check must immediately get out of check. If he cannot do so he is checkmated and the game is over.

There are three ways to escape check:

(1) By capturing the attacker, either with the King, if the opponent's man is unguarded on an adjacent square, or with another man.
(2) By interposing a man between the King and the attacker.
(3) By moving the King to a square that is not under attack.

It follows from this that opposing Kings cannot stand on adjacent squares since they would then be attacking each other. Figure 22

Figure 22

shows a situation where whoever plays first can give checkmate. If White moves, the game is over immediately with the Pawn moving one ahead on to the eighth rank when it promotes to a Queen or, in this rather exceptional case, to a Bishop; or by taking the Bishop with the Pawn and promoting to Knight. In each case the black King is in check, the attacking piece cannot be taken, Black cannot interpose and there is no square to escape the check because all the squares round the King are attacked by the white King or Queen.

Black cannot give checkmate in one move, but he can do so in two. First he plays his Queen up the white diagonal to the top of the board, attacking the white King. White would now like to promote his Pawn and give checkmate but he cannot do so as he is in check himself. White cannot capture the black Queen, nor can he take the Bishop with his King because the King would still be in check from the Queen. Also, White cannot move his King out of check (now it is the black King that restrains the white) so he has no alternative but to interpose his own Queen when Black will simply take it off with his Queen and White is checkmated.

Once in a game the King together with one of his Rooks can make a joint move subject to certain conditions. This is known as castling and has the dual purpose of removing the King to safety and bringing a Rook into play. The requirements are that neither the King nor the Rook must have previously moved, the squares between the two pieces must be vacant, the King is not in check at the time and the King does not cross nor arrive on a square attacked by an enemy man. The alternative castling moves for White are shown in Figure 23.

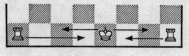

Figure 23

They are, of course, the same for Black.

Draws in Chess are frequent. Both sides may have inadequate forces to give checkmate, moves may be repeated, or, most commonly, both players agree to draw, usually when there appears to be no winning prospects for either side. Another way to draw is by stalemate. This is the situation where a player whose turn it is to move and whose King is not in check has no legal play. Stalemate is quite common between beginners, rare between strong players.

To start a game, men are arranged on the board as in Figure 24. Notice that each player has a black square in his near left-hand corner and that the two Queens face each other and occupy squares of their respective colours.

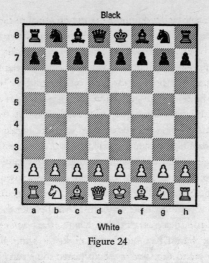

Figure 24

A notation is used to record games. Two notations are in common use in Chess, the abstract algebraic and the more logical descriptive. The algebraic is used here, since it is common to other games. Files are lettered a–h from left to right, and ranks 1–8, both from White's point of view. The combination of a letter and number will identify a square. A man is identified by his initial – N for Knight to avoid confusion with the King.

Most moves are recorded simply by an initial (the man moved) and a square (where the move ends). Any ambiguity (e.g. both Rooks can move to the square) is removed by giving the rank or file of the man moved. A capture is indicated by an '×' and a check by a '+'. In annotation, a '!' is often used to indicate a good move and a '?' a doubtful or bad move. Slight variations are found, but they are all self-explanatory.

Strategy

It is impossible to grant even elementary justice to the beauties and complexities of Chess in a page or two. Go back to Figure 22 for an example of simple tactics. Suppose in this position it is Black to play and he overlooks the winning check and instead plays Pawn takes Queen (P × b4). White could now play Pa8 = Q+ when the black King would move out of check while continuing to guard his Queen by Kc5 when, with a Bishop and Queen on each side, the game would be drawn with correct play. Or, more subtly, he could try Bg2, hoping for Q × g2 (notice the Queen cannot move off this diagonal because the King would then be exposed to check – an illegal move). Now White would promote Pa8 = Q+, and after the King moves away, Q × g2 would allow him eventually to win. The correct Black reply to Bg2 is B × a7 when White will be obliged to take the Queen and the game will be drawn as Black has insufficient force to mate. White would lose if he promoted by capturing the Bishop. If he promoted to a piece other than a Knight, the black Queen could mate at once; if to a Knight, giving check, the white King would move to safety and the Queen would prove too strong for Knight and Bishop.

Which brings us to relative values. The Queen is the most powerful piece (equivalent to about 9 Pawns), then the Rook (5 Pawns), with Bishop and Knight about equal (3 Pawns), but much depends on the position. The Rook and Bishop work well on open lines, the Knight in blocked positions. At the start of a game, however, the Knights are active, whereas the Rooks cannot easily be brought into action until some exchanges have taken place. It takes experience to evaluate the strength of a piece in any given position, and in particular to determine whether its potential is temporary or permanent.

A game of Chess divides roughly into three stages: the opening, the middle game and the end game. The opening has been extensively analysed and books on opening variations are constantly being published. The middle game is a theatre of general principles while the end game, that stage of the game when most men have gone from the board and the immediate aim of both sides is often pawn promotion, has again been exhaustively researched. A game may be won in the opening or the middle game. The shortest game of Chess has just two moves on each side from the starting position. White always plays first. This unlikely game runs 1. Pf3, Pe5; 2. Pg4, Qh4 mate (Figure 25) – White exposed his King to attack. Both White and Black could have played slightly differently with the same result.

Figure 25

Consider the most common of all opening attacks, exclusively the tactics of beginners. 1. Pe4, Pe5 (remember these Pawns do not attack each other: neither can now move); 2. Bc4, Nc6; 3. Qh5, Bc5; 4. Q × f7 mate. Again, variations are possible. Black must protect f7 (see Figure 26).

A chess game is a synthesis of three elements – force, space and time. Force is represented by the chessmen: if you have the stronger force, you are more likely to win. Aim to exchange pieces to increase your advantage. As the weaker side, you should avoid exchanges and try to complicate the game. Space is represented by the board: the greater your area of control, the greater your freedom of movement. If your men are cramped, they cannot realize their potential and are liable to obstruct one another. Time is represented by the moves. Economy of movement marks a good chess-player. A beginner's error is to march the Queen about early in the game. Since the Queen is the most valuable piece, she will be obliged to move if attacked – with advantage to the opposition who will attempt to combine threats to the Queen with developing moves.

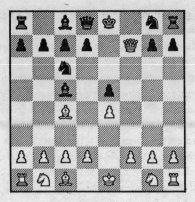

Figure 26

Judgement in Chess is an appreciation of the relative importance of these three elements in any given situation, coupled with an evaluation of the position (i.e., the interaction of the pieces). This should indicate your strategy.

The end game calls for precise calculation – the player who promotes a Pawn first usually wins. An end-game concept that occurs frequently is the 'Opposition', which corresponds to the 'Move' in Draughts. In Figure 27, with no other pieces on the board, White is

Figure 27

said to have the Opposition if it is Black's turn to play and *vice versa*. With the Opposition, White wins, for he can promote the Pawn which will be sufficient to force checkmate; if Black has the Opposition, however, the game is only drawn because the Pawn cannot be promoted. Follow the play with Black playing first. 1. ... Kd8 (Kb8 would allow the Pawn to promote in two moves); 2. Pd7, Ke7 (the only legal move); 3. Kc7 (White continues to guard the Pawn but now covers the promotion square so that the Pawn will 'queen' next move). Now consider White playing first. 1. Pd7 + (in reply to any other move Black would simply move his King in front of the Pawn), Kd8. Now the only square to which White can play his King and retain his guard on the Pawn is d6 – but then Black is stalemated.

Finally, a few general hints. Be adventurous – this is the fastest way to learn. The player who is thrifty of ideas sees little. Concentrate on the centre until the end game is reached: pieces at the side of the board, with the exception of the Rook, control fewer squares than in the middle. In the end game, use your King as a fighting piece; he is usually in little danger of getting checkmated.

Never move randomly. Any plan is better than none. Look for weaknesses in your opponent's position and try to exploit them. If you cannot see any, set about making them. Get all your men working as soon as possible and do not attack without preparation. Beginners tend to undervalue Pawns, which should be used in both attack and defence. When you begin to see their potential you are beginning to understand chess.

Variants

Books have been written on chess variants, sometimes referred to as Fairy Chess games. One of the best variants is Progressive Chess, described elsewhere in this book. Losing Chess is popular too. The rules are the same as for the game except that capturing is compulsory, the player having a choice where there is more than one capture available. There is no checking: the King is taken like any other piece. The object is to lose all your own men. The game is skilful but tends to be stereotyped.

Rifle Chess is another popular variant. Again, the usual rules apply, except that capturing pieces do not move (captured pieces are simply removed from the board) – all men are assumed to be armed with rifles (the use of missiles in Star Chess is a similar concept). King of the variants is Kriegspiel, but since this requires an umpire it is outside our scope.

Over the years attempts have been made to establish some variants as games in their own right. Modern Chess and Three-dimensional Chess are two of the more recent. See also Hexagonal Chess.

• CRIBBAGE •

- Card game
- Standard pack
- Fifteen minutes
- A pub and club game

Background

Cribbage dates from the start of the 17th century and was derived from an earlier card game called Noddy. It retains widespread popularity as a pub and club pastime. A peg board is used for scoring (Figure 28); like the chess clock, it is commonly used in other games and is familiar to most of us.

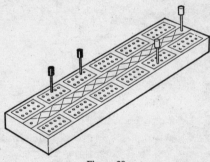

Figure 28

Play

Ace ranks low. As in Gin, court cards count 10, Aces 1, other cards pip value. Suits are equal.

Cut for deal, lower dealing. Five cards, distributed singly, are given to each player.

Each player starts by discarding two of his cards face down on to the table. These cards form the *crib*, which belongs to Younger Hand (dealer). Elder Hand (non-dealer) at once marks 3 points 'for last' as part compensation. He then cuts and the Dealer turns up the top card of the lower packet. If the card is a Jack, dealer scores '2 for his heels'.

The object is to form point-scoring combinations without, and also in conjunction with, opponent's cards and to notch certain bonuses. The game takes place in two stages, rather like Piquet. Play starts by Elder putting one of his cards face up in front of him and announcing the pip value. Dealer now does the same but announces the total value of the two cards and also any points claimed (see below), which he immediately pegs. Play alternates in this manner, each player announcing the cumulative point total as he puts down, until all six cards are on the table or the point count nearest but not in excess of 31 has been reached, where neither player can put down without exceeding 31.

Points scored during play are as follows:

Pair – 2 points
Pair-Royal (three of a kind) – 6 points
Double Pair-Royal (four of a kind) – 12 points
Run (from three to six cards in sequence) – 1 point for each card in run. A run is scored regardless of the card order, provided that the sequence is uninterrupted: 6, 7, 5 earns 3 points; 6, 3, 7, 8 does not.

If a card is played that brings the cumulative pip total to 15, the player notches 2 points. A player who cannot put down a card without exceeding a pip total of 31 must check, when the opponent may play again if he can. 1 point to the player of the last card; 2 points if it brings the total to 31 exactly.

The hands are now picked up and scored independently – the 'show' – starting with Elder. The 'up-card' is now included with the hands, so that each player has effectively four cards. Scoring is the same as in the first phase for matched cards and runs; also for every combination totalling 15. If a player has the Jack of the same suit as the up-card he scores 1 ('for his nob'). If all three cards in a hand are of the same suit, this is a Flush, scoring 3; it scores 4 if the up-card is also of this suit.

Combinations are scored in every possible way. If the up-card is, say, ♥5, and you hold ♠5, ♣5, ♥J (a fine hand) you score 'fifteen-eight' (2 points for each of the four combinations that total 15), 6 for a Pair-Royal and 1 for his nob – a total of 15.

Dealer now scores his hand and when he has done so, he picks up the crib and does likewise. A Flush can only be scored in the crib if the up-card is of the same suit – 5 points, since the crib has four cards.

Scoring

The cribbage board has two sets of double lines, each line of thirty holes, divided into tens and fives for easy reckoning. Each player uses his own double lines, moving his peg (or burnt matchstick!) every time he scores, up the outer line, down the inner line and into the central hole to finish on 61.

Strategy

The Dealer's advantage is not so big as it seems. First, Elder scores 3 'for last'; second, Elder is sure to throw two poor cards into the crib; and third, the game ends when a player notches 61 points – and since Elder's hand is scored first, he may have a decisive advantage in the last deal.

It will be apparent that some cards are better than others. A Five is always good since with sixteen *tenths* (court cards and Tens) in the pack, the chances of notching 15 at least once are excellent.

As Dealer, remember that there is a lot more scoring potential in the crib than in hand, because of the extra card. Therefore it is often wise to discard good cards into the crib. A Five is a natural candidate; so are two cards in sequence. Conversely, Elder should contribute worthless cards – Kings and Nines qualify here.

A good lead is a low card (below a Five) which does not allow

Dealer to mark up fifteen; also one of a Pair, for if opponent scores for a Pair, you score for a Pair-Royal.

Elementary tactics are quickly learnt. If you bring the count to 21, the chances are high that your opponent will peg out with a tenth. At 22, however, you are fairly safe (a Nine may well have been discarded into the crib if you are Dealer). Cribbage centres on Fives and tenths, which tend to dominate the play by their presence or by their absence. Consider them carefully.

In an average game, Elder will score about 9 points and Younger about 11.

Variants

These are many and good, including the less popular six-card and seven-card Cribbage. 'Muggins' is widely played. If a player overlooks a scoring combination, his opponent calls 'Muggins!', often with relish, and pegs the score for himself.

• DRAUGHTS •

- Abstract boardgame
- Board and men
- Thirty minutes
- A game deserving of more attention

Background

Draughts is younger than Chess but is still very old. Although widely played both in Britain and more particularly in North America (where it is known as Checkers), Draughts has rarely excited public enthusiasm and gets little attention from the media. In Britain the game has a plebeian image, which it shares with Darts, and it is in public bars and working-men's clubs that it is most often seen.

Draughts is an excellent game of great depth but unfortunately suffers from a bad press. Its appearance is not encouraging: Draughts *looks* dull. It also suffers from comparison with Chess – an unfair comparison, as apart from using the same board the two games have little in common. Draughts also carries the stigma of being classed as a children's game, an injustice probably caused by the simple rules and because generations of youngsters have had the game thrust upon them by their parents at an early age.

But serious Draughts is played, if not widely. Between well-matched players draws are common and it is often the practice in tournaments to ballot the opening moves. Draughts may never fire the world, but if studied and played intelligently it can give off a lot of warmth.

Play

Each player has 12 men of uniform pattern, the two sides being of contrasting colours, usually black and white.

The board is the standard 8 × 8 chequer board. Play is only on the black squares, the board being placed between the players so that each has a black square in the near left-hand corner with the 'double corner' as it is called on the right. In diagrams, however, board and play are reversed for the sake of clarity, so that the action is on the white squares, which are numbered for reference (Figure 29). The starting position is shown in Figure 30.

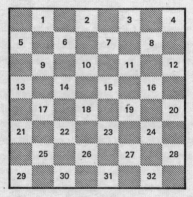

Figure 29

Black moves first. The men move diagonally forward only, one square at a time. On reaching the end rank, a man is promoted to a King and the opponent caps the promoted man with a like draughtsman to signify this. A King may move backwards as well as forwards, again one square diagonally.

Capture is by leaping. A man may take an opposing man that is adjacent and diagonally in front of it provided there is a vacant square immediately beyond which the capturing piece then occupies. A King captures in like manner but in any direction. Multiple captures are permissible and are compulsory if the first capture of a series of

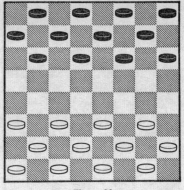

Figure 30

two or more possible captures is made. There must be a vacant square between each captured piece. A man promoted in the action of capturing may not continue to capture as a King in that turn. Capturing is compulsory, but the player has the choice, if an option is open to him, and he is not obliged to take the longest capture. Captured men are removed from the board and take no further part in the play.

If a player fails to capture when he is able to, his man is *huffed* (removed from the board) as a penalty. Alternatively, the second player can require that the capture be made. In some circles, failure to capture loses the game outright. Huffing is a controversial rule that is often dispensed with.

The object of the game is to take all the opponent's men, but (as in Chess) a game is normally won by one side giving up. A player can also lose by having no legal move when it is his turn to play – 'stalemate' is a draw only in Chess. Draws are by agreement and are common.

Strategy

The immediate aim of both sides is to get a King while preventing the opponent from getting one. This is explained by the considerable powers of an unopposed King. His range is short, but his influence extends across the whole board; if he can capture but a single man, the position otherwise being equal, this should be enough to win the game.

It is evident that your opponent cannot promote a man unless you vacate one of the back-rank squares, but you will be obliged to do this sooner or later and indeed may choose to do so in some circumstances. The single corner is the least important of the back-row squares, since the only approach to it is covered by the adjacent defender; for this reason, the first move off the back row is often out of the single corner.

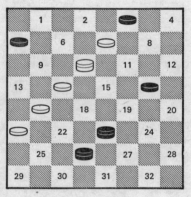

Figure 31

Position is at least as important as in other strategy games: a co-ordinated deployment with emphasis on control of the centre is the ideal. Avoid play to the sides without good reason, particularly the forward edge squares – the 'dog holes'.

Zugzwang – the discomforting situation of having to move where every move available will lead to a worsening of your position – is much more common in Draughts than in Chess. Look out for opportunities to manoeuvre your opponent into *zugzwang*.

Sacrifices are common in Draughts; even multiple sacrifices, beloved by problem composers. A sacrifice is an effective weapon to disrupt a position or get a man through to become a King, because it may not be declined – you force an opponent's play. Figure 31 demonstrates this well and breathes some of the excitement of the game. Men are equal, but Black has two Kings and White's position appears vulnerable. Black played 26–22, a natural-looking move. There followed 7–2(K)! (as in Chess, an '!' is used to indicate a good move, while a '?' indicates a bad move) which forces Black's reply – 22–13. White now plays 21–17 – another sacrifice – followed, after 13–22, by a third one: 14–9. Again Black is compelled to accept, 5–14; White then cleans up four black men to end on 12, when the last black man is doomed.

Figure 32

There is a whole armoury of text-book strategems similar to this that come up frequently in one form or another and are familiar to the expert. Openings have been deeply analysed: there are about fifty of them, a surprising number, perhaps, in view of the apparent limitations on movement.

End games too are well researched. We said earlier that an extra man in an even position should be enough to win. Theoretically this situation should reduce to a two-to-one King fight and a beginner's first task is to learn this nursery ending where the lone King has reached the temporary sanctuary of the double corner (Figure 32).

Black to play wins easily with 27–24, 32–28; 23–19, 28–32; 24–28, 32–27; 28–32, 27–31; 19–15, 31–26; 15–18, 26–31; 18–22.

An important concept in Draughts is the 'Move'. This is not easy to define but corresponds roughly to the Opposition in Chess. It has been described as being in a position to check the advance of the opponent's men beyond a certain point. Tactical considerations may render the Move irrelevant, but it assumes particular significance when there are only a few men left on the board. One reason is that a simple exchange (sometimes called a one-for-one cut) can reverse the Move, and exchanges are harder to come by when there are not many men around. However, one is available for White in Figure 33. Black

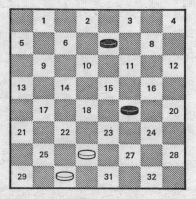

Figure 33

theoretically has the Move, but White reverses this with 26–23 and after 19–26, 30–23, Black is clearly lost.

To show that Draughts is not as simple as might be inferred from the above examples, Figure 34 shows a deep and pretty win for White (to move). White is admittedly two men ahead, but his position is precarious and Black, of course, has a King. White plays 9–6, a surprising sacrifice. There follows 2–9, 27–23; 18–27, 20–16; 9–18, 10–6; 1–10 (now White is two men *down*!) 26–23; 19–26, 30–7 (Black has no less than three captures and White is going to make him take them

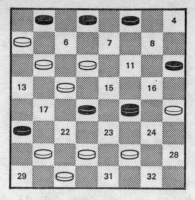

Figure 34

all. The order is not important); 3–10, 5–1(K); 12–19, 1–6; 21–30, 6–31(K) and White has the Move and the win.

Variants

Losing Draughts is what a lot of us play, but this is a different game. You win if you are the first to lose all your men or are left without a move. Capturing is obligatory (no huffing!).

There are other variants in which the powers of the men or the Kings or both are increased.

Draughts is played world-wide in many versions, of which Continental (or Polish) Draughts is one of the best and best-known.

• FANORONA •

- Abstract boardgame
- Board and counters
- Forty-five minutes
- A game of strange procedures

Background

This is a Madagascan game, developed about three hundred years ago from Alquerque, a family of games that was introduced into Europe by the Moors and which was probably known to the Ancient Egyptians.

Fanorona has an unusual form of capture and, even more remarkable, a rule whereby in alternate games the previous winner is required to sacrifice men.

The board and men are simple and are easily prepared. As in Alquerque before it, the board is commonly incised in stone or drawn on the ground.

Play

The Fanorona board consists of forty-five points in a 9 × 5 array. Each side has twenty-two men of contrasting colours which are arranged on the board at the start to cover forty-four of these points. The central point is empty (see Figure 35).

Movement is to an adjacent empty point along any line. Capture may be by approach or withdrawal. An *approach capture* is made by moving a man to a point adjacent along a line to an enemy man in the same direction of movement. This man, and any enemy men in unbroken sequence behind it in the same line, are captured 'by approach'. A *withdrawal capture* is the reverse of this. A man standing

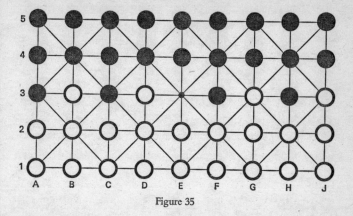

Figure 35

next to an enemy man on any line moves back one point in the reciprocal direction. The enemy man and any enemy men in unbroken sequence behind it on the same line are captured 'by withdrawal'. As in Draughts, capture is obligatory, including successive captures if any, but the player may choose between alternatives.

Thus in the starting position White, who begins, has the choice of four plays, all of them captures. These plays, and the men captured by them, are: 1. f2–e3 (d4, c5); 2. e2–e3 (e4, e5); 3. d2–e3 (f4, g5) and 4. d3–e3 (capture *either* f3 by approach *or* c3 by withdrawal).

There are a few other rules. Only one man may be moved on a turn. On the first move by each player only one capture may be made. Every move in a *sequence* (a succession of two or more captures) must be along a new line: a player cannot after a capture retrace his move to make a second capture. either immediately or after succeeding captures in the same sequence. A game ends when one player loses all his pieces.

In the second game between the same players a *vela partie* is played. In this, the loser of the preceding game takes White and Black must, on successive plays, sacrifice 17 of his men. On each move White takes only the one man he approaches or withdraws from and not any other men on the same line. Only on his 17th move may Black capture; thereafter the game is played in the normal way. White's advantage is not as staggering as it looks but should still be decisive. After a *vela* game, a normal game is played; thereafter *vela* and normal games alternate.

Strategy

The game has two main phases, the opening, when men are massacred in decimating sequences, and the closing, where a few men face each other across open space. Here is the opening of a typical game. 1. e2–e3 (e4, e5); f4–e5 (g3, h2, j1). 2. h1–h2 (h3, h4, h5); g5–f4 (e3, d2, c1) f4–g3 (h2) g3–h4 (f2, e1) h4–g5 (j3). 3. d3–e3 (c3) e3–e4 (e5) e4–f4 (d4, c4, b4, a4) f4–e3 (g5) e3–d4 (c5) d4–d3 (d5) and now White cannot again play d3–e3, so his turn ends; he has apparently gained a handsome bag of nine men, but his position is now critical; f3–e3 (d3) e3–f2 (g1) f2–e2 (g2) e2–d2 (c2, b2, a2) d2–d3 (d1) d3–c3 (b3) c3–b2 (a1) b2–b3 (b1) and Black must win despite the impending loss of his men on j4, j5 (Figure 36).

It is important to appreciate the peculiarities of the board. A man on any of 16 of the 24 perimeter points has a maximum of three moves at his disposal; on the remaining 8 points, however, he has a maxi-

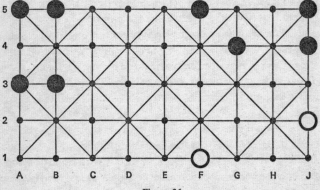

Figure 36

mum of five. Of the 21 internal points, 11 have eight connections each and the other 10 only four.

Consider a black man on f1, one of the weak perimeter points. In this position, a white man on any of the nine points d2, d3, d4, e4, f4, g4, h4, h3, h2 has only to move to e3 or g3, as appropriate, to trap the black man. White is now threatening to move f2, when the black man falls.

The openings have not been analysed, but experience with the *vela* game suggests that position is more important than material, since a good position will lead to the win of material and perhaps the game.

Notice that the starting position is asymmetric. There are a total of 17 different Black responses to White's opening play. After White's second turn, about 100 different arrangements are possible and after Black's second turn these have increased to perhaps 1,500, which gives an idea of the scope of the play.

In terms of the highest number of prisoners taken on the second move, White's most promising openings seem to be 1. d2–e3 (f4, g5) and 1. d3–e3 (f3), but one then has to ask how many of the resulting positions are favourable to Black – a happy problem for a computer but not for a human being.

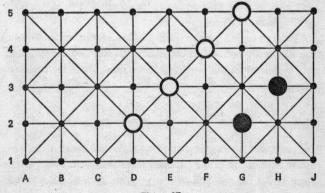

Figure 37

Draws are theoretically common, since an advantage of one man is often not enough to force the win. Figure 37 shows a favourable position for White (to play), who has four men against two. White goes here d2–e1 and Black is in *zugzwang*. Notice that all the white men are a Knight's move removed from one or both of the black men – an ideal deployment for the attacker.

The danger of the point with only four connections is demonstrated economically in Figure 38. White has only two men to one but the

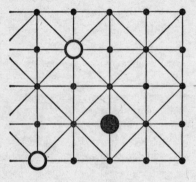

Figure 38

black man is on the weak point and has nowhere to go. Again notice the Knight-move separations.

A good general rule for the ending is that it is preferable to move a man diagonally rather than orthogonally, except on the perimeter, since in this way it will keep maximum flexibility as it travels only through points having eight connections.

Variants

One researcher has suggested allowing a man to capture along a line used in the same sequence provided that the move is in the reverse direction, but this does not seem to be in the spirit of the game and, more important, does not appear to improve the strategy.

Boards of different sizes with different starting arrangements are of course possible, but one would need a good reason for change and I know of none.

• FOOTSTEPS •

- A psychological game
- Pencil and paper
- Five minutes
- A little game of surprising subtlety

Background

This simple-to-play psychological game combines mind-reading with bluff, mental arithmetic and just a little luck. A proprietary version is marketed as Quo Vadis (Invicta).

Play

The 'board' consists of seven circles or marks in a straight line, spaced so that each circle is large enough to accommodate a small token. A line is drawn through the central circle. The three circles on each side of it belong to the respective players (see Figure 39).

Figure 39

Each player starts with 50 points. On each turn, both players write down the number of points that they wish to spend. The minimum allowed is 1. Numbers are then compared and the player with the larger number advances the token, which is placed at the start of each game in the central circle, one space into his opponent's territory. If the numbers are equal, the token is not moved. Both players now deduct the points they have used from their allocation of 50 to give their remaining total of points, and the next turn starts. The object of the game is to get the token on to your opponent's end circle; or, put another way, to win three more turns than your opponent. If one player uses up all his points, the other can have successive plays. If both use up their allocations, the game can either be agreed drawn or a half-victory awarded to the player in whose territory the token does not lie. And that is all there is to the game – but don't underestimate it.

Strategy

The subtleties of Footsteps will not become apparent until you have played a few games. The ideal to be aimed at, of course, is to win each turn by a single point. To allow your opponent a big lead on points is to face certain loss. In the early stages a margin of 5 or 6 points is acceptable, but later this could be severe. An extreme case is where you have got the token to within one space of victory but have used up all your points. Your opponent, however, has 5 points left. Clearly he has only to play 1 point each turn to win.

Be frugal with your points until danger threatens. Consider the situation where the token is on the centre and you have each used 30 points. You decide to allocate 9 to your next turn (you wouldn't do this if you'd played the game twice!) and you find that your opponent has only allocated the minimum permissible of 1. Now you are two spaces from victory but your opponent has 19 points left to your 11. If you now play 6, for example, your opponent may again play 1, and although this puts you within a space of home, you have only 5 points left to your opponent's 18 – an unacceptable margin. Your opponent next plays 5 (in case you gambled all your remaining points) and thereafter will force a win by a series of low plays: remember that you are obliged to use at least 1 point on each turn. It will now be clear where the mind-reading comes in. Some people seem to have second sight at this game, particularly when playing with close friends or relatives.

Psychic players could claim that it is an advantage to let the opponent write his number down first. The way round this is to keep the action concealed with, say, a one-minute time limit per move.

Good advice for Poker is good advice for Footsteps: never play routinely. If you always play low your opponent can advance quickly by pitching a few points higher each time. If he reaches the penultimate space you are obliged to equal his point count, so it is better to stop him one space further back. But he may read your thinking on this and – well, as I said, the subtleties of the game will soon become apparent.

Variants

The seven-space board and the fifty-point allocation give a quick and balanced game, but you may prefer other parameters.

Incidentally, a couple of pocket calculators are a useful aid for Footsteps. Start with 50 on the display and at each turn compare negative inputs.

• GIN RUMMY •

- Card game
- Standard pack
- Forty-five minutes (game)
- The favourite American game

Background

Two-handed Gin Rummy is the most widely known and played of the large family of Rummy games, though not perhaps the best. Originally called Gin Poker and probably derived from the Mexican game Conquian, it reached its zenith of popularity in the 1940s.

Play

Cards rank from King down to Ace and are valued by pip count, with court cards counting ten and the Ace one. Suits are equal. The winner is the first to score 100 points.

Cards are dealt singly, 10 to each player; the pack then acts as stock, the top card being turned face up beside it. Players strive to make *sets* – either *sequences* of three or more cards of the same suit or *melds* of three or four cards of the same rank. Cards which are not part of sets are called 'deadwood'. When the deadwood of his hand totals 10 or less, a player may go out (*knock*).

At the start of play, the up-card may be taken into hand by the Non-dealer who discards to make a new up-card. If he does not want the up-card, the Dealer may take it and discard. If neither player wants it, Non-dealer takes the top card off the stock pile and discards face up on top of the first up-card. Play now alternates, with each player having a choice of the other's discard (top card of the up-pile) or the concealed card on top of stock. Players endeavour to improve their hands by making sets and by reducing the value of unmatched cards.

A player may only knock after he has picked up a card. He then lays his hand face up on the table and discards. Now the second player exposes his hand and *lays off* any deadwood that fits his opponent's sets.

The reason for reducing deadwood is that it counts against one. Scoring is simple: if declarer's penalty cards sum to less than those of his opponent after he has laid off any that he is able, then declarer wins by the difference of their scores. If declarer goes out without any unmatched cards, then he announces 'Gin' and scores his opponent's unmatched cards plus a bonus of 25. The second player may not lay off on a Gin call. If, however, the second player's deadwood equals or totals less than declarer's, whether or not cards were laid off, then the second player scores the difference between the two totals (if any) and earns a 25-point bonus. Sets do not score. The hand is now over and the deal changes.

Here is a simple example of scoring. Player *A* has:

Sets: ♣10 9 8 7♠4 ♦4 ♣4
Deadwood: ♦7

and knocks with a remainder of 7. Player *B* is fortunate to have:

Set: ♠Q ♥Q ♣Q
Deadwood: ♣J 6 5 ♥5 4

and can lay off the Five, Six and Jack of Clubs on *A*'s sequence and the Four of Hearts on *A*'s Fours, leaving him with a penalty score of only 5. This is 2 less than *A*'s total, so *B* scores $2 + 25 = 27$ points on this hand.

The first player to reach or pass 100 is the winner. He collects 100 extra points for this and doubles his new total if his opponent has failed to score. Both players score 25 points for every *box* (or deal) won and these are added to their respective scores. If stakes are played for – which is usual, for Gin is a gambling game – then settlement is now made.

It is customary that the last two cards of a stock pile are not used. If a hand reaches this point with neither player having knocked, the deal is abandoned as a draw.

Strategy

There are two major factors to be considered: the opponent's hand and the laws of probability. A good Gin player quickly gets a feel for his opponent's holdings, or at least what cards he wants. Every discard has a message. Some are easy to read: for example, if your opponent discards a Jack and later picks up a Jack that you discarded, he most probably wants it for a sequence. Memory is a great asset at Gin, for discards are quickly buried. If you have a card you know your opponent wants, hold it as your final discard on knocking. When faced with a decision on what to throw out, consider the probability of getting the card(s) you want. If a desired card has a high point value, for example, the chance of your opponent discarding it is increased.

Generally it is good to knock early, but sometimes it may pay you not to declare but to go for Gin instead, with the alternative hope that your opponent will knock and you will under-score him.

High scores are made by knocking early; for this reason do not hold on to unmatched cards for too long, unless you believe your opponent needs them or you will be able to lay them off on his sets if necessary. Go for Gin only when the odds look good: when, for example, your deadwood is a single card and play has just started.

A few statistics will help. The average hand of Gin is eight to nine turns (not too long to remember those discards!). After the first pick-up, it is even chances that one player holds a set. When you make your first discard, the odds against completing a set for your opponent are:

King or Ace: 5–1 against
Queen or Two: 4–1 against
Any other card: 7–2 against

The middle-value cards are the most useful, as they can make sequences up and down.

Variants

There are many variants. Bonus scores tend to vary. For example, a *shut-out* or *Schneider* (game reached without the second player scoring) sometimes earns but 25 points – fairer, perhaps, than the vindictive doubled score. In Oklahoma Gin, in which game is often 150 points, all scores and bonuses are doubled if the dealer's up-card is a Spade. It's a variant for gamblers.

• GO •

- Abstract boardgame
- Go board and stones
- One hour upwards
- An absorbing but demanding game

Background

Go comes from China where it is known as Weiqi (literally 'surrounding Chess'). Its origins go back nearly three thousand years, but the game can have changed very little through its long history. In the East, Go is the game of the educated as Xiangqi and Shogi are the games of the people. Nevertheless it has an enormous following, particularly in Japan, where centuries of official patronage under the Shogunate created a foundation for the present-day army of experts, many of them professionals, who have reached degrees of skill that parallel those of the chess grandmasters of the West.

Go undoubtedly ranks with the world's best games and has great intellectual appeal. In recent years it has attracted interest in the West but has still to gather a universal following. There is a large literature, increasingly becoming available in English.

It is necessary, to understand Go, to abandon the western concepts inherent in games like Chess. Here is a game with few and simple rules yet a profound strategy; a wargame, at least in the abstract, that has no movement, no prime objectives, no front lines and no leaders and where tactical success can lead to strategical débâcle; a game that can sometimes even throw up situations that seem not to be covered by the rules. A game, in compass, that has none of the familiar certitudes to which we are conditioned.

Play

The board is marked out with a regular lattice of 19 × 19 lines. Nine points, known as star points, are marked for use in handicap games (Figure 40). Each player has a bowl of counters, called stones, one

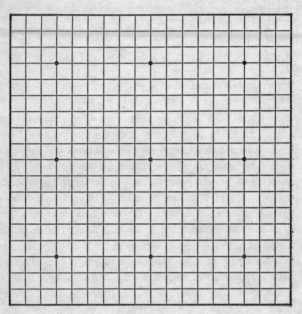

Figure 40

player black, the other white. There are 181 black stones and 180 white stones equivalent in total to the number of intersections on the board, but the numbers are not significant: they are enough for their purpose.

The game starts with the board empty. Play is on the intersections. Black starts; each player in turn places one of his stones on any vacant intersection (often called a point). Stones once placed are never moved. The object of the game is to enclose territory (vacant points).

Stones may be captured in the process. The game ends when neither player can make a useful move, because all available territory has been secured. The winner is the player with most territory in his possession after deduction of stones taken prisoner.

There are two basic principles, both easy to grasp.

Territory – a single point or perhaps 100 points – belongs to the player whose stones totally surround it. The board edge may be used as part of the perimeter so fewer stones are required to enclose a given area in the corners and along the sides of the board than in the centre.

Two or more stones that occupy adjacent points or a series of adjacent points are called a group or army. Figure 41 shows two rival

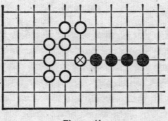

Figure 41

armies and also a single white stone (marked X) which is not strictly part of the white army since it is not directly linked to any stone in it.

A single stone or a group is captured when all adjacent points, including any internal points in the case of a large group, are occupied by hostile stones. The process is one of suffocation and a vacant intersection adjacent to a stone or group is sometimes appropriately called a breathing space (*me* in Japanese). A stone has two adjacent points in the corner, three on the edge and four elsewhere on the board. The number of adjacent points to a group will depend on its size and configuration.

In Figure 42(a) the surrounded black group has only one remaining breathing space. White makes his next play there (42(b)) and the whole group is captured. Captured men are at once removed from the board (42(c)) and are kept by the captor for accounting at the end of the game.

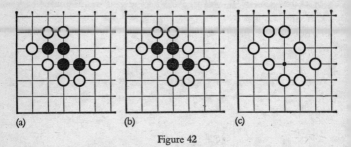

(a)   (b)   (c)

Figure 42

It is a rule of Go that no man may be placed on a point that is surrounded by enemy stones nor on the last remaining breathing space of a friendly group *unless* such a play simultaneously effects a capture. Consider Figure 43. White may legally (though not wisely!) play at *A* in (a) because his group would still have one breathing space left. A White play at *A* in 43(b) would however be suicide and therefore illegal. In 43(c), a White play at *A* would be legal because, although the point is surrounded by enemy stones, the three black stones on the left would simultaneously be surrounded and taken prisoner. The position in 43(d) would be the outcome. Notice that the capturing stone has, as a result of the capture, acquired a breathing space.

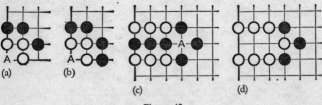

(a)   (b)   (c)   (d)

Figure 43

The doubt as to who is encircling whom, particularly where stones are widely spread, is often a problem for the beginner.

It will now be clear that control of territory can only be achieved by a wall of stones that is invulnerable to capture. Similarly, a territory cannot be effectively disputed by occupation where the attacking forces are vulnerable to capture. Which takes us to the heart of the game structure: how immunity from capture can be gained.

Look now at Figure 44. Black's territory consists of two separate intersections. White cannot play into both at once and a play into one would not result in a capture and so would be illegal. The black group is invulnerable. Unless Black were so stupid as to fill one of these points himself, he has secured two indisputable points of territory.

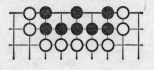

Figure 44

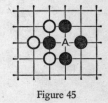

Figure 45

Now we have a clear guide. Stones that form part of a group that has two or more secure breathing spaces – points that an enemy stone cannot occupy without committing suicide – are immune from capture. The smallest possible live group consists of six stones.

One of the few rules of Go concerns the situation shown in Figure 45. If White plays at A and captures the black stone on the left, Black could in theory recapture the white stone and play might continue in this wise indefinitely. The situation is known as *ko*, and the rule of *ko* states that if a single stone is captured, the second player cannot take the capturing stone until he has made at least one move elsewhere. Notice that *ko* only applies to a single stone. If more than one stone is captured on a turn the situation cannot repeat itself.

Another situation which sometimes arises is illustrated in Figure 46. The 5-stone white and black groups in the centre assist in the

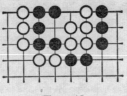

Figure 46

encirclement of each other and share two breathing spaces. If either side occupies one, the second side will occupy the other and capture 6 stones. This is a stalemate situation known as *seki*. Neither side will play here and the two points of territory belong to neither player.

At the end of the game it is the practice to use prisoners to fill in territory (white in white, black in black) and then to rearrange configurations to facilitate counting. Between well-matched players the winning margin will be only a few points.

Go is favoured with a handicap system that is close to perfection. It allows players of varying strengths to play on equal terms without – and this is where it differs from systems in most other games – distorting the strategy.

The weaker player takes Black and places between two and nine stones on the board before play begins. Stones must be placed on prescribed points of strategical significance – the star points, accentuated on the board.

Figure 47 illustrates the various handicaps (Black is assumed to be sitting at the bottom of the board):

2 stones: Black stones on 1 and 2
3 stones: 1, 2 and 3
4 stones: 1, 2, 3 and 4
5 stones: 1, 2, 3, 4 and 9
6 stones: 1, 2, 3, 4, 5 and 6
7 stones: 1, 2, 3, 4, 5, 6 and 9
8 stones: 1, 2, 3, 4, 5, 6, 7 and 8
9 stones: all nine points

It is common in Go, as in similar games, to use a letter/figure grid notation to record games and positions.

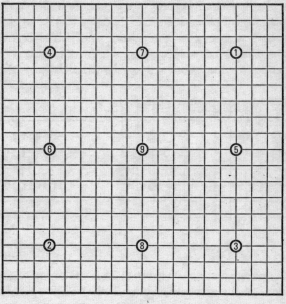

Figure 47

Strategy

Early play should be directed at sketching out potential territory by placing stones a few points apart. Only when a tactical challenge is threatened should defences be consolidated. A policy of establishing safe territory in the opening stages is disastrous, since such territory will necessarily be small and meanwhile your opponent will be laying claim to large areas that later may prove difficult to penetrate. In short, use your stones economically to serve in both attack and defence. If your opponent concentrates his play in an area, it is probably best to seek compensation elsewhere.

A primary principle is not to pursue the inevitable. If you have doomed an enemy group, do not hurry its demise: leave the position until the end when such situations are normally agreed and prisoners surrendered. Another example of this principle is illustrated in a tactical situation known as the *ladder*. In Figure 48(a) the white stone is trapped. A direct attempt to evacuate will fail. The sequence of play in (b) shows why: the white group is driven to the board edge to perish. Note that black 8 at 9 would have had the same effect.

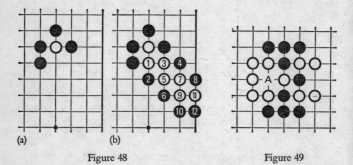

(a)   (b)   Figure 49

Figure 48

The sacrifice is a common feature of Go. It is often wise to give up a stone or two to retain the initiative. This is well exemplified in *ko* fights, another feature of the game. Consider Figure 49. A lot is at stake here, and it hinges on the *ko*. Black to move captures the single white stone with a play at *A*. White now cannot immediately recapture and if Black on his next play continues by filling the *ko*, he will consolidate his position and win much ground. So White must force Black to play elsewhere and he does this commonly by a sacrifice in another part of the board. If Black responds to the attack (because there is more at stake there than in the *ko*), White recaptures the single black stone and now it is Black who must seek compensation elsewhere or allow White to consolidate. Play can go backwards and forwards like this for many turns.

Opening plays in Go have been well studied. These are almost always confined to the corners of the board as it is easier to stake out territory there and form secure groups. Because of the board's symmetry this means that every game has four openings (*joseki*), not one. A *joseki* in one corner is as valid as a *joseki* in another, but because each corner influences by extension every other corner (though beginners have difficulty in appreciating this) it is usual to play a different *joseki* in each corner for positional balance. Play that involves linkage between corners – the board-wide opening strategy – is also studied and is known as *fuseki*.

Figure 50

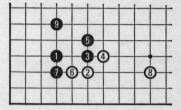

Figure 51

It is less important to know your openings than in Chess, where the consequences of weak play can be direful, but it is essential to grasp the principles of sound play, which include subtleties of extension and shape too involved to discuss here. It is broadly true that in a *joseki* one player controls the corner while the other seeks to contain him and in compensation develops strength down the sides and towards the centre. Two sample *joseki* are illustrated in Figures 50 and 51. If you play these through, move by move, you will discover, at least in general terms, the purpose of each play. You will see that neither side plays close to the edge of the board since little territory can be made there; nor too far from it, for it is hard to surround points away from the edges to begin with. Most opening play is centred around the third and fourth lines of the board.

This brief advice barely introduces the extraordinary tactical and strategical profundities of Go. If the game appeals to you, turn at once to a primer.

Variants

It is quite common for beginners to start with a quarter-size board, and this is recommended. Other variants are little more than curiosities.

• GOLOMB'S GAME •

- Abstract boardgame
- Set of pentominoes and board
- Fifteen minutes
- A contest of visual dexterity

Background

This game was invented by Solomon Golomb a quarter-century back. Pentominoes are well-known to mathematicians and, in a different form, to Go players concerned with forming eyes (the interrelationship of unlike games is always a pleasing discovery). Pentomino sets can be bought cheaply, but it is an easy matter to make your own out of card; use a chessboard as the playing area.

A set of pentominoes numbers 12 – all the different ways in which five identical squares can be joined regularly in one plane. The appeal of pentominoes lies in their number (tetrominoes total five, hexominoes thirty-five) – enough to both manage and perplex. Pentominoes, lettered for identification, are illustrated in Figure 52. (Golomb's notation is used; there are others.)

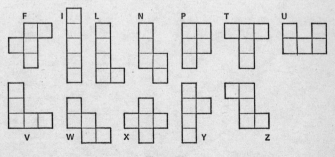

Figure 52

Play

The twelve pentominoes are between the players who take it in turns to put one on the board. The object is to leave your opponent without a move.

The minimum number of plays possible is five, for that is the number of selected pentominoes that can be placed so that none of the remaining seven can be played. At the other extreme, all twelve pentominoes can be placed – a pleasing array is shown in Figure 53.

| Figure 53 | Figure 54 |

The second possibility will never occur in practice, because, of course, the players are conspiring not to make the pentominoes fit together. An ordinary game will therefore take between about six and nine moves, and there will always be a winner. An end position is illustrated in Figure 54 – the last player has just placed one of the seven pentominoes and no further play is possible.

Strategy

This is hard to find, let alone define, but two precepts will help:

(1) If you are the first player, you will want the game to finish with an odd number of pieces on the board; if you are the second player,

an even number. Keep this in mind throughout so that at each move you can conjecturally leave space for the appropriate number of pieces – neither more nor less.

(2) Golomb recommends that if the position is unanalysable, complicate it. As the board fills, the mental task will diminish and precept (1) will become easier to apply. The last few plays should, of course, be completely foreseen.

The first few moves are often played, as David Parlett has observed, more with an eye to balance and symmetry than with any clear-cut objective. My own experience is that the seven-move game is the most common, if the pieces are spread, so perhaps the second player should aim to crowd just a little and to open up if the first player crowds. Again, this is a game which has been little explored.

• HEX •

- Path-forming game
- Pencil and paper
- Twenty minutes
- A modern classic

Background

Hex was invented by the Danish poet Piet Hein during the Second World War and has since inspired a number of structurally similar games, including Sid Sackson's Network and Alex Randolph's Twixt.

Hex is basically a race game with the novel feature that the players are following independent routes to mutually exclusive goals. A draw is not therefore possible, unless neither side tries to win.

Hex can be played with pencil and paper (isometric graph paper is suitable), on a board with counters or on a plastic-covered board using felt pens.

Play

The lozenge-shaped playing area is marked with a regular three-way grid, giving 121 intersections on which the game is played. This can be seen in Figure 55.

Each player adopts a pair of opposite board edges and the players take turns to occupy any vacant intersection using contrasting marks or colours. The object of the game is to link your pair of edges with a continuous chain. Men are considered to be connected when they occupy adjacent intersections. A corner intersection may be used as a baseline point by either player. The number of links in the chain is unimportant and the number of plays is limited only by the inter-sections available.

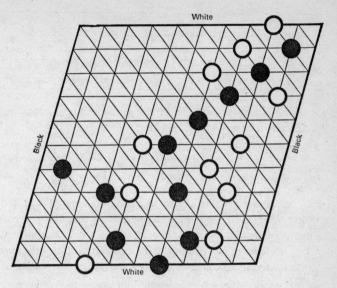

Figure 55

Figure 55 shows a win by Black using a simple technique. Although he has yet to establish any firm connection, he has two ways in which to link each pair of men. Whichever point White now attacks, Black will occupy the twin. White has no way through Black's embryo chain.

Strategy

It is known mathematically that the first player has a forced win, but a winning strategy has not, to my knowledge, been discovered. Some players redress (?) the bias by not allowing the first play to be made on the centre intersection. This is the key point, since it is the hub of the central area, where prospects for chain development are optimal.

Strategy is similar to that of Go. This can be briefly described as establishing a presence in as large an area as possible. This is done by prudent spacing of your points. Do not connect points unless it is essential to do so and then only when you have to – i.e. when under close attack. It is not necessary nor even desirable in your opening plays to space your men so that they can be considered safely connected (opposite sides of a parallelogram, as the black plays in Figure 55); these are 'small' plays that will allow your opponent to take a lot of ground. It is better to keep your men about three or four intersections apart, always provided there are no enemy points in the vicinity, in which case they will have to be closer together.

The first player has the initiative and should force the play. A viable strategy for the second player is to keep at a distance, roughly match the first player's deployment and hope for an opening. It is common for one player to make a series of forcing moves to each of which the second player has only one reply, but if the attack is halted, the game can quickly turn round.

Here is the score of a game that may give you a few ideas. Black opens. 1. E6, G7; 2. H4 (Black occupies the open area), G5 (Black was threatening to come here); 3. F3, F9 (White joins his 1 to the top edge, but the second player cannot afford himself this sort of luxury early in the game. He needed to play lower centre); 4. H2 (shutting White out from the lower edge), E4 (attempting to find a way through); 5. F5 (with the double threat of F4 and G4 – Black has succeeded in linking lines *E* and *H*. He can afford to attack directly because of White's weak third play), C7 (White is on the defensive but has faint hopes of running up the left-hand side); 6. D5 (reaching for the left edge. Notice that the promising-looking C4 with the double threat of D5 and E3 is nicely met by 6. . . . D4! This is a useful idea that comes up often: an intersection that is common to both threats is occupied – and both threats fail), B6; 7. C4 (and Black is through to the edge), K2 (otherwise Black wins at once by playing here); 8. J5, G4; 9. H3 and White resigns (see Figure 56).

Variants

Almost limitless. Many different sizes of board have been tried. A 7 × 7 is a good one to start on while 15 × 15 makes for a game of

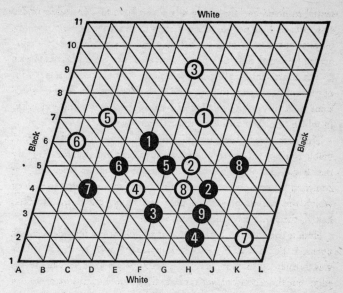

Figure 56

deep calculation. The larger the board, the less Black's opening advantage.

Between strong players meeting on equal terms, restrictions on the opening play can be extended. Two handicaps that have been used forbid this play to be on:

(1) The centre, plus the six adjacent points on the central hexagon
(2) The short diagonal A11–L1.

Boards of different shapes offer interesting possibilities. One is a triangular board, on which players try to form a chain that touches all three sides.

• HEXAGONAL CHESS •

- Proprietary chess game
- Hexagonal Chess set and board
- One hour
- Novel strategies with traditional pieces

Background

Hexagonal Chess is the invention of Wladyslaw Glinski. Although first launched in Britain (in 1973), the game has attracted a greater following in his native Poland.

The inventor is at pains to stress that Hexagonal Chess (Hex Chess for short) is not a chess variant but a game in its own right; even so, the close affinity of the two games cannot be escaped.

Hex Chess has been brilliantly and vigorously promoted and is now played in a number of countries. However, it has failed to make a significant impact, in part, perhaps, because of marketing problems, in part, I feel, because it looks complicated (the eye has some difficulty travelling along the lines of contrasting hexagons) and in part because it really is in competition with Chess even if the inventor would wish otherwise.

A number of championships and international team matches have been organized.

Play

The game is played on a board composed of 91 regular hexagons (cells) of three alternating colours. Each player has an army of 18 men as in Chess but with the addition of an extra Bishop and Pawn. The starting position is shown in Figure 57.

White begins and the object, as in Chess, is to capture (checkmate) the opponent's King.

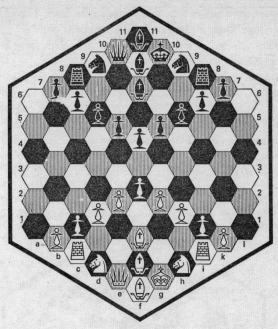

Figure 57

Vertical rows of hexes are called *files* and rows of hexes that run diagonally are referred to as *oblique files*. On all files the hexes are of alternating colours. The longest files have 11 hexes. *Lines* consist of unconnected hexes of the same colour and are either *cross lines*, which run horizontally across the board, or *oblique lines*, which run at a slant. The longest lines have 6 hexes.

The movements of the various men parallel those in Chess but are modified by the nature of the board. Capture is by displacement.

The *Rook* moves in straight lines along files over any number of hexes that may be vacant. *Bishops* move on lines in a like manner. A Bishop cannot leave the hexes of the colour on which it stands in the starting position. A *Queen* moves as Rook and Bishop combined.

The *King* can move to any adjacent hex and to any of the hexes one removed from him of the colour on which he stands. Except at the edges of the board a King attacks 12 hexes.

The *Knight* moves directly to any hex three steps away from it except a hex of the colour on which it stands.

Pawns have the same properties as those in Chess; they move only straight forward along the files one cell at a time with the option of moving two hexes on their first move. Pawns capture one cell forward along the oblique files and on reaching the end of the board promote as in Chess. Notice that despite the V-shaped array of the Pawns in the starting position each has the same distance to travel to promotion. If a Pawn makes a capture which leaves it on its initial oblique file (i.e. a capture towards the centre of the board) it retains

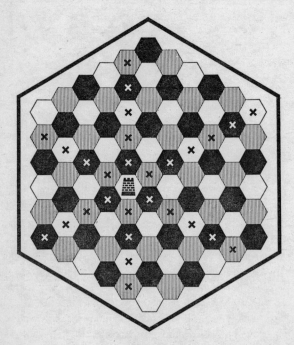

Figure 58

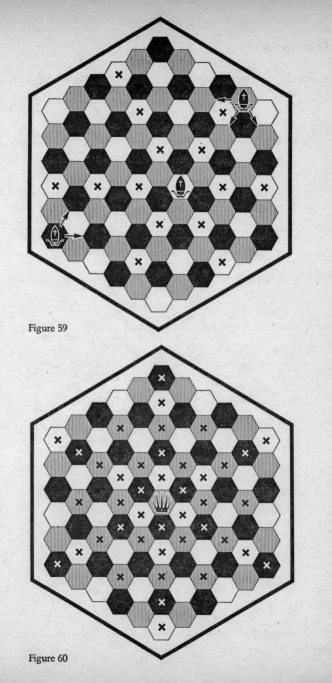

Figure 59

Figure 60

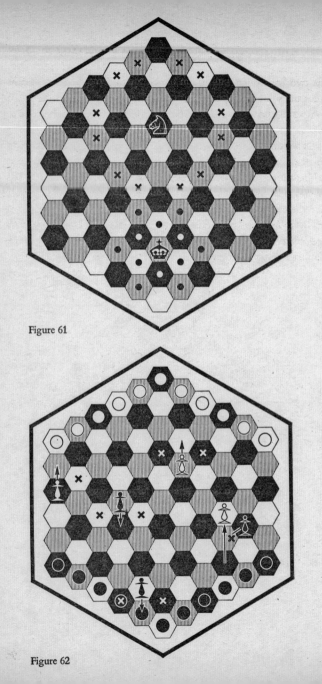

Figure 61

Figure 62

the two-hex option. An outside Pawn can in theory make four captures and subsequently take the two-hex option, but the centre Pawn forgoes this privilege as any initial capture will take it one step nearer promotion.

En passant is as in Chess and there is no castling. Stalemate is a win for the player who gives it. Perpetual check is a draw.

The moves of the various men are shown in Figures 58–62. The crosses in Figure 62 indicate squares on which captures could be made and the circles mark the promotion squares.

Check and checkmate pose no special problems in Hex Chess; they are governed by rules analogous to those in Chess (q.v.). In Figure 63 the black King is mated.

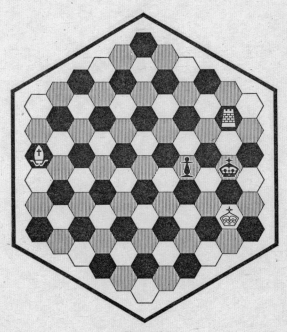

Figure 63

Strategy

Again it is hard to escape comparison with Chess. In Hex Chess the relative powers of the pieces are different. The Rook is more powerful: at the centre of the board it commands 30 cells though less near the edges. The King and Knight have increased powers too and the Queen is a shade stronger. The power of the Bishop is little changed. The only man to suffer is the Pawn; its scope is not increased and its powers on the larger board are correspondingly reduced.

The opening, middle game and end game form distinct phases and the strategy of Hex Chess varies little from that of Chess. The old dicta are valid: strive for development, space, time. Seek command of the centre and keep your King protected. Several openings have

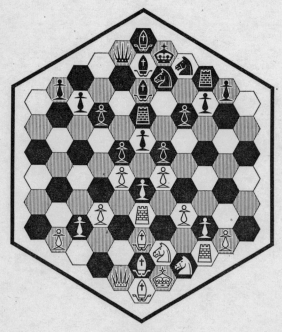

Figure 64

been developed but have been little tested. Because of its novelty the game is mercifully free of the minutiae of chess opening analysis. Notice that every man is free to move from the outset. Here are the first moves of the Rook's Opening – there's nothing like it in Chess! 1. e4–e5, e7–e6; 2. g4–g5, g7–g6; 3. Nd1–g2, Nd9–g9; 4. Rc1–f4, Rc8–f8 and Figure 64 is reached.

Sadists will appreciate the 'Fool's Mate' – one of several games of the shortest possible length. 1. i2–i4, Kg10–h8; 2. Qe1–b4, Kh8–i6; 3. Qb4–k4 mate.

• LABYRINTH •

- Maze game
- Pencil and paper
- Thirty minutes
- An imaginative but undemanding game

Background

Man's preoccupation with the labyrinth, apparent in the legend of Theseus, recurs in unnumbered ways through history. Recently there has developed an intelligent interest in mazes that has raised to an art-form what a decade ago belonged exclusively to children's puzzles. Several games marketed in the past few years have made use of the theme, the best-known being the fantasy 'free' game, Dungeons and Dragons, whose possibilities are only circumscribed by the players' imaginations. Labyrinth is less ambitious: it is an uncomplicated pencil-and-paper maze game, not the best game in this selection, but one in which there is more scope for skill and psychology than is at once apparent.

Play

Both players first draw two 6 × 6 grids and enter some convenient notation for square reference (say, files A–F and ranks 1–6). On one of his two grids each player marks a 'start' square and a 'finish' square, which may be anywhere on the grid, and then creates a maze by thickening the sides of squares to form walls, in the manner of the barred-line crossword. No more than three walls may be linked in a continuous line, whether straight or stepped, and it is not permitted to isolate any square or squares. Thus it must be possible, following an orthogonal path, to reach every square on the grid.

The number of walls that may be built is agreed beforehand – 20 is a good number. An example of a completed grid is shown in Figure 65. Notice that the linked walls round F2, though five in number, do not extend to more than three in a continuous line in any direction and are therefore legal. The object of this rule is to avoid a maze like that in Figure 66. Here, chance is in command. If the player steps on the right path he is led home by his nose; if he fails to find the door he is likely to be wandering around for some while.

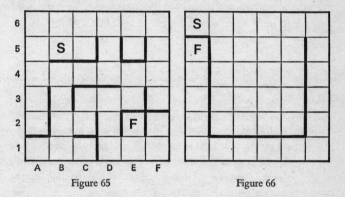

Figure 65   Figure 66

Each player now has a maze, which his opponent will attempt to negotiate, and a blank grid, which the player will use to chart his own progress through his opponent's maze. Both players announce the start and finish squares of their respective mazes and annotate the blank grids as appropriate.

Play alternates. A player on his turn first asks if a wall exists between two adjacent squares. The answer must be truthful. For example, in Figure 65:

'B5/C5?' ('Is there a wall between B5 and C5?')

'No.'

The same player now attempts a move, which may be of one, two or three squares in length:

'Move B5–C5?'

'Yes.'

The player now moves to C5 (he may not opt not to do so) and his turn ends. Instead of moving safely, he might have gambled on a longer move:

'Move B5–C5–D5–D4?'

'No.'

In that case, the player does not move and his turn ends. Notice that it would have been ambiguous merely to have asked to move from D5 to D4 as there is more than one way of doing this.

Play continues in this fashion, the two questions being asked in the same order on each turn, until one player wins by reaching the finish first.

Strategy

There are two phases to consider: constructing the maze and un-ravelling the opponent's maze.

A devious mind, I imagine, is a help in devising a devious maze. If you have not got a devious mind, here are a few ideas. A start and/or finish square boxed in on three sides should buy a little time. Clear ways, unless they go nowhere, should be avoided, as they increase the chance of your opponent making ground with a multiple move. There is no logic in this, but a lot of people seem to think in terms of straight lines. It is not always wise to construct a tortuous path, for if your opponent starts along it he may have few opportunities to go astray. By contrast, small deserts of unwalled squares where he can move freely can be rewarding.

Negotiating a maze calls for calculation, divination and luck in good measure. If your opponent is nearing his goal you will have to gamble on long moves; otherwise a combination of the bold and the cautious is probably best.

Variants

Different size grids offer different length games; other (or no) limits on wall-building are alternatives. The questions can be varied too.

For example, the player could be allowed to choose the order in which to put his questions, ask two questions of the same type or even ask different kinds of question ('How many walls has F4?').

A variant popular in France uses a 10 × 10 grid, up to forty walls and start and finish squares in opposite corners. A player advances orthogonally one square at a time until stopped by a wall. On his next turn the player may start from any square (including the start square, if appropriate) traversed on his previous turn; he is not obliged to start from the last square of that turn.

• LASCA •

- Abstract boardgame
- Lasca board and men
- One hour
- An almost unknown septuagenarian game

Background

Lasca, sometimes known as Laska, was invented by Dr Emanuel Lasker, a former world chess champion and man of genius who was interested in boardgames generally. The game is seventy years old but has never been popularized.

Reversi, certainly a no better game, was successfully refurbished for the mass market. Why not Lasca?

The game's affinity with Draughts will be apparent, but the strategy is quite different. Sets are easy to come by in Lasker's native Germany but are not so easily found elsewhere. Fortunately a draughts set can readily be adapted.

Play

Each side has eleven men similar to draughtsmen in contrasting colours. They carry a mark on one side to signify promotion.

The board is a 7 × 7 chequerboard with the four corner squares white. Play is on the white squares only and the men are arranged in the starting position across the first three ranks of each side (Figure 67). The board can also be presented as 25 contiguous circles in the same arrangement. White moves first and play alternates.

All men start as *Soldiers*, plain side uppermost. The Soldier moves exactly like a draughtsman, diagonally forward only. Also like a draughtsman, he is promoted (to an *Officer*) if he reaches the end rank;

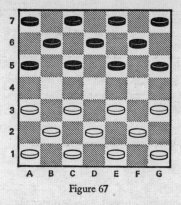

Figure 67

he may then move backwards as well as forwards, still diagonally and one square at a time, just like a King in Draughts. A Soldier is turned over on promotion to display his rank.

Officers and Soldiers also capture in the manner of draughtsmen by leaping over an adjacent opponent to an empty square immediately beyond. Capturing is compulsory, but the player has the choice if more than one capture is available.

If, after a capture, a second capture can be made with the same man, this must be done; so must any third or subsequent capture. A Soldier who is promoted on making a capture may not, however, continue to capture as an Officer on that move. The move is ended by promotion.

All this, of course, is still exactly like Draughts, but now comes the difference. A captured man is not removed from the board but is picked up by his captor to become the bottom piece of a column of two. The captor is now referred to as a *Commander* because, if you'll allow the pun, he has men under him. No special powers are conferred on the Commander – he remains, for the purpose of movement and capture, either a Soldier or an Officer. However, wherever a Commander moves – allow another pun – his column goes with him. A simple capture by a white Soldier is shown in Figure 68 (a and b).

Columns increase in size as further captures are made, captured men being placed beneath the pile each time.

When a column, however high, is jumped, the capturing man only removes the Commander, leaving behind a pile reduced by one with a new Commander. An example of this is shown in Figure 69. The white column captures the black Commander and effectively promotes the white man beneath to be the new Commander of the column. This is a double gain for White since he has acquired a piece and at the same time Black has lost one.

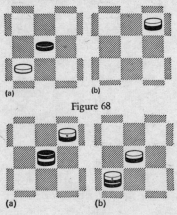

(a)　　　　　　(b)

Figure 68

(a)　　　　　　(b)

Figure 69

It is not permissible for a piece to attack the same piece twice in a single move; thus an Officer cannot jump back and forth over a column picking up its Commander each time. Notice that an Officer, once promoted, cannot be deprived of his rank however long he languishes at the foot of an enemy column. Notice also that all twenty-two men remain on the board throughout the game.

The game ends when one player cannot make a legal move. This can come about in two ways: either all the pieces are commanded by his opponent or he is unable to move because he is blocked; in both cases he loses. It is in Lasca's favour that a drawn game is impossible unless the players succumb to tedium – and Lasca is far from being a tedious game.

Strategy

Strategy cannot be considered without first appreciating tactics. A few examples of tactical play will go far towards an understanding of the game.

In theory it is possible for all the men to end up in a single column. This does not happen, but columns comprising six or seven men often arise.

Figure 70 shows two columns both headed by white Commanders. The left-hand column is weak because if the Commander is captured it reverts to being a black column. The right-hand column is strong, since it will remain a white piece even if it is jumped three times. From White's viewpoint, the left-hand column is valuable because it ties up four black men, over a third of the enemy force. White will want to preserve this column and because of its weakness will need to protect it well. The right-hand column, by contrast, may also be considered weak, in that a number of white men are demonstrating muscle but are not using it. This column should now, in view of its near-immunity, be used aggressively to capture enemy men. This is a paradox of Lasca – strong columns are often weak and weak columns are often strong.

From this simple example, it will be obvious that the strength and value of a column depend on its composition. Since a column with a single control is always vulnerable it will be the object of attack. In Figure 71 White sacrifices with D2–C3; Black takes D4–B2 and White recaptures A1–C3. Instead of two Soldiers, White now has a strong three-man column and a second column with a black prisoner.

Figure 70

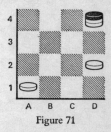

Figure 71

Two columns can successively attack each other where they can both move in the same direction. If the board is clear down a diagonal, this can produce an amusing combination (see Figure 72a). White plays C1–B2, a temporary sacrifice for a long-term gain. Black must capture when White captures and so on until the position in 72b is reached. White has captured both black Officers, reversing the column at A1 in Figure 72a.

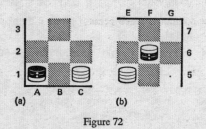

Figure 72

A noticeable feature of Lasca is the lack of space to manoeuvre – only 25 squares as against 32 in Draughts. This means that blocked positions and in particular *zugzwang* often arise. Space to move and control of the centre are as important in Lasca as in Draughts and Chess. One interesting feature of Lasca that is not found in the other games is the occasional sudden reversal of fortune. A single capture can release a powerful column to bring the losing player back into the game.

A final point to observe, and one on which many of the subtler strategies are based, is that you can only add enemy men to your columns. The only way in which you can get strong columns is to allow your opponent to build them and then to remove his Commander. In other words, we have another paradox: you must give up men to build a strong column.

• THE L GAME •

- Abstract boardgame
- L-game set
- Three minutes upwards
- A quick and uncomplicated game

Background

This ingenious little modern game has an interesting origin. Its inventor, Edward de Bono, perhaps better known for his work and books on lateral thinking, was sitting next to the mathematician Professor Littlewood at a dinner. Talk got round to games and the two agreed that Chess achieved difficulty through complexity and that this was aesthetically unsatisfactory. As a challenge, de Bono set out to design a simple game that could still be played with skill. The L game was the result.

Play

The board is marked with sixteen small squares (4 × 4). Each player has a flat L-shaped piece that exactly covers four squares. In addition, there are two circular neutral pieces slightly smaller than square width. The starting position is shown in Figure 73.

Figure 73

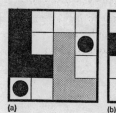

(a)   (b)

Figure 74

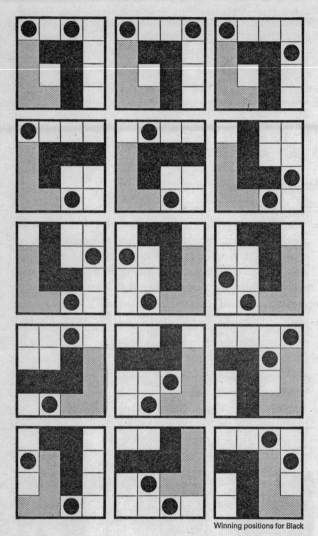

Winning positions for Black

Figure 75

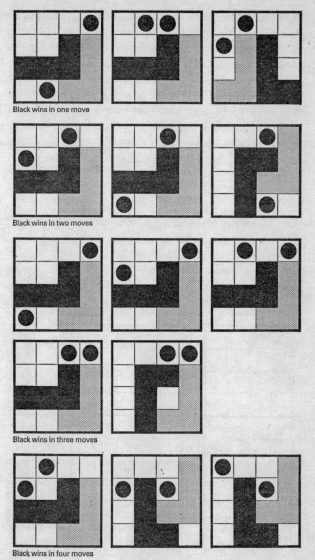

Black wins in one move

Black wins in two moves

Black wins in three moves

Black wins in four moves

Figure 76

Play alternates. In the basic (or 'classic') game, each player on his turn picks up his L-piece and replaces it on the board to cover four empty squares, at least one of which must be different from the four squares just vacated. The piece may be turned round or over if desired. After the L-piece has been re-sited the player may optionally move one (but not both) of the neutral pieces to any vacant square. The object of the game is to leave your opponent without a legal move for his L piece. Figure 74 shows the close of a game. Black is to play in 74(a). He repositions his piece and then a neutral man as shown in 74(b). Now White is unable to move and so loses.

Strategy

The L game is amenable to precise analysis, but so arguably is Chess, and the game is not spoilt by this.

There are a total of 2,296 distinct board positions (18,368 if rotations and reflections are included). There are 15 basic winning positions – that is, where one L-piece is unable to move. There are 10 different arrangements of the two L-pieces, 4 of them allowing

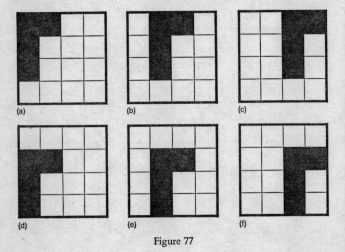

(a)　　　　　　　　(b)　　　　　　　　(c)

(d)　　　　　　　　(e)　　　　　　　　(f)

Figure 77

alternative placings of the neutral piece(s). These 15 positions are illustrated in Figure 75.

A further 14 positions are known to be wins (Figure 76) and it is also apparently possible to force a win after five moves, which is claimed to be the maximum, but there is probably scope for more research.

Analysis of these winning positions is revealing. First, consider the six fundamental ways, each a translation of another, in which an L-piece can be placed on the board (Figure 77). Any other position is a rotation or reflection of one of these six positions. You will see that in every winning position the loser has his L-piece covering a corner square – that is, it is in one or other of the fundamental positions 77a, 77c or 77d. You will also see that in 22 of the 29 winning positions the trapped piece is in position 77a, and that in all but one of the 29 cases the winner's L-piece is occupying one or other of the three fundamental positions where the piece does not cover a corner square (77b, 77e, 77f).

Now a sound strategy becomes apparent:

(1) Do not cover a corner square with your L-piece and, in particular, do not play your piece where it has total contact with the board edge (77a).
(2) Use the neutral pieces to stop your opponent occupying one of the safe positions.

A more positive strategy will require memory of the known winning positions and the ability to plan ahead. Planning requires spatial perception, however, and most people find this difficult (I do). Try working out, without moving the pieces, how to force the win in the three-move examples given (Figure 76) and you will see what I mean.

One may conclude that the basic game should always be drawn between good players (but again, that is theoretically true of Chess too!).

Variants

Fortunately, there are a number of good variants of the L game, some suggested by the inventor, that rescue it from rote play. In the scoring game, the four squares in one corner of the board are marked. The game proceeds exactly as in the basic game except that a player scores a point every time he covers a marked square. Thus, if position 77a is open, three points may be gained at the risk that the piece may get trapped. Five points are earned for blocking the L-piece (I would award more); the starting position is then resumed. The winner is the first to reach an agreed total or who has the most points at an agreed time.

In another variant, play follows the basic game, except that the winner is the player who is able to place his L-piece in a position symmetrically equivalent to that of his opponent's. In this version, only one position of the L-piece (Figure 77e) is safe and the neutrals are of greater importance.

Other variants may suggest themselves, perhaps using different shapes and boards (compare Golomb's game of Pentominoes), but the essence of the L game is its simplicity.

• MANCALA •

- A unique family of games
- Board and counters
- Thirty minutes
- A game for the mathematical

Background

Mancala is not a specific game but a large family of games that are found across most of Africa and the surrounding islands, parts of the Middle East and Asia. These games are characterized by a board containing a number of holes or cups, in which counters are distributed and redistributed in a succession of plays with the object of taking prisoners.

Mancala is very old: Mancala-type games were being played at least three thousand years ago. Little can have changed, because playing procedures and rules are uncomplicated.

About two hundred different regional Mancalas are known. The version described here is the West African Wari, chosen because it is one of the best-known and best of the two-player Mancalas.

Equipment can be basic. In Africa, commonly holes are just scooped in the ground, with seeds, shells or pebbles for counters. A permanent board is carved of wood, but a satisfactory set can easily be assembled from materials at hand.

Play

A Wari board has fourteen cups or shallow holes: two parallel rows of six with a large hole at each end (Figure 78). Players have the board lengthways between them. Before play starts the board is dressed by distributing four stones or similar small and easy-to-handle objects

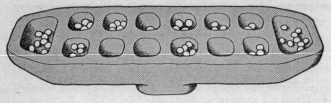

Figure 78

(dried peas or beans are ideal) into each of the twelve small cups. The two large cups are for prisoners, one for each player.

One player starts by lifting all the stones from one of the cups on his side of the board and *sowing* or distributing them one at a time into successive cups, starting with the next cup anti-clockwise and continuing in this direction. For example, if White (it is convenient to call the players Black and White) first picked up the stones from his end cup, F, then he would drop them successively in cups f, e, d, c (see Figure 79). The second player now picks up all the stones from one of the cups on his side of the board and sows them anti-clockwise in the same manner. Play alternates like this until one player puts the last stone from one of his cups into one of his opponent's cups that has exactly one or two stones in it. These stones (now two or three as the case may be) are prisoners and are transferred to the player's storehouse (large hole). If the preceding cup also has precisely two or three stones in it these too are prisoners, and so on until a cup is

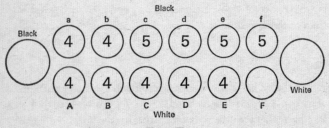

Figure 79

reached which has less than two or more than three stones in it or is on the player's side of the board, when the turn ceases.

A few rounds of a game will clarify this procedure. If we designate the cup emptied by its letter and indicate the number of stones in it as a check, the distribution of stones is straightforward. For example, E4 means that White has picked up the four stones in cup *E* and sown them in cups *F*, *f*, *e* and *d*. Remember that a player can only lift stones from a cup on his side of the board, that he must lift and distribute all the stones in the cup, and that prisoners may only be taken from opponent's cups. White starts this undistinguished but typical game: C4/b4; C1 (a play of D5, E5 or F5 would allow Black c5 winning two prisoners)/f5; B5/b1; D7/b1; C1/f2 (another play would have given White three stones with A6); D1/c6 (Black assures himself of two prisoners); C1/d7 (× 3, i.e. he removes 3 stones); C1/c1 (threatening b3); E8 (threatening A8)/d1; F8/b5 (× 2); A10/d2; C2/e10; B6 (now White must take prisoners)/f4; E4 (× 6 – cups *d* and *e*)/b4 (× 3) and Black eventually won (position at this stage is shown in Figure 80).

The game ends when the player whose move it is has no stones left to sow; his opponent then picks up any remaining on his side of the board and adds them to his prisoners. It sometimes happens, when there is only a stone or two left on each side, that neither player can make progress. In this event each player picks up the stones on his side of the board and the game is over. The player with the most prisoners is, of course, the winner.

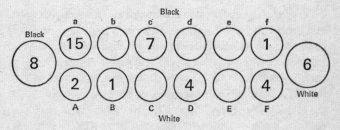

Figure 80

There are one or two other rules which may be considered optional (there is no Mancala authority to enforce them). If a cup is emptied that contains 12 or more stones, some players leave that cup empty; thus the 12th stone will be dropped in the same cup as the first stone and any additional stones in subsequent cups as usual. The second rule requires a player to leave at least one stone on his opponent's side of the board. Only when he is unable to do this does the game end.

Strategy

Mancala is a game entirely of skill – skill exercised solely in deciding which cup to empty at each turn. Logic dictates that there must always be a best move, or a choice of best moves, and there are at most six moves to choose from. However, the calculations necessary to reach the right decision each time may well be within the powers of a computer but hardly those of a mortal, unless there are only a few stones left on the board.

Tactical wrinkles are soon acquired. If one of your cups has only two stones in it, it is vulnerable to attack. The attack may be defeated by (1) emptying the cup, or (2) emptying a cup that will cause a stone to be added to the threatened cup, or (3) playing so as to add a stone to any of your opponent's cups that are threatening yours.

An empty cup is also vulnerable, but less so. A stone may be dropped in it so that on the next turn the cup can be taken – provided that there are two cups with the right number of stones in them to take advantage of the situation.

The ideal is to build up your cups so that every one of your opponent's cups is threatened. This will rarely be possible, but you should be able to keep several of your opponent's cups under attack. Avoid where you can the situation where the number of stones in any of your cups will, if distributed, cause the last stone to be sown on your side of the board, since such a cup poses no threat.

The rule that you must, if possible, leave at least one stone on your opponent's side of the board may seem benevolent (it prevents a strategy which tries directly to deprive your opponent of a move and thus favours the player who is losing), bu', on examination, it indicates a cunning end-game strategy: contrive to get all the stones on your side of the board and distributed such that no cup has enough stones to feed the opponent's side. A maximum of 15 stones can be so arranged, but this is remarkably unlikely to happen.

The easiest way to win prisoners is by setting up a multiple threat. As in most games, you can op' to play adventurously, with correspondingly high rewards or penalties, or cautiously, giving priority to defence.

Variants

Instead of both players picking up the stones on their respective sides of the board, when no progress can be made, it is better to divide the stones equally (casting out an odd one), since the timing of the pick-up may favour one player and disadvantage the other.

Other variants are different games with, in particular, different numbers of stones sown in different ways. A book is waiting to be written about them.

• MASTER MIND •

- Code-breaking game
- Boxed proprietary game (Invicta Plastics)
- Ten minutes (pair of games)
- Deduction at the double

Background

Master Mind is the proprietary version of an old code-breaking game known to children as Bulls and Cows. In Bulls and Cows a short series of figures (or letters) is written down by one player (the Code-maker) and the second player (the Code-breaker) has to discover them, in correct sequence, by nominating a like number of figures which the Code-maker 'marks' by stating how many (if any) are correct and are correctly placed, and how many (if any) are correct but incorrectly placed. The Code-breaker, deducing what he can from this information, makes a second attempt, which is again 'marked', and so on until the code is broken. The aim is to discover the code in the least number of attempts. The players then change roles.

Master Mind was the invention – if that is the word – of an Israeli, Mordecai Meirowitz. It was launched in 1973 and in one year sold $1\frac{1}{4}$ million in Britain alone. With Scrabble and Monopoly it must rank as one of the three most popular proprietary games.

The magic of Master Mind lies in its presentation – symbols have been replaced by coloured pegs and pencil and paper by a board. The difference is striking, even though the purist might protest that it is the same game. The visual appeal, the increased ease of identification, the subconscious pleasure (Freudian?) of putting pegs into holes, transform an unpleasing game into a pleasing and social one – Master Mind can be enjoyed by onlookers.

There are regular championships, where the top players frequently break a code mentally within a minute.

Standard Master Mind is neither trivial nor deep and is enjoyed most when it is not played too often. Some newer versions are more challenging (see Variants).

Incidentally, Master Mind is often spelt as one word – even the makers don't discriminate!

Play

A Master Mind set consists of a peg board, a shield at one end to screen the code pegs, an adequate supply of these pegs in six different colours and small black and white pegs to serve as markers.

Players take it in turns to be the Code-maker who, after he has set his code, acts as referee. The code is made up of four pegs; these pegs may be in any combination of colours, and indeed can be all of one colour if the Code-maker wishes (an unintelligent choice, by the way, as it is quickly discovered).

The Code-maker announces that the code is set and the Code-breaker puts down four pegs of his choice along the first row of the board. The Code-maker now checks the row and inserts at the end of the Code-breaker's line one black marker peg for each peg that matches, in colour and precise position in the line, a peg in the hidden code, and a white marker peg for each peg in the Code-breaker's line that is of the same colour as one in the hidden code but in the wrong position. For example, if the hidden code were BLUE, RED, GREEN, GREEN and the Code-breaker's first line was RED, YELLOW, GREEN, RED, the marking would be one black peg for the Green and a white peg for one of the Reds. Note that both Red pegs would not score since there is only one in the code. If one of these Red pegs had been in the second position the Code-breaker would have earned two blacks. If none of the Code-breaker's pegs match any of the colours in the code, that line, of course, gets no marker pegs.

The Code-breaker now has information which he will use in planning his second attempt. The game continues in this wise until the

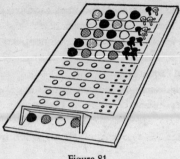

Figure 81

code is broken – i.e., when the Code-breaker's line is marked with four blacks. A completed game is shown in Figure 81. The Code-breaker has taken 5 lines, which is the average for a game. The minimum number of lines necessary to break a code depends on the code in combination with the Code-breaker's first attempt, which is a guess. The good player will achieve the minimum, or perhaps 1 more; the beginner may well take 3 or 4 extra lines.

Strategy

The strategy for the Code-maker is minimal. Possibly the hardest line to break is one using three colours, but it is as well to vary with four-colour and two-colour lines.

The precise choice of colours and their placings bring into question the significance of psychological factors. Some players are convinced of the importance of these; others argue that they are irrelevant. It probably depends on the type of person your opponent is – emotional or logical. I have noticed that John Searjeant, twice world champion and undefeated king of Master Mind, has an uncanny knack of putting down a first line that gathers a lot of information.

The strategy for the Code-breaker must depend on the context in which the game is being played, as Dr Austin has pointed out. (For example, is it important to try and win by the largest margin, simply to win, or to not exceed a certain number of lines?) If the aim is to break the code in not more than 5 lines, a strategy devised by Professor Knuth of Stanford University guarantees this – in theory, anyway, unless you are able to memorize columns of computer print-out. If the aim is to maximize the chance of breaking the code in the minimum number of lines, a different strategy is called for, which runs the risk of exceeding 5 lines on occasion. Work on this second strategy has been done by Robert W. Irving and others. None of which is of much practical help, except that in Knuth's strategy the first guess by the Code-breaker uses two pairs of colours and in Irving's strategy, three colours.

After the first line has been marked, the Code-breaker's task is one of deductive reasoning. The strategy he follows will depend on the nature of the contest. For example, if he has to beat his opponent's 6 lines, he will play safe; but if he has to match or even beat 4 lines, he will have to gamble.

Here are a couple of problem games taken from championship events.

The Code-breaker has the following lines on his board. Black marker pegs are indicated by an X and white pegs by an O.

(1)	BLUE	GREEN	WHITE	RED	XO
(2)	RED	RED	BLACK	YELLOW	XX
(3)	WHITE	BLUE	GREEN	GREEN	OO

The code can now be broken. The reasoning process goes like this: lines (1) and (3) have the same pegs except that (1) has a Red and (3) an extra Green. Since both lines have two correct pegs, Red is out, unless the code uses a Red and two Greens. But in that case line (3) would put the two Greens in the first two positions, which cannot be reconciled with line (2). As Red is out, line (2) immediately tells us that Black and Yellow are correct. Now the coded pegs in first and second positions must be two from the colours Blue, Green and White. If Green were correctly placed in line (1) (to earn the black marker), then White would have to be the second colour, otherwise Blue would deserve a black marker too. But White is in first position in line (3) and there is no black marker for that line. Hence, from line (1) Blue is correct in first position and White must be in second position. So the hidden code is BLUE, WHITE, BLACK, YELLOW.

Here is another example:

(1)	BLUE	RED	YELLOW	WHITE	OO
(2)	YELLOW	GREEN	WHITE	BLACK	OOO
(3)	WHITE	BLACK	BLUE	BLUE	OO
(4)	RED	BLUE	BLACK	RED	X

The approach to this sort of game problem is to establish one fact and to use this in deducing others. From line (4), only one of the colours Red, Blue and Black is correct. Line (3) has two marker pegs, so one of the colours in the code must be White, or a second Blue, if Blue was correct in line (4). But two Blues are excluded by line (2). So there is a White peg in the code. Now things are easier. Lines (1), (2), (3) have White in three different positions but score no black markers. So there is one White in the code and it must be in position two.

This eliminates Blue from line (4) and hence the two Blues in line (3). So Black must be the second colour in line (3) and must be in the third position from line (4). This puts Red out from line (4), so the second colour in line (1) is Yellow, and Yellow must be in fourth position, since in line (2) it does not earn a black marker in first position.

There remains one position to fill – the first. Since Green is out (from line (2)), all colours have been accounted for, so the fourth peg must duplicate one of the other three (Yellow, White and Black). But Yellow cannot be in first position nor can there be two Whites (already proved), so the hidden code must be BLACK, WHITE, BLACK, YELLOW.

Variants

A time limit is desirable to put players on level terms; it also sharpens the play. A chess clock is ideal; start with six minutes and come down to three. The setting for the Code-maker's time is of course irrelevant. The clock runs only during the time the Code-breaker is thinking and placing his pegs.

The chance element of the Code-breaker's first attempt can be neatly eliminated by the Code-maker not setting his code until the first 'attempt' has been made; he then marks the attempt in the usual way. This makes for more player interaction since the Code-breaker by his choice of pegs influences the Code-maker's selection.

Invicta have marketed a number of different versions of Master Mind following the electric success of the standard game. One is Grand Master Mind, which introduces shapes as well as colours.

The standard game can be made more difficult by the inclusion of blanks (empty holes), which has the same effect as introducing a seventh colour. The latest version of the game, and likely to become the standard one in the future, uses four holes and eight colours.

• NAPOLEON AT WATERLOO •

- Wargame
- Boxed proprietary game (Simulations Publications)
- One hour
- An introduction to wargaming

Background

This is one of the simplest board wargames and one of the shortest to play. It is an ideal introduction to the 200-odd sophisticated games of this type now available.

Play

The board represents the field of Waterloo with its several villages and level, open terrain. As in almost all wargames, the board is in fact a map and is overlaid with an hexagonal grid to regulate positioning and movement.

The pieces are small cardboard counters, coloured and treated, representing units of divisional size. Each unit is identified by a symbol and marked with two numbers, that on the left being the combat strength of the unit and that on the right the movement factor.

Figure 82 shows a unit occupying a clear terrain hexagon (called *hex* for short). The crossed box identifies it as infantry and the surrounding symbols as the First Guards Division. The unit has a combat factor of 7 – high, but to be expected of an elite corps – and a movement factor of 4, which is standard for infantry in this game. Its colour (red as it happens) declares it to be British. If it were occupying the adjacent wood or village hex, the unit's defence strength, though not its attack strength, would be doubled, giving it a combat factor of 14. This is quite realistic if you think about it.

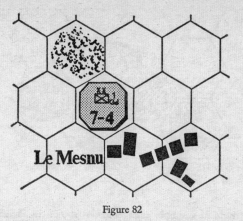

Figure 82

To start the game, the British and French armies assume their historical deployment as indicated on the board. The Prussians are not deployed but enter the battlefield from the east after the first clashes. The hour is 1 p.m. on 18 June 1815, and each turn represents an hour of historical time. The battle lasts 10 hours (10 turns).

On his turn, a player first moves all or any of his units. A unit with a movement factor of four, for example, may be moved up to four hexes in any direction (subject to any local restrictions). After all desired movement is completed, combat takes place between adjacent units (at longer range in the case of artillery) at the choice of the player. It is permissible to concentrate one's forces, perhaps four or five units attacking a single enemy unit, but no unit may take part in more than one engagement in any one turn.

In each engagement, the total combat strength of the attacker(s) is compared with that of the defender. The player then rolls a die (which reflects the element of chance in war) and enters the appropriate odds table to determine the outcome of the engagement. At favourable odds, the chances are that the defender will be forced to retreat or may perhaps be eliminated; at unfavourable odds (and the attacker may be obliged sometimes to engage under these circumstances) the reverse is likely.

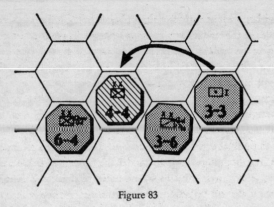

Figure 83

An example of a simple engagement is shown in Figure 83. A French cavalry division combines with an infantry division and an artillery division (attacking from a distance) to engage a Prussian infantry division. The attackers have a total combat strength advantage of 12 against 4, odds of 3 to 1. At those odds, a die roll of 1 would eliminate the defender, while a die roll of 6 would eliminate the defender but also an attacker of at least equal strength. Thus the French player would have to give up either his infantry division (the 6–4 piece) or his two supporting divisions, as he has no unit of combat strength 4 engaged. Any other die roll would require the defender to withdraw a hex.

In wargames, as in war, the opposing sides have different objectives. In Napoleon at Waterloo the Allies attempt to bar the road to Brussels, while both sides strive to inflict casualties on the other. In certain circumstances the Allies can become demoralized, when their combat effectiveness is reduced.

The French win if they can exit seven units off the board towards Brussels – in short, if they break through.

Strategy

Like most board wargames, Napoleon at Waterloo is a simulation, historically accurate in every important respect. This aspect of wargaming has great appeal for serious players, who will study accounts of battles in the search for a superior strategy. There is a lot of satisfaction to be had in master-minding a quick French victory, for example – it is quite a thought that if you had been Napoleon, the course of history could well have been changed!

A strategy that takes in the whole board over the whole period of the game is essential for both sides. This has to be said, as there is a natural tendency to concentrate on tactical engagements. There is much to think about. Reserve units must be positioned to anticipate events; conflict must be sought under the most favourable circumstances; withdrawals must be co-ordinated so that stray units don't get cut off and cut up; contingency plans must be ready should the main battle plan fail – in short, all the problems of generalship.

A strategy for the Allied player is to try and hold the French attack, yielding as little ground as possible, until the Prussians arrive. An alternative plan is to attack against the odds and hope that Prussian reinforcements arrive before the French break out.

For the French player, an aggressive strategy is essential; he will strive for an early break-through for his cavalry, while he has local superiority. The detailed planning of the strategy – the thrusts, the feints, the outflanking manoeuvres – coupled with the realism of the movement and engagements is what gives wargaming its special appeal.

Variants

One of the attractions of wargames is that they can often be played at different levels. The advanced game of Napoleon at Waterloo uses the same board but with units at brigade rather than divisional strength and with refined rules of play. This makes for a longer, more complex but also more challenging game, even though strategy tends to be similar.

• NINE MEN'S MORRIS •

- Game of alignment
- Morris board and men
- Twenty minutes
- Adult Noughts and Crosses

Background

Nine Men's Morris belongs to a family of games of alignment (see also Renju) widely played in the ancient world. A board identical to that shown below is incised in a roofing slab at Kurna (Thebes) and it may be presumed that a very similar game was played at that time (1300 B.C.).

It is not known when Nine Men's Morris reached Britain, but it was widely played here during the Middle Ages and then, together with similar alignment games (Three, Six, Twelve Men's Morris), it plummeted from favour and has been little heard of in the last hundred years or so. There is a small revival going on at present in the wake of the games' boom, but I would not be surprised if it did not soon drop again into limbo. This is not to condemn it: it is simply that the competitition is fierce. Morris has nothing to do with Morris dancers; it is a corruption of *merels*, from the Latin *merellus*, a counter.

Nine Men's Morris is currently in favour as a coffee-table game. If you don't want to buy a morris board it is easy to make one – and any tokens will do for the men, provided the two sides are in contrast.

Play

Nine Men's Morris uses a square board marked with a grid (Figure 84). Play is on the intersections, known as points, of which there are

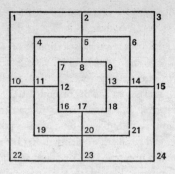

Figure 84

twenty-four. These are numbered for reference, but there is no accepted notation.

Each player has nine men, usually black and white. Black plays first and places one of his men on any point on the vacant board. The object is to form a straight line of three men of one's own colour, known as a *mill*, along any of the sixteen lines. When a player completes a mill he removes one of his opponent's men from the board. There is one restriction: you may not take a man from an opponent's mill unless there is no option when you may take any man. Play now alternates.

When all the men (less any captives removed) have been entered, the second phase begins. Play continues to alternate and at each turn a player moves one of his men. The move must be along a line to an adjacent point. If the move forms or re-forms a mill, an enemy man is removed as in phase one. If the player whose turn it is is unable to move (*stalemated*) the opponent continues to play until the block is relieved.

When a player is reduced to three men, a third phase is entered. The player with three men is allowed, on his move, to play a man to any vacant point on the board, not just to an adjacent point. It is possible for both players to reach this position. The capturing rule is still in force in phase three and the first player who is reduced to two men is the loser.

Strategy

First thoughts might suggest a wide selection of opening moves, but in fact there are only four: 1, 4, 10 and 11. All others are just orientations or reflections of these basic four.

The initiative is paramount and the first move a decided advantage. As might be expected in a game that is fundamentally simple in structure, the number of possible configurations is not great. Patterns repeat themselves and familiarity quickly makes for competence.

Trevor Truran has researched the openings and has named them. Because of the symmetrical board it is easier to consider these as ideas rather than sequences of moves at designated points.

A play which has as its aim the formation of a mill is an Attack; that which aims to prevent it, a Defence.

The Simple Attack. An attempt to form a single mill by occupying three points directly, e.g. 8, 5; 1, 2; 20, 21.

The Junction. Occupation of points on two lines with the threat of occupying the common point and so forcing a mill; thus 4, 12 with the threat of 11 or 1, 8 with the threat of 2.

The Diagonal. Occupation of opposite points on a square such as 9, 16 or 1, 24. The threat is to occupy one of the remaining corners to force a mill.

The Zigzag. Occupation of, say, 4, 9. The threat is 5 or 8 followed, when the mill is stopped, by the other.

The Doubleback. Occupation of the same corners of adjacent squares e.g. 4, 7. The threat is the same as in the Zigzag.

Attacks are combined to retain the initiative and force the opponent into unfavourable positions. When a mill is formed, care should be taken in selecting the victim – the aim must be to retain the initiative.

Superficially it may appear that Black's advantage is decisive; but as in several other games the initiative can easily change hands. The defender will always, where he has the choice, occupy a point that enhances his attacking chances.

Beyond this, it is difficult to advise White, since Black dictates the play. An adjacent play is usually sound since it cuts off part of the board and destroys any attack that could be developed there.

A material factor to note is that the points 5, 11, 14, 20 can be extended in four directions whereas all other points are confined to three.

Variants

Two common variants concern the rules of capture. In one, a player is free to take any of his opponent's men on completion of a mill; in the other, a man may not be taken if it forms part of a mill, which means that if all the opponent's men form mills, no capture is made. Another variation is to count stalemate a loss for the blocked player. This rule effectively gives the game a second objective and introduces new strategy.

These are offered as variants, but in fact there is no generally recognized set of rules. The version given here is commonly played but cannot be considered definitive.

Trevor Truran proposes a scoring system for Nine Men's Morris akin to that of Backgammon. If the winning player has only three men left, he wins one game; between four and eight, two games; and if he has all nine men, a treble game. I prefer a scoring system where the winner's score is the number of men he has left at the end. A match can then be, say, 25 up.

• PIQUET •

- Card game
- Standard pack from Sevens up to Aces (thirty-two cards)
- Forty-five minutes
- An elegant, elaborate, excellent game

Background

Piquet has a history almost as old as cards themselves; it is mentioned by both Shakespeare and Rabelais. It remains one of the best card games for two.

Play and procedure are rather elaborate, so I have chosen to rationalize a few of the obscurities. Piquet is not a game that can be absorbed in five minutes and enjoyed within ten, but it is decidedly worth trying.

Play

Piquet can be broadly described as a concord of Poker and Whist – points are scored for combinations of cards and subsequently by trick-taking. There is a lot of luck in the game, but skill tells in the long run.

A game, or *partie*, consists of six hands, deals alternating. The object is to get the higher cumulative score. Cards rank from Ace down to Seven; suits are equal and there are no trumps.

Cut for choice of deal, higher card winning. Twelve cards are dealt either in twos or threes to each player, and the remaining eight are fanned face down on the table to form the *talon*. Elder Hand (non-dealer) now discards between one and five cards from his hand. These are put face down in front of him and he may look at them during play. A corresponding number of cards from the top of the talon is taken into hand. If less than five are exchanged, Elder Hand may also look at those cards in the talon to which he was entitled (which may subsequently be taken by Younger Hand).

Younger Hand (dealer) can now exchange cards up to the number left in the talon. Unlike Elder Hand, he may elect to exchange none. Any that remain in the talon may be looked at by both players or left concealed, at Younger's choice, after the first lead.

Combinations are now compared and scored. These are of three kinds and are declared in this order:

(1) *Point*. The player with the most cards in his longest suit scores as many points as he has cards in that suit. If both players have the same number of cards, highest pip value scores (Ace counts 11, court cards 10 each). If pips are equal, neither player scores for point.

(2) *Sequence*. The player with the longest sequence (cards of the same suit in order) scores for that and any other sequences he holds. If the best sequences are of equal length, higher sequence scores; if still equal, neither player scores and any other sequences are disregarded.

(3) *Sets*. These are three or four cards of a kind. Any four beats any three. If best sets are equal, higher wins. Winner also scores for any other sets

Elder Hand starts by announcing his longest suit, thus: 'Point of six' (his longest suit has six cards). Younger Hand now replies: 'Good' (if his longest suit has less than six cards), 'No good' (if his longest suit has seven cards or more) or 'Equal' (if he also has a six-card suit), when Elder Hand replies with his pip count. Longer suit (or higher pip count) scores. Elder Hand then declares his best sequence and the same procedure is followed; similarly with sets. Either player may require his opponent to prove any declaration for which he has scored. A statement is usually sufficient.

There is no obligation to declare any combination, or one's best combination (four Kings, for example, could be declared as a set of three, or not at all – 'no set'). Strength is concealed in order to score better in the trick-taking stage. Naturally, one only scores what one declares and you need only prove your call.

Notice that only one player can score for each type of combination, and it is possible for neither player to score point or sequence.

Declarations completed, Elder Hand leads to first trick. The second player must follow suit if possible. The highest card of suit led wins, the winner leads to the next trick, and so on until the hands are exhausted.

Scoring of Combinations

(1) Point – one point for each card in longest suit

(2) Sequences: the names and scores are:
Tierce (3 cards) – 3 points
Quart (4 cards) – 4 points
Quint (5 cards) – 15 points
Sixième (6 cards) – 16 points
Septième (7 cards) – 17 points
Huitième (8 cards) – 18 points

(3) Sets
Trio (3 of a kind, As, Ks, Qs, Js or 10s) – 3 points
Quatorze (4 of a kind, As, Ks, Qs, Js or 10s) – 14 points

Notice that sequences must be of three cards or better and that Sevens, Eights and Nines cannot form sets.

Scoring of Tricks

Elder Hand gets 1 point for first lead. Each trick lead to and won earns 1 point, and if not lead to, 2 points. There is a bonus of 1 point to the winner of the last trick, a bonus of 10 ('for the cards') to the player who takes seven tricks or more, and a bonus of 40 (but excluding the 10 for seven or more and the 1 for the last trick) if all twelve tricks are taken. This is called *capot* and is rare.

Other bonus scores

A player who picks up a hand without a court card can declare *carte blanche*, which scores 10 points. The declaration is made before play starts and the declarer must prove his claim by exposing his cards rapidly one after another face-up on the table, then taking them back into hand.

If either player scores 30 in hand before his opponent has scored, he announces *repique* and collects 60 points. For repique, declarations are taken strictly in order: carte blanche, point, sequences, sets. Once play starts, if Elder Hand reaches 30 points before Younger scores, he adds 30 for *pique*. Thus if Elder scored 7 for point, 4 for a quart, 17 for quatorze and a trio (total 28) and won the first trick (1 point for the lead, 1 for the trick), he would have 30 points and score pique, provided, of course, Younger had not first declared carte blanche. (In some schools, equality in point or sequence debars pique or repique.)

It is normal for each player to announce his progressive score every time he earns points, but any other method of recording the score may be used.

At the end of the partie, the winner is the player with the higher score. If both players have scored over 100, the winner adds 100 to the difference between their scores; if neither player has scored 100 after the sixth hand, or the loser has scored less than 100, then the winner's score is 100 plus the sum of the two scores – the loser is said to have been *rubiconed* or *lurched*.

Strategy

The deal strongly favours Elder Hand; so if you win the cut, elect to deal first, as this will give you Elder Hand in the important last game, when it may be necessary to take risks to avoid being rubiconed. Elder Hand's advantage means that he should play an attacking game – voiding a suit, for example, to make point and also possibly capot. It almost always pays him to exchange five cards; Younger Hand too will normally change the maximum.

Notice the scoring: in particular, the difference between quart and quint and between trio and quatorze. Pique and repique pay handsomely and are not too difficult to achieve. Younger should try to keep a guard in each suit to avoid being overrun. He should play to avoid heavy penalties, and generally he cannot afford to be so ambitious as Elder.

Exchanging is the critical part of Piquet. Thereafter, scoring for combinations is a formality and the trick play largely predestined. In a sense, exchanging at Piquet corresponds to bidding at Bridge. It is difficult to offer good advice on this stage of the game, for demands are in conflict – one wants to build a hand that will score well in combinations and also one which will command most if not all of the tricks; at the same time there is the defensive requirement of avoiding heavy penalties. The good player calculates his chances of drawing a certain card and acts accordingly; it is not always policy, for example, to discard low cards and retain high ones. Much, naturally, depends on the hand one is dealt, but skill can minimize the ill-effects of chance.

Variants

There are many, but none deserving of serious attention.

• PROGRESSIVE CHESS •

- Chess variant
- Chess set and board
- Five to ten minutes
- An exhilarating and eye-developing game

Background

To call a game instructive is inviting rejection, but Progressive Chess, arguably the best of a hundred or so practised chess variants, develops tactical sense in the parent game quicker and more enjoyably than any other way. It is also an excellent quick game in its own right; any charge of triviality is easily refuted.

Play

Rules are as in Chess except that players make an increasing series of moves. White opens as in the game, Black then makes two moves, White makes three, and so on until one side is mated. The only restriction is that one may not give check until the last move of one's turn. Similarly, if you start your turn with your King in check, you must get out of check on your first move. The moves you make in a turn may be all made by the same man or by different men. Naturally, you may not, within your turn, permit your own King to be in check even for a single move.

If White were allowed four moves to start with (absurd, but it shows how you can co-ordinate ideas), few players would miss the Scholar's Mate 1. Pe4; 2. Bc4; 3. Qh5 (or f3); 4. Q (or B) × f7 mate. An alternative would be to move the Queen out before the Bishop.

Strategy

Piece values are of little importance; development is everything (lesson 1). Weaknesses in the enemy position and particularly un-defended squares round the King, must be identified (lesson 2). One's own forces must be co-ordinated to exploit the enemy weaknesses (lesson 3). Over-commitment to attack, however, can leave one's own position vulnerable. Attack and defence must be combined, un-less it can be foreseen that all-out attack will result in mate.

Here are a few guidelines. If you believe there is any danger of being mated next turn, give check on your last move, since this will deprive your opponent of one of his moves while he gets out of check. An essential for defence is to allow your King plenty of air, particularly after the first few turns. A King tucked away is easy to mate, but a King in the open with half a dozen escape squares round him is a different matter. Indeed, the King can often be used boldly, for in the open he can limit the attacker's options because of the 'no check until last move' rule.

If you cannot find a mate at your turn, give your King plenty of room and destroy as many of the opponent's dangerous men as pos-sible. In Progressive Chess, a Pawn can queen in just five moves, per-haps picking up a piece or two on the way, amply demonstrating that normal piece values have little validity. Good players often get past move ten and rarely miss a mate. Odd moves are White's, evens Black's.

Here is a typical game with commentary: 1. Pe4; 2. Pd5, Pe5 (Black opens the game to give his pieces scope); 3. Pd4, Bg5, B × d8 (White sees he cannot mate so destroys Black's strongest piece); 4. Nf6, Nc6, K × d8, Bb4 + (Black finds no mate so develops his men and checks White); 5. Pc3, P × e5, P × f6, P × g7, P × h8 = Q + (Black is now two Queens and a Rook in arrears and has to get out of check, yet he is certainly not losing. White has omitted defence); 6. Ke7, Bg4 (the order of moves is not now material), Rd8, P × e4 and now Black even has a move to spare before he plays R × d1 mate.

Variants

This is another game where you can make your own rules, e.g. that no man may move more than twice in a turn. I prefer the game as it is.

• RENJU •

- Game of alignment
- Go set and stones
- Thirty minutes
- The aristocrat of five-in-a-row games

Background

Five-in-a-row games are to be found in many parts of the world. The aim of them all is the same: to align five of your men in a straight line (compare Nine Men's Morris and Tic Tac Toe, where the object is to align three). In most of these games the line of five can be orthogonal or diagonal; in a few, orthogonal only. Boards vary in size; sometimes men can be moved after all have been placed, sometimes not.

Go-moku is probably the best-known of the five-in-a-row family. It comes from Japan, where, although popular, it is not considered of consequence. Proprietary versions have appeared in the West under a number of names: Five-in-a-Row, Go-bang, Pegity. The weakness of all these games is the large advantage conferred by the first move.

Renju is also of Japanese origin but has not yet been exported. It is a modern version of Go-moku, in which certain restrictions are placed on the first player to balance the advantage of the move. The game has supported a number of professionals during its short history.

Play

Renju is played on a board which has a lattice of 15 × 15 lines, but a Go board is convenient. Each side has fifty stones of contrasting colours – again, Go stones are ideal though the two games have very little in common. Moves are on the intersections (most five-in-a-row games use the cells but clearly this does not affect play).

Black moves first and places a stone on the centre intersection. White then plays a stone on any other intersection and so on alternately until one side has five in a row or until the stones are exhausted, when the game is drawn. There is no movement and no capturing.

The restrictions put on the first player are severe:

(1) He cannot make a play that simultaneously creates two or more *open threes*. An open three is defined as three stones in a row, not necessarily connected, which can be converted into an *open four*. An open four is in turn defined as four stones in a row unblocked at either end (= open) which can be converted into five in a row.

(2) He cannot make a play that simultaneously creates two (or more) *fours*. A four is defined as four stones in a row, not necessarily connected, that can be converted into a five and therefore open at least at one end or in the middle. Neither of the above restrictions apply, however, if a winning line of five contiguous stones is simultaneously created.

(3) He cannot make a play that results in a line of six (or more) contiguous black stones. This could only result from five or more stones divided into two groups being linked by the play of a single stone and is known as an *overline*.

There are no restrictions on the second player, who is free to form his line of five in any way he can.

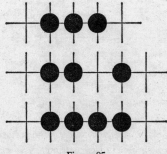

Figure 85

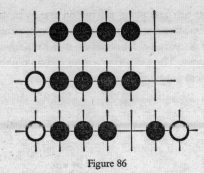

Figure 86

All this is a little complicated and certainly detracts from the game's appeal, but it ensures equality of chances.

Two examples of open threes and an open four are shown in Figure 85. In Figure 86 are the three types of four, of which the first is, of course, an open or straight four.

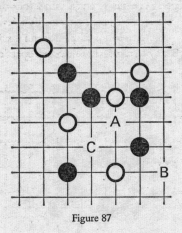

Figure 87

Strategy

This deserves a book, which is why the game is rated so highly.

The first player will strive to get a *four-three* (meaning a four and an open three), which is legal. The four will have to be stopped when the three can be converted into an open and unstoppable four. Figure 87 shows this tactical play. Black fills in at *A*, creating a four–three. White must now stop at *B*, when Black plays at *C*; now White cannot block both ends of Black's open four.

Black must retain the initiative from the outset. If he is forced to defend, his handicaps will doom him. White can rarely afford to be bold early in the game but will try to exploit Black's restrictions. The normal pattern of play is for Black to have his forces concentrated and capable of expansion in several directions, whereas White's stones occupy the perimeter of the play stopping potential fives. Eventually enough of White's stones may be grouped to enable him to take over the offensive.

An open three must be stopped at once or it will convert into an open four, but single threats pose no problems: it is the double (even triple) threat that forces the win, and here White is at an advantage, for two open threes are easier to attain than a four-three.

A short game between beginners may clarify a few points (Figure 88). White 2 is pointless whereas Black 3 forms a solid base for expansion. White 6 is a bad error: the threatened open four should have

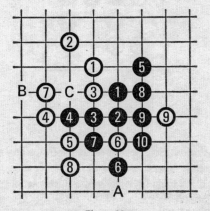

Figure 88

been stopped by a play at *A*. Notice that in moves 4 to 8 White is compelled to block a series of open threes. After his seventh move, White would dearly like to be able to play at *B* or *C*, but he is now lost. Black could not have reversed the order of his moves 8 and 9, as his second play would have then produced two open threes. After 10, Black's five cannot be prevented. Notice the concentration of Black's stones in the final position. By contrast, White's are split and ineffectual, thanks largely to his wasted play at 2.

Played at an advanced level, Renju has a unique strategical feature. White aims to force Black into a position where he can only avert defeat by making a prohibited move; conversely, Black's strategy is to avoid this situation.

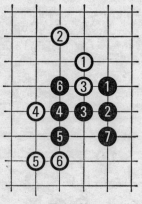

Figure 89

Variants

These have already been mentioned. Between unequal players, the restrictions can be dropped and the weaker player takes Black. In the above game Black could have won more quickly without the 'three-three' rule – see Figure 89.

• REVERSI •

- Abstract boardgame
- Chessboard and reversi men
- Thirty minutes
- A game enjoying a revival

Background

Reversi first appeared 100 years ago. As with so many games, there is dispute about its origin. Apparently a 'player', Mr Lewis Waterman, claimed to have invented it, but this was contested by a 'gentleman', John W. Mollett Esq., B.A., on the grounds that Reversi was merely an adaption of his game Annexation, which had been marketed a few years previously.

An early set of rules claims that 'it may now fairly be said to have taken its place as one of the – if not THE – most popular of indoor games'. A less ambitious claim is made for the game itself: 'Whilst requiring on the part of each player a considerable amount of calculation and skill, no such concentration of thought and study is demanded as in some of the more time-honoured games, such as Chess etc.'

Enthusiasm for Reversi went out with Victoria's reign and it seems to have been little played until recent years. It was marketed with minor modifications as Exit, Chain Reaction, and again, with great success, as Othello (1976). Othello has a strong following in Japan (abstract games have great appeal to the Japanese – see Go, Shogi, Renju) and international championships are played.

Play

Reversi makes use of a normal chessboard though the colours of the squares have no significance in the game. A plain 8 × 8 board is preferable.

There are sixty-four men, which have the appearance of draughts-men but are black on one side and white on the other. Sometimes other contrasting colours are used.

Players decide on colours, then each takes 32 men and places them, own colour uppermost, to hand. White plays first and places a man on any of the four central squares of the empty board. Black and White then play alternately to fill these squares. Only two formations are possible (Figure 90). The board is now said to be *dressed* and the game proper begins.

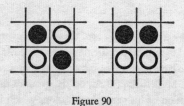

Figure 90

White must now place a man on a vacant square next to a black man such that the black man is trapped between two white men in a straight line, either orthogonally or diagonally. It can be seen that White has a choice of four possible plays in either of the base formations.

The trapped black man is now turned over and becomes a white man for the time being. There are now four white men on the board and only one black man. It is Black's turn to play and he must similarly place a man so as to effect a capture. The line must be unbroken: that is, there must be no empty square(s) anywhere between the two captors. Even with only one man on the board, you will find that Black can, on his third turn of play, always make a capture.

Play continues in this way until the board is full or there is no legal play for either player (if you cannot make a capture, you miss a turn). The winner is the player who has most men of his own colour on the board at the end. Notice that only vacant squares may be occupied and that a capture must be made on each turn of play.

There is no movement on the board and no man is removed, although men may change colour many times during the course of a game.

More than one man may be trapped in a single play, often on more than one line. Look at Figure 91. A White play at (1) simultaneously captures the five marked black men which are all now turned over, transforming the picture (Figure 92). It is only the last man played that determines captures: men turned over cannot assist in taking further prisoners.

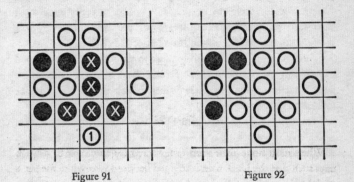

Figure 91   Figure 92

Strategy

There is at present new thinking on the correct strategy in Reversi, challenging some of the older beliefs. One thing is clear: a strategy of capturing as many men as possible on each turn, though superficially appealing, is quite unsound. The game is a fight for control of important squares, for, as you will quickly discover, squares have different values – some it is wise to occupy, others not. Only the four corner squares are secure for the occupier, since there is no way in which a man in a corner can be legally captured. These are consequently strong squares and a corner man acts as an anchor in three directions simultaneously.

Men on any of the other twenty-four perimeter squares can only be trapped in one direction, horizontally or vertically. However, these squares are not all of equal value. Perimeter squares adjacent to the corners are weak, since occupation of one of these could cede one of the strong corner squares to the opponent. Weakest of all, however, are the four squares diagonally adjacent to the corners since they not only suffer the influence of the corners but are also open to attack from all other directions. The twelve central squares – one may ignore those used for dressing – are unstable, as their ultimate control will most probably depend on the men outside them; for this reason, they appear to offer fairly safe plays. I say 'appear', because no-one has yet analysed the game in sufficient detail as to really understand their relative importance. It does seem probable, however, that the four corner squares are the strongest of the twelve.

Figure 93 gives rough relative values to the squares. Like all good games, Reversi has no inviolable rules. Positions will arise where tactical factors will upset these values, which should therefore be looked on only as a guide.

Here is one of the shortest games possible. Algebraic chess notation is used. White starts. Men in brackets are turned over. 1. e5, e4; 2. d5 (the side-by-side formation is favoured by the experts), d4; 3.

1	4	1	3	3	1	4	1
4	5	3	3	3	3	5	4
1	3	1	2	2	1	3	1
3	3	2	2	2	2	3	3
3	3	2	2	2	2	3	3
1	3	1	2	2	1	3	1
4	5	3	3	3	3	5	4
1	4	1	3	3	1	4	1

Figure 93

d3(d4), c4(d4); 4. b5(c4), e6(e5); 5. f5(e5, e4), d6(d5); 6. d7(d6, d5, d4, e6) – and as all the men are now White's, the game is over.

The Reversi player has a number of possible strategies which include gaining as much territory as possible or securing strong squares as a basis for territorial expansion later. A strong position can be defined as one in which a significant number of contiguous cells are occupied to the edge of the board, preferably a corner. (Such a chain will consist of cells which are safe in at least one direction.) Once a corner is established, progress can be made along both edges. Control of three corners virtually guarantees victory. In the later stages of the game territory-taking moves are paramount. Beware isolated enemy men within your forces: these should be eliminated if possible, as they can be often used to devastating effect by your opponent.

Some work has been done in programming computers to play Reversi – most abstract games can be taught to the electronic brain. Here is a game in which Dr N. J. D. Jacobs, who has been experimenting in this field for some time, is vanquished by his brainchild. The figures in brackets denote the number of men to be reversed at each turn. Dr Jacobs is White. 1. e5, d5; 2. d4, e4; 3. e3(1), f3(1); 4. f4(1),

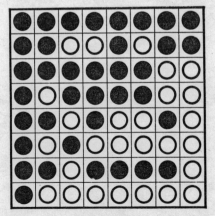

Figure 94

d3(2); 5. c3(1), f5(3); 6. f6(1), e6(1); 7. d6(2), c5(2); 8. g3(5), c2(1); 9. c4(3), h3(3) – capturing a good edge cell; 10. c1(1) – likewise, b3(1); 11. c6(1), d7(4); 12. e2(2), e1(4); 13. d8(4), b4(2); 14. d2(1), g4(1); 15. a4(1), a2(1); 16. a5(2), f7(1); 17. b5(1), b6(5); 18. a6(1) – at this point the computer assessed White ahead, f2(1); 19. f1(1), g1(1); 20. h5(2), g5(1); 21. g6(7), c8(3); 22. b8(1), h7(1); 23. g8(2), f8(2); 24. e8(4), c7(2); 25. b7(2), e7(1); 26. g7(3), d1(7); 27. h1(4), a8(2); 28. h2(2), h8(9) – the computer had analysed to the end from here and had calculated it would win by at least 10 points; 29. h4(2), g2(2); 30. h6(1), b2(1); 31. a3(7), a7(5); 32. b1(1), a1(2). The computer wins by 10 points. (See Figure 94.) Notice that Black has control of three of the four corner squares.

Variants

A smaller board may be used: a 6 × 6 board is big enough to be interesting, makes for a quicker game, and is a good way to start.

• SCRABBLE •

- Proprietary word game
- Scrabble board and set
- Ninety minutes
- The most popular of all word games

Background

Scrabble Crossword Game, to give it its full title, is the most popular of all word games and perhaps the most popular of all proprietary games. It was invented in the 1940s by an American, James Brunot, and is now marketed world-wide with different letters and letter combinations for different languages.

The annual National Scrabble Championship, sponsored by J. W. Spear and Sons, the U.K. copyright holders, attracts several thousand entries every year. Regular Scrabble tournaments are also held in the U.S.A. and elsewhere.

Play

Scrabble is a crossword game played on a board marked out with 225 squares (15 × 15). Certain squares, regularly distributed like the black squares on a crossword puzzle, are marked and distinctly coloured and are known as premium squares. Premium squares are of four types: double and triple letter scores, double and triple word scores.

The game is played with 100 letter tiles. Each tile has a value between 1 and 10 according to the approximate frequency of the letter in the language. Thus common letters like *A*, *E*, *T* and *S* score 1, while scarce letters like *Q* and *Z* score 10. Distribution of letters in the set also corresponds to usage. So one finds, for example, twelve

E tiles but only one *X* tile. Two tiles are blank and may be substituted for any letter but do not score.

Play begins by shuffling the tiles face down. Each player then draws seven tiles, which he examines but does not reveal to his opponent. The first player puts down on the board a word of from two to seven letters (assembled from his hand), crossword fashion, and sums their value. This score is doubled, as the central square, which must be covered on the first play, is a premium square. The player then makes his hand up to seven tiles by drawing from stock and his turn ends. Thereafter, each player in turn puts down tiles such that at least one new word is formed and scores appropriately for each word made. If all seven tiles can be put down in one play, there is a bonus of 50 points.

At least one tile of each word must interlock with the letter grid and all tiles must form words, as in a crossword. It is usual to keep progressive scores so that both players are constantly aware of the state of the game.

Instead of playing to the table, a player has the option of exchanging any or all of his tiles. He would not want to do this, since he does not score, unless he had an unbalanced or awkward hand. Tiles are discarded face down into the pool and a like number drawn.

The game ends when one player exhausts his tiles and there are none left in stock (when he adds the value of his opponent's unused letters to his own score) or when the stock is exhausted and neither player can put down a word. The winner is the player with the higher score.

Strategy

If Scrabble were simply a matter of making the highest possible score each turn it would be a rather poor game – a combination of chance, vocabulary and memory. Certainly there is a fair amount of chance in the game – and this is an attraction – but the stronger player will come out on top most of the time. Bear in mind anyway that if you draw bad tiles you can always exchange them.

A good vocabulary is an asset and top Scrabble players roll out words like *yclept* and *zho*, but it is equally important to be able to create situations in which they can be used.

Several factors govern strategy. If you consider only your own score you are likely to open premium squares for your opponent and if you always put down high-scoring words you will often find yourself left with a poor selection of letters for the next round or two.

Good players strive for the 50-point bonus. They do this by conserving blanks and useful letters like *S* (which will pluralize most nouns) and getting rid of duplicated and awkward (but not necessarily high-scoring) letters in short low-scoring words or exchanges. One word using common letters is really worth getting: IRATE. Add an *N* or an *S* to make the six-letter words RETINA and SATIRE respectively, and most letters of the alphabet will now combine with either set of letters to earn a 50-point bonus, provided there is somewhere on the board where your word will fit.

Scrabble can be played offensively by opening up the game (i.e. extending the grid in different directions to give access to the premium squares), but this usually means helping your opponent as well as yourself. Or it can be played defensively, by denying your opponent access to useful letters and squares and by keeping the scores down. It is enough to have a higher total than your opponent at the end, although few would deny that there is satisfaction in scoring well even if your opponent does better. Experts combine both modes of play, viewing the whole situation and not just the immediate scoring opportunities at each turn. It is impossible to say what makes a good score at Scrabble. A score of 250 might be considered good in one game and a much higher score poor in another. It is possible to construct artificial positions in which breathtaking totals are possible – over 1,500 points *in a single play* – which, however fanciful, demonstrates the breadth of the game.

Proficiency at Scrabble, as at most things, is achieved with practice, but there are one or two short cuts to success. Perhaps the most useful, since it's the most practical, is to learn all the two-letter words in the dictionary. (The vexed question of word usage besets Scrabble as much as other word games; if playing seriously, it is as well to agree on a dictionary before you start.) There are probably twice as many two-letter words as you thought. It is not just that you sneak a few extra points; two-letter words allow you to put down words where no other link is available. A store of words that use letters like *J* and *X* is another practical asset, as is a knowledge of letters that combine – for example, a *U* always follows a *Q*.

Another powerful weapon is memory. If you can recall what letters have been played, especially the scarce ones and the vowels, you can in the later stages of the game form a fair idea of what your opponent holds and what is left in the pool. You can always check the board if in doubt, but I don't recommend a census at every turn unless you are planning new friendships.

Scrabble can have one serious drawback: the tedium of waiting for your opponent to play. As a chess master once remarked, the slowness of genius is hard to bear, but the slowness of mediocrity is intolerable. The answer is to agree a time limit, each player being allowed, say, an hour for the whole game. A chess clock looks after this. The system whereby an egg-timer is used on each move is much less satisfactory – a clock allows a player to spend more time on difficult situations and less on straightforward plays.

Variants

There are a dozen or so variants of Scrabble that have attracted interest. In one, a blank tile on the board may be picked up by either player and replaced by the letter it represents. In this way the blanks are constantly re-employed, which makes for more 50-point bonuses.

Postal Scrabble is popular. This allows dictionary-hunting, which is a good way to improve one's vocabulary, but requires someone to act as game controller.

· SHOGI ·

- Japanese Chess
- Board and men
- Two hours
- One of the world's best games

Background

Shogi (Japanese Chess), like Xiangqi (Chinese Chess), is a derivative of Chaturanga, the Indian game from which Chess developed. Its most striking feature, which sets it apart from all other chess games, is that captured men can re-enter play.

Shogi is little-known outside Japan, where there are millions of players, a corps of professionals and good media coverage. Its popular acceptance in the West is inhibited by its appearance – it looks difficult to learn and to play. The effort is worthwhile: Shogi is without dispute one of the world's best games.

Play

The game is played with two armies on an uncoloured board marked with a grid of eighty-one rectangles (hereafter called squares for simplicity) in a 9 × 9 array. Four thick spots on the board mark the promotion zones.

Each army consists of a King, Rook, Bishop, 2 Lancers, 2 Knights, 2 Gold Generals (commonly called simply 'Golds'), 2 Silver Generals (called 'Silvers') and 9 Pawns. The men are flat and wedge-shaped, vary in size according to rank and are identified by ideograms. All pieces, other than the King and Golds, can be promoted and have the appropriate ideograms on the reverse – pieces are turned over on promotion.

Figure 95

The men are illustrated in Figure 95. When you get a set they probably won't look like this, as every manufacturer has his own design; however, recognition should not be difficult.

The men are not distinguished by colour; in play, a man's side is shown by the way he is pointing. For convenience, the players are referred to as Black and White.

Play is on the squares and the object, as usual, is to capture (checkmate) the enemy King. The starting position is shown in Figure 96. Black opens.

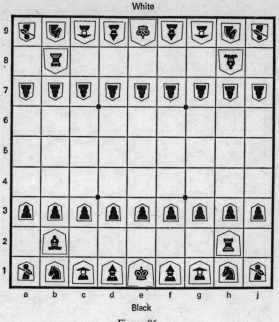

Figure 96

The moves of the *King*, *Rook* and *Bishop* are identical to those of the corresponding pieces in Chess. The *Knight* also has a move similar to its chess counterpart but only forward. The behaviour of these four pieces is shown in Figure 97.

The *Lancer* moves like a Rook but forward only on the file on which it stands. The *Gold General* behaves like a King except that it may not play to either of the squares diagonally adjacent to the rear. The *Silver General* also moves like a King except that it can move to neither of the adjacent horizontal squares, nor to the one directly behind it. It can be seen that the Generals attack the three squares directly in front of them; otherwise their command of adjacent squares is complementary. The *Pawn* moves one square forward only and captures in the same way that it moves. Movements of these men are demonstrated in Figure 98.

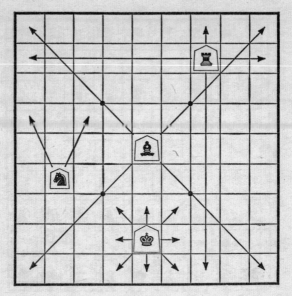

Figure 97

Promotion is made at the end of a move in which a piece enters, leaves, or is wholly within the opponent's first three ranks. Promotion is optional unless the piece could not otherwise legally move again, when it is compulsory. For example, a Lancer played down to the ninth rank must promote. A piece that is not promoted on first moving into the zone retains the option to promote on a later move, provided it starts its move within the promotion zone. Promoted Rooks and Bishops extend their normal powers to include control of all adjacent squares; other men promote to Gold.

Pieces that change their powers, like Knight and Silver, may often be more effective unpromoted, whereas pieces that add to their powers, like Rook and Bishop, are normally promoted on entering the promotion zone.

A promotion is shown by turning the piece over to display the appropriate ideogram. The ideogram for a promoted piece is peculiar

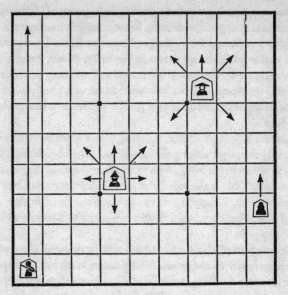

Figure 98

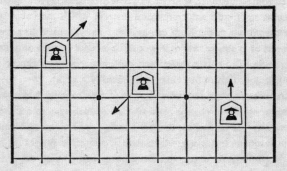

Figure 99

to that man, which means that a piece with the power of Gold may be represented in any of five different forms according to whether it is a Gold or a promoted Pawn, Knight, Lancer or Silver. Legal promotion moves for Silver are shown in Figure 99. Pawns, Knights and Lancers, since they cannot move backwards, can only promote on entering the promotion zone or when their move is wholly within it. A promoted man retains his new powers wherever he moves about the board.

Capture is by replacement. A captured man is removed from the board by the player making the capture and placed beside him. This man is said to be 'in hand'. Men in hand are shown in diagrams on their captor's side of the board next to a blank piece symbolizing the player's colour. Promoted men that are captured revert to their original rank. Thus a promoted Pawn taken into hand becomes a Pawn again.

On any turn of play a man in hand may be dropped, like a paratroop, on to any vacant square. A drop counts as a move. A dropped man may give check but cannot be promoted immediately if dropped within the promotion zone. There are a few restrictions on dropping apart from the obvious one that a man may not be dropped if one's King is in check unless the dropped man interposes between the King and his attacker.

A Pawn may not be dropped on any file on which the player has an unpromoted Pawn nor may a Pawn be dropped to give immediate checkmate. This does not prevent a drop in which the Pawn gives check from which the King can escape. Finally, a man may not be dropped on a square where it would be subject to the compulsory promotion rule. This is logical and can only apply to a Lancer (9th rank), Knight (8th or 9th ranks) and Pawn (9th rank).

An interesting and important feature of the dropping rule is that it allows a Bishop to change from one set of diagonals to another, a Pawn to appear on the first or second ranks, and Knights and Lancers to reach squares forbidden to them in their original identity. Not least, the drop effectively debars draws: Shogi is a game you win or lose.

Strategy

Shogi exhibits most of the elements of strategy and tactics that belong to all chess games.

But Shogi is shaped by certain features that are unique to the game. First among these is the drop. The presence of pieces in hand, or the threat of capture to take pieces in hand, dominates the play. It would be unwise, for example, to exchange a Gold for a promoted Pawn which, although it has the same powers as a Gold, will revert to a Pawn in your hand, while your opponent will be richer by a Gold.

Another feature of Shogi is the aggressive profile of most of the pieces. Only the King, Rook and Bishop are omnidirectional; three pieces, the Knight, Lancer and Pawn, move only forward, whilst both Generals can more easily advance than retreat. In consequence, the rear ranks are vulnerable, particularly to penetration by a Rook.

The shortage of long-striding pieces might appear to make the game slow-moving, but since Pawns are often taken in hand in the first few moves, and sometimes Bishops too, tactical complications can quickly ensue.

The thrust of opening play is to find room for the major pieces to operate – indeed, after 1. c4, g6 the two Bishops attack each other. As an example of tactical play in the opening stages, here is an early disaster for Black. Remember, Black plays first: 1. c4, g6; 2. h4, g5; 3. h5, Rg8; 4. h6, P × h6; 5. R × h6, g4; 6. P × g4?, B × b2; 7. S × b2, (and now not B drops g7 attacking both Silver and Rook because Black can reply 8. Rh2, moving the Rook back to defend the Silver, but) 7. ... B drops j5, attacking King and Rook simultaneously and so winning the Rook and, theoretically, the game (Figure 100).

A few examples of tactical situations and mates will reveal something of the possibilities of this fascinating game.

In Figure 101 Black can mate immediately in one of three possible ways. In the tradition of the 'back rank' mate in Chess, Black can play Re9, with or without promotion; the Silver attacks the King's flight squares on the eighth rank. The other two mates are more typical of Shogi play. Black can advance the Silver to c8 promoting

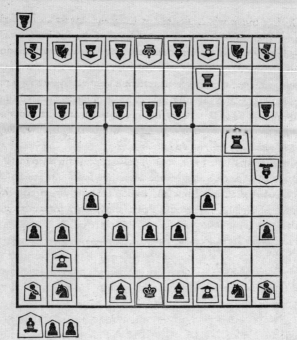

Figure 100

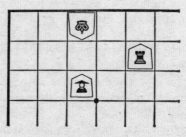

Figure 101

to Gold, a move which attacks the King and covers all his flight squares; the promoted Silver cannot be taken by the King as it is defended by the Rook. Or Black can play the Rook to the same square, promoting. Now it is the Rook that covers all the King's flight squares and it cannot be taken as it is guarded by Silver – a case of reversible roles frequently met in Shogi. Notice that Sc8 (does not promote) fails, as the King can escape at b8, and Rc8 (does not promote) does not immediately mate, as the King has two flight squares available, at b9 and d9.

In Figure 102a, Black with a Gold in hand drops on c8 to mate. In 102b, Black mates with Rg9 (promotes). In 102c White finishes the game with P × a2 check, S × a2 (forced), and now White has a Gold in hand which he drops on b2 to mate. In 102d White has a Silver in

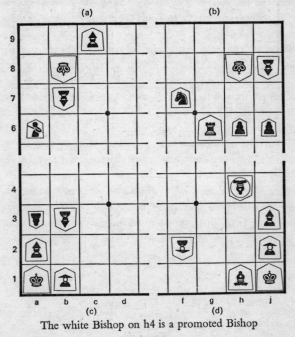

The white Bishop on h4 is a promoted Bishop

Figure 102

hand, but Black with a Pawn in hand looks fairly safe, for PBg3 (the P here means *promoted*) is met by P drops h2. White however forces the King out with S drops h2, and after K × h2 (forced) moves his promoted Bishop to g3 to mate. These examples underline the danger of vacant squares round the King. A useful defence is often to occupy a square on which your opponent threatens to drop a man. Protection of the King is paramount and Generals make good defenders. It is customary to move the King towards one side of the board accompanied by a General or two.

Drops may be made defensively as well as offensively, and a Pawn in hand can prove a useful block against an intruding Rook or Bishop.

Opening play is mainly concerned with finding space for the major pieces and has been heavily analysed. The end game as understood in Chess does not exist; there is only the end of a game – the successful attack on the King.

Evaluation of the pieces is complicated greatly by their promotion and 'in hand' values and these in turn will depend much on the position; for example, a Silver in hand may prove much more useful to one player than to the other. That said, it is obvious that a general assessment can be made, based on the powers of the pieces. The Rook is the strongest and is worth about three Generals; next is the Bishop, followed by the Gold, which is slightly stronger than the Silver. Knight and Lancer are worth about the same and together equal a Gold.

Shogi has an extensive literature, most of it in Japanese, though there are a few books in English. But what is wanted in my view is a redesigned set in which the pieces are instantly recognizable – that is, if Japan wants to share her favourite game with the world.

• SKIRRID •

- The 'Shapes' game
- Skirrid set
- One hour
- An excursion into spatial mathematics

Background

Skirrid is a new boardgame that was energetically marketed as a baby by its inventors, Mark Eliot and Brian Taylor, who put their savings into the enterprise.

Skirrid is still in its childhood but has undoubted potential for growth. It is possible that, like many other good games, it will fail to reach maturity – certainly its presentation leaves a lot to be desired – but I do not think so. Skirrid lacks the originality that has contributed so much to the success of, for example, Black Box, but it is nicely balanced with just the right depth of strategy, which permits forward planning yet denies the players total control. It also has simple rules – sure sign of a good game.

Spatial perception is important in Skirrid, as well as a facility with figures, features that should attract complementary talents.

Play

The Skirrid board has 361 regular squares. Half the squares are blank and the rest are valued between 1 and 25 (see Figure 103). Each player has eighteen pieces in six different shapes, which correspond in size to between one and six squares. These are named for ease of reference (Figure 104). There are three pieces of each shape; one blank, one marked with a 2 and the third with a 3. These numbers are bonus multipliers which can be compared with the double and triple letter/ word squares on a Scrabble board.

Figure 103

Black plays first and places any one of his pieces on the board so that it covers the central square. He scores the aggregate of all numbers covered. If any number is covered by a bonus number, the two are multiplied. Play now alternates. At each turn a player puts one of his pieces on the board adjacent, at least along one side of a square, to any piece or pieces previously played, and scores appropriately. The object of the game, predictably, is to have the highest score when all the pieces have been played. Pieces once placed on the board are not moved. There are only two other rules, both of which add depth to the game. No black square may be covered until an individual score of 75 has been reached. This has the effect of distributing the play and

The Eye   The Rod   The Quoin   The Snake   The Door   The Gun

Figure 104

also adds to the game's skill as the first player able to cross from the white to the black arena is in richer territory. The other rule concerns blocking. A player may, on his turn, play one of his pieces upside down. This bars his opponent from placing a piece next to it on the next move but halves the score of the piece played (odd numbers are rounded down).

Strategy

It is too early yet for definitive judgements. A natural first step must be to arm oneself with the potentials and limitations of each piece. Some, it will be found, are best used as blocks, others as high-scorers; some are better employed in the white arena, others in the black; some shine in defence, others in attack. There is great scope in planning to get the maximum potential out of each piece. Also, certain pieces tend to combine well, others do not.

An obvious anomaly to be considered is the asymmetrical distribution of square values (though the numbers in each black quarter sum to the same total). A lesson quickly learnt is that if you reach for a big number by playing a block (and thus depriving your opponent of the prize) he is free, without sacrifice of a half-score, to reach for another big number – you cannot take both. Consider Figure 105. White has played his Gun as a block to capture the 10 on the left next move. Score: 4 halved = 2. This gives Black the opportunity to go for the 10 square upper right. He also plays his Gun but does not block.

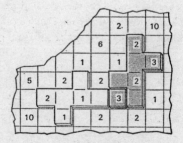

Figure 105

Score: 7. Now if White takes the 10 upper right, Black can take the 10 on the left, as the block is only effective for one turn. Result: Black has made a substantial gain. Moral: don't block unless you can see a clear profit.

The key piece is the Door, since it can cover the pairs of high-scoring squares in the corners. However, it can be overrated, and it must be remembered that no piece can be played in isolation; high scores are reached by effectively combining the pieces, one's own and one's opponents. One of the inventors – Brian Taylor – visualizes the placement of all the pieces from the outset and modifies this notional array according to his opponent's reactions – quite a mental feat! Certainly looking ahead as far as possible is something to be aimed at.

Variants

It is early days for these. The game itself may be modified as a result of accumulated experience, but keen Skirrid players are likely to introduce their own house rules anyway, as happens with most proprietary games. A reallocation of the numbered squares is an obvious direction of experiment, though it may lead nowhere. There is great scope for research into strategy, not in order to find solutions to specific situations but to discover general truths that have practical value. I suspect several exist.

• SPROUTS •

- Topological game
- Pencil and paper
- Five to ten minutes
- A curious game of spatial perception

Background

Acclaimed shortly after its invention at Cambridge University a couple of decades ago, Sprouts is still little-known except among the bright boys. It is a strikingly original game, ideal for odd moments.

Play

To start, a number of points are marked at random on a sheet of paper. Experience will dictate how many: four is a good number to begin with; the tendency is then to increase the number (and the size of paper!). Play alternates in the usual way. On each turn a player must draw a line linking two available points and mark a new point somewhere along it. The player who, on his turn, is unable to link two points loses.

There are only two rules:

(1) No more than three lines may connect at any point;
(2) No line may cross itself or any other line.

Figures 106–8 all show illegal plays (dotted). In Figure 106 play crosses a line; in Figure 107 the lower point cannot be used, as it is already connected to three lines; while in Figure 108 play joins three existing points (only two may be used; the third must be created).

The sequence of play in Figure 109 shows a simple tactical situation, which gives a glimpse of the possibilities of the game. In 109(a) the

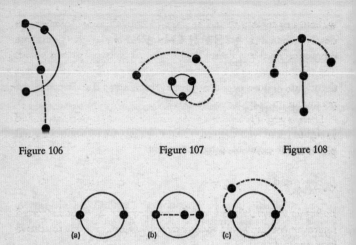

Figure 106   Figure 107   Figure 108

Figure 109

first player has used a single vacant point to start and finish his line and has added a new point on it. In 109(b) the second player has joined the two points directly so that his new point (in the centre) cannot be used. He could, if he had so wished, have joined the same points outside the ring, making his new point available for a further connection – 109(c).

Sprouts has only one slight hiccup: it is possible to reach cramped positions, in which play poses a physical problem. The way round this is to space the points well and not stint on paper.

Strategy

I have yet to hear of any sound strategy being evolved for Sprouts. It is not even clear whether it is an advantage to start or not. Theoretically, perhaps, this should depend on the number of points used; theoretically, too, it should be possible to define best or equal plays under all circumstances. Practice is a different matter. Sprouts resembles the old school game of Boxes in this respect: a mass of paths without a signpost in sight. The closing stages of a game, however, are clearly a contest of skill. Every point *created in play* offers only one connection since it is already by definition connected to two points. The total number of turns during a game cannot exceed three times the original number of points less one (example: with seven points, the maximum number of turns is twenty).

There is a strong suggestion of creativity about Sprouts that should appeal to those with a feeling for abstract art; what prompts a good player is not known to me.

Variants

Invent your own. It is just possible that the game has an undiscovered improvement that would widen strategy – a chance for you to achieve immortality?

• STAR CHESS •

- Electronic game
- Proprietary game (Videomaster)
- One hour
- Chess with chance

Background

It seemed right that a place should be found in this book for at least one of the proliferating field of electronic games. In many so-called electronic games the microprocessor's sole function is to replace otherwise tedious procedures like rolling dice or making calculations. Pocket calculator games also have this disadvantage and I've yet to come across a good one.

However, there are a few good electronic games that exercise mental rather than physical responses. Tomorrow we have been promised chips with everything, but we cannot assess tomorrow's games; meanwhile we have Star Chess, which is perhaps the best game currently available in the field; it is also compact and not outrageously expensive.

Star Chess was conceived by Peter Gebler and is unashamedly built round Chess. How long it will be with us I would not like to predict.

Play

The pack consists of a console, an adaptor and two command modules. The equipment is plugged into an ordinary TV receiver, colour or black and white. The players face the television and each takes control of a command module. The playing area (board) is projected on the screen with men arranged for play. A cursor (light spot) on the screen indicates whose turn it is to move. A move is made by directing the cursor from the command module and activating the appropriate key; the play is instantly reflected on the board with, if appropriate, special effects for 'realism'.

Each side has an army and the object is to eliminate the opposing Commander. The different men with their chess equivalents are listed. Each player has:

1 Commander (= King). Missile and shield strength: 7
1 Destroyer (= Queen). Missile and shield strength: 7
2 Supercruisers (= Rook). Missile and shield strength: 4
2 Starcruisers (= Bishop). Missile and shield strength: 4
2 Superfighters (= Knight). Missile and shield strength: 4
8 Starfighters (= Pawn). Missile and shield strength: 2

The starting position is shown in Figure 110. The men occupy the same squares as their chess counterparts, except that the Commander and Destroyer are reversed (the Commander stands on the square of its own colour). The two squares occupied at the start by the Commander and the Destroyer are known as the Star Base. All the pieces move exactly as their chess counterparts except for the *Starfighter* which moves one square orthogonally – forwards, backwards or sideways. Starfighters do not promote, there is no castling and no check – the Commander must be eliminated.

Capture is by displacement, as in Chess, but there are two additional elements that introduce a chance factor into the play and complicate it considerably:

(1) *Missiles.* Every man is armed with missiles and a corresponding number of shields. A player on his turn may, instead of making a move or capture, use one of his men to fire a missile at an enemy man within range (compare the chess variant known as Rifle Chess). A probable hit factor is applied, depending on the distance between the men; a missile that misses, however, 'explodes' in the vicinity of the launcher with probable self-damage. A random element is also applied, which determines how many shields you destroy on a hit. This varies between one (100% chance) and seven (1% chance).

Figure 110

A spaceship whose shields are exhausted is destroyed and disappears from the screen.

A piece may re-arm by staying a few turns in its Star Base, but shields cannot be replaced. The opponent's Star Base cannot be occupied, so a Commander who does not move away from it can only be destroyed by missiles.

(2) *Time warp.* If you have a piece in danger of capture or one which is obstructing a line of attack (e.g. a Starfighter in front of a Supercruiser) you can, on your turn, despatch it into *hyperspace*. It disappears from the board and re-enters a few moves later, announcing its coming with a suitable galactic whine. A warped spaceship will return to a random location. If the square is occupied, the piece on it is des-

troyed – which is fun if it happens to be your opponent's Commander, but not so much fun if it's yours.

Strategy

This is a new game and I know of no research that has yet reached any definite conclusions.

Clearly chess openings and strategy have a general application to Star Chess, but they can be of little direct value. For instance, the ability of a Starfighter to manoeuvre sideways or backwards removes one of the principal concerns of every chess-player – weak Pawns.

The chance element makes this a not-too-serious game which also perhaps gives us a glimpse of the what-will-be.

Variants

Star Chess can be made more skilful at the expense of a little entertainment by excluding the warp facility. Other variants suggest themselves; for example, both players could agree that missiles cannot be replenished.

• TABLUT •

- Wargame
- Do-it-yourself board and men
- One hour
- A little-known game of unusual strategy

Background

Tablut is a Norse game of the Tafl family. An earlier version known as Hnefatafl was brought by the Vikings to Britain and was, according to Professor Murray, the only boardgame played by the Saxons.

The Tablut/Tafl family is identified by distinctive kinds of movement and capture; only the boards and men change in the different games. However, this is partly conjecture as existing records are fragmentary.

A modern French version has Romans fighting Gauls.

Play

The game is played in the cells of a regular 9 × 9 board with two armies, one representing the Swedes and the other the Muscovites. The Swedes have a King, who occupies the central square (the *konakis* or throne), and eight Soldiers. No Soldier of either side may occupy the *konakis* though any may pass through it. Opposed to them are sixteen Muscovites. Most boards have the squares occupied by the two sides in the initial position decorated in contrasting patterns. The starting position is shown in Figure 111. It is not known which side started in the game as originally played, but I recommend the Muscovites.

All men move in the same manner – orthogonally, over any number of vacant squares, exactly like the Rook in Chess.

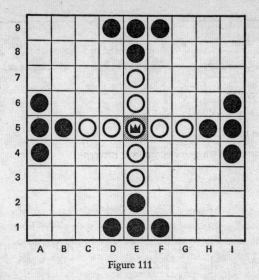

Figure 111

The objectives of the two sides are different, a feature, interestingly, that is common in modern wargames but rare in traditional games. The aim of the Swedish player, who is besieged, is to get the King to the perimeter of the board. The Muscovite player wins by capturing the King.

The King is captured in the same manner as a single stone in Go: by the occupation of all adjacent cells. Figure 112a shows a Muscovite moving to win. The King is also captured if the konakis occupies one of these cells (Figure 112b); nor does the seclusion of the konakis save him (112c).

Other men of both sides are captured by the custodian move: two men flank the victim. In Figure 113a the Muscovite moves to capture. Standing next to friendly men does not save the Swede – 113b is also a capture. Two or more men cannot be captured together, however: Figure 113c is not a capture. If the men are separated, more than one man may be captured on a move; in 113d all three Swedes are captured. A man, however, may safely move between two opposing men (Figure 113e).

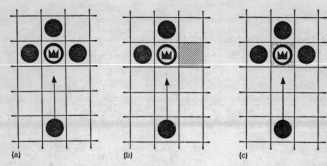

Figure 112

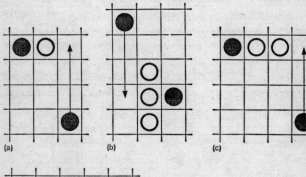

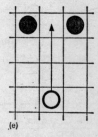

Figure 113

Strategy

Tablut in its orthodox form is an unbalanced game, as it chauvinistic-ally favours the Swedes. No matter: it makes for a good contest between unequal players; anyway, the fault can be easily overcome.

The strategy for each side is fairly straightforward, the aims of one being the reverse of those of the other. The Swedish player's strategy is to make space for the King to move around. As in many other games – for example, Renju – it is often a double threat that decides the game. Probing moves should be made to try and force weak-nesses among the Muscovites or to draw them away from a sector to which the King then switches. If two open paths to the board edge can be created simultaneously for the King, this wins at once.

There are just enough Muscovites to contain the Swedes, so early moves must activate the under-employed men on B5, H5, E2 and E8. These are best moved into the open area in the corners. Strategy for the Muscovites is to advance like a police line. Early casualties cannot be borne, since the King will then escape easily through one of the gaps. For this reason, the attackers must not let a Swede through

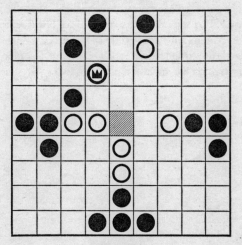

Figure 114

their lines, for the defender will quickly find victims from behind.

Since it is essential to restrict the movement of the King, it is usually not a good strategy to capture defenders. The more men the King has around him, the harder he will find it to move about. However, there are not enough Muscovites to seal off every rank and file, even if no casualties are suffered, so the attacker must anticipate the King's manoeuvring and try to operate his fire-brigade actions so that a little ground is gained each time. Here is the score of a brief disaster, a good example of how *not* to play the Muscovites. In this game the Swedes move first. 1. E6–B6 (threatens E4 –B4), A4 –B4 (correct was I6–E6); 2. E5–E6, D9–C9 (threatens C9–C6)? 3. E6–D6 (threatens D6–D9), E9–D9; 4. D6–D8 (threatens D8–A8), C9–C8; 5. F5–F8 (captures E8), I6–C6 (captures B6); 6. E7–C7 (captures C6), A6–C6 (captures C7)??; 7. D8–D7 wins. The final position is shown in Figure 114.

Variants

One kind of Hnefatafl – already referred to – uses a large board with forty-eight besiegers and twenty-five besieged deployed in an elaborate array. Play is on the intersections of the board rather than the cells. It is recommended when you have mastered Tablut.

A possible improvement for Tablut, since it gives a more balanced game, is to restrict the move of the King to four squares in any direction.

• WAR IN EUROPE •

- Wargame
- Boxed proprietary game (Simulations Publications)
- Two hundred hours (full scenario)
- The ultimate in wargames

Background

This is what is known as a 'monster' and is without doubt a classic of its kind.

The game embraces the campaigns of the Second World War in the European theatre. It is in two main parts, which are also sold separately: War in the East (the Russian front) – don't get the first edition by the way, it's faulty – and War in the West.

'Monsters' are popular despite their monstrous cost because their size allows every aspect of the hostilities to be simulated and because they offer reduced scenarios that can be played out in, say, an evening. In War in Europe there are a number of separate campaigns that can be played as separate games (for example, Poland, France 1940, North Africa, Stalingrad).

A monster requires both space and time. For this one you will need a billiard room without a billiard table or a large wall. The maps are superbly produced and, when put together, make an impressive tableau that can do a lot for a room. Once the maps are firmly in place, the time factor is less important.

War in Europe was designed as a three-player game (Allies, Axis, Soviet Union) but can equally be played as a two-player game with one player controlling both the Allies and Russia. And perhaps *played* is the right word, for the rule book cautions: 'Ideally, several hundred hours of sweat, toil and trouble should result in utter frustration as *no* player finishes a winner. Indeed, War in Europe is designed not to be *won* but to be *played.*' Don't be put off by the disclaimer; the game is a real experience even if you don't know what is happening most of the time.

Play

A pleasing feature of War in Europe is the simplicity and playability of its rules, although the collected rule books run to 56 three-column pages (!).

A good idea of the scope of the game can be gained from a review of the number and diversity of the units involved. The playing area covers nine maps and nearly 20,000 hexes, each hex spanning thirty-three kilometres.

Game units are of three different types: Combat Units, Support Units and Markers. Combat Units are mainly of divisional size or equivalent; Support Units include mobile supply and railroad repair; while Markers are used to indicate hexes used for fortification, air interdiction, entrainment and so on.

The Soviet Union has 1,200 separate units; the Axis, which includes Bulgarian, Hungarian and Rumanian elements as well as the main German and Italian forces, has the same number; a further 1,200 units are divided between the British and Commonwealth forces, the United States and a number of smaller combatants and armed neutrals: France (3rd Republic, Vichy and Free French), Poland, Yugoslavia, Turkey – indeed, every country in Europe including Switzerland. (The point of the armed neutrals is that if a player decides to invade one of them – say, Switzerland – their forces at once declare for the other side.)

All the vast complex of Second World War forces and operations are to be found: airborne landings, strategic bombing, amphibious assaults, U-boats, partisan units, cavalry divisions . . .

The principal factors that influence military operations are there too: production (the Soviet player, for example, has to consider how he can best use his industrial resources to meet the German onslaught), weather (mud and snow can halt the panzers in the Ukraine), terrain (there are fifteen types of terrain hex, each imposing its own restrictions on movement).

There are also a number of charts, including combat resolution tables that are used in conjunction with dice rolls (see Napoleon at Waterloo). Part of one chart, the Soviet Production Cycle, is reproduced here (Figure 115).

As you can see, this is not a game to be hurried.

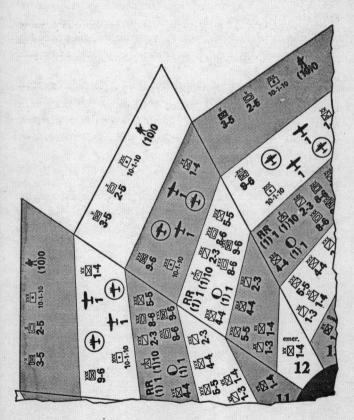

Figure 115

Strategy

It is impossible in so short a space to give the flavour of the game. The problems facing the players, as in most simulation wargames, are those of the political and military leaders of the nations at that time engaged ('Should country X be invaded?', 'How can production capacity best be apportioned?') and of the commanders in the field ('How can lines of communication be maintained?', 'Is a tactical withdrawal necessary on front Y?'). The possibilities are intriguing: the historical decision-makers may have overlooked opportunities which the player perceives, with the awesome thought that had he been in command at the time, the course of events might have been very different.

Wargames fascinate by the richness of their play and can easily become addictive. To enjoy them fully, be sure you have plenty of free time – they demand quite a lot to set up before you can even start to play.

Variants

Wargames are frequently improved by player research and come out in new editions with modified rules, as happened with War in the East. Wargamers frequently make their own house rules (adjusting the combat tables, for instance), a healthy indication that they are thinking about the game. By all means amend the rule book if it suits you.

Single-theatre scenarios, of which War in Europe offers many, may be considered as variants, although of course they are not. It is quite a good idea to try these out separately before blending them in the full game – it is better to spoil an evening's endeavour with a crass mistake than to shatter, with the same mistake, a continent-wide strategy you have spent weeks implementing.

• WORD SQUARES •

- Word game
- Pencil and paper
- Ten minutes
- A much underestimated game

Background

The true word square, in which words are formed both across and down, was a popular Victorian pastime, whose best-known practitioners were probably the Reverend Dodgson (Lewis Carroll) and the puzzle master Hugh Dudeney.

Word Squares is a competitive form of the true word square, a game that has been around a long time (I can recall researching it over forty years ago) and under many different names. It is commonly and wrongly considered a shallow time-filler. It is one of the best of all word games, particularly if one of the more elaborate variants is played.

Play

Each player draws a grid of 5 × 5 squares. The first player calls out a letter; both players then enter it in any square on their respective grids, which are kept concealed. The second player in turn nominates a letter; again both players enter this letter in a vacant square on their grids. This continues until the grids are filled, the last letter, of course, being named by the first player.

The object of the game is to make words across and down. At the end of play grids are exchanged for marking. A good scoring system is 10 points for a five-letter word, 5 for a four-letter word and 3 for a three-letter word. The usual rules for word games (no proper nouns etc.) apply and, I suppose, the usual disputes about validity occur. No letter may form part of two words on the same line – i.e., only one word may be scored on any one line.

There is no reward for high scores in themselves. To win, one has simply to get a better score than one's opponent.

Strategy

A surprising number of different strategies are possible and it is wise to vary your play. Naturally you will wish to confound your opponent by giving him awkward letters – letters that are awkward for him, of course, not for you. At the same time, you will wish to use your opponent's letters to the best advantage; with forethought these can often be anticipated. Try to visualize his thought processes and how he is distributing the letters in his grid. This is not as difficult as it sounds, as he is likely to be building five-letter words.

In your own grid you should aim for flexibility – skeleton words that can be completed by the addition of any of a number of letters maximize your chances of finding useful homes for your opponent's letters.

As in Scrabble, it is possible to play offensively, with the aim of getting a high score by using the more common letters (like *A*, *E*, *N*, *T*, and particularly *S*: plurals can proliferate in this game), or defensively, by using awkward letters aimed primarily at keeping down your opponent's score. A few of the simpler strategies can be enumerated. Plan words with uncommon letters like *J*, *Q*, *X* and *Z*. Give your commoner consonants first and let your opponent provide the vowels (here flexibility will allow you to accommodate perhaps two of each vowel), then bring out your nasty ones. Another strategy is to concentrate on words requiring a lot of vowels and let your opponent provide the consonants. Repeated use of a single letter after the first few turns can be devastating – *L* is a good one for this purpose. Again, you form your skeleton words first with help from your opponent.

Useless letters (and however skilled you become, your opponent will oblige with one or two of these) should be confined to the eight squares round the centre.

If your opponent gives a *U*, watch out for a *Q* to follow at some stage. A little word like ATE in the middle of a line is easily converted by any of a dozen consonants into a four-letter word, and an *S* (or perhaps a *D*, an *R* or even an *X*) will promote it to a five-letter word. Never be in a hurry to complete a word; since you know how many turns you have left, you can easily allow for essential letters. Always give your opponent every opportunity to help you.

In the closing stages it is often unwise to make a three-letter word by giving a common letter – you may be handing your opponent something better. It is sounder to present him with, say, a *J* and sacrifice your three points.

Here is the score of an average game to show how things can work out (Figure 116).

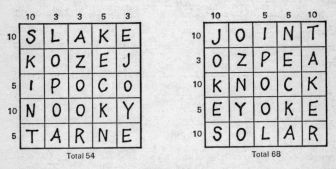

Figure 116

The first player has used a couple of obscure words (a wide vocabulary is an asset, as in most word games), but the second player has deployed his letters much more skilfully. It is difficult to give an average score – so much depends on the strategy that each side adopts – but 65 can be considered good.

• XIANGQI •

- Chinese Chess
- Board and men
- One hour
- Tactical game of the chess family

Background

Xiangqi, or Chinese Chess, as it is better known to us, is played in Chinese communities everywhere but hardly anywhere else. The game compares unfavourably with Chess in many respects but has two distinct recommendations: an emphasis on tactics, which tends to make for incisive games, and the incorporation of a piece – the Cannon – whose behaviour gives rise to remarkable play.

Xiangqi, like Shogi, is derived from the Indian game of Chaturanga, the antecedent, according to historians, of the chess family, which includes many games not given here (Burmese, Korean, Siamese and Tibetan versions of Chess, for example).

As with Shogi, Chinese chessmen are identified by ideograms, the calligraphy tending to vary from maker to maker. Recognition should not be difficult, however, and purchase of a set should prove something of a pleasure, as your nearest Chinese emporium is likely to have a range of plastic and wooden sets at pocket-money prices.

Play

Xiangqi is played on a board, commonly of paper, marked out as in Figure 117.

The rival forces face each other across a *river* (the central band); there is a *fortress*, sometimes called a palace, at either end, marked with large crosses, whilst other markings merely indicate the position of pieces at the start.

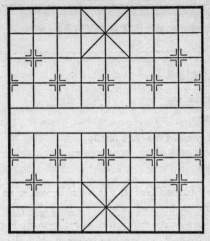

Figure 117

Each side has an army of 16 men, shown in Figure 118. Notice that the Cannons, Chariots and Horses are denoted by the same ideograms whether white or black, whilst the other men are distinctively marked.

Traditional Chinese design		Symbol used for diagrams		
兵	卒	🛡	🛡	Soldier
車	車	⚙	⚙	Chariot
砲	砲	◎	◎	Cannon
馬	馬	🐴	🐴	Horse
仕	士	🛡	🛡	Mandarin
相	象	🐘	🐘	Elephant
帥	將	🛡	🛡	General

Figure 118

This is of no significance in the game. Although referred to as 'white' and 'black', the men may be in any contrasting colours – red and blue are popular.

Play is on the intersections of the board and the starting position is shown in Figure 119. The object of the game, as in all chess games, is to capture (checkmate) the opposing King (General).

The *Chariot* moves exactly like the Rook in Chess (q.v.). The *Horse* is similar to the Knight except that it may not jump. Its move is one square orthogonally, then one square diagonally to left or right. This can give rise to interesting situations. In Figure 120, for example, the white Horse attacks the black Horse but not the reverse: the black Horse is blocked by the Soldier. In the same manner, a Horse entering the enemy position can find its retreat cut off.

The *Elephant* (or Bishop) moves two points diagonally; the intervening point must be vacant. The Elephant may not cross the river

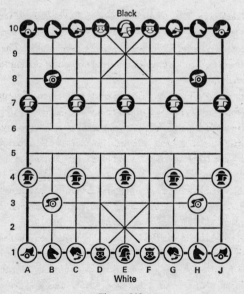

Figure 119

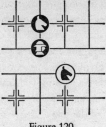

Figure 120

and is thus restricted to a maximum of seven stations. Elephants can defend each other.

The *Soldier* (or Pawn) moves straight forward one point at a time. The step across the river counts as one move; once across, a Soldier may also move sideways, again one point at a time. There is no promotion. A Soldier reaching the end rank may only move sideways.

The *Mandarin* (or Guard) moves one step diagonally and is confined to the fortress; thus the two Mandarins have a choice of only five stations between them. They readily defend each other. The *General* is also confined to the fortress and moves one point orthogonally but not diagonally.

All these pieces capture by displacement, as in Chess. Captured men are removed from the board and take no further part in the game.

The *Cannon* is unique in that it captures in a different way from which it moves. Its move is identical to that of the Chariot, but to capture it must have one man of either colour (known as the screen) between it and its prey, which may be anywhere along the same line beyond the screen. (If you consider the Cannon an anachronism, you are right: Xiangqi was being played before Cannons were invented. The old term for this piece was *Ballista*.)

Figure 121 demonstrates the Cannon's powers. Here two are working together – a formidable combination. For the position to be legal it must be Black to play as he is in check from the Cannon on rank 5. The Elephant is the screen. However, Black cannot move the piece away to escape check because then the Cannon on rank 5 would serve as a screen for the Cannon on rank 3 – and the black General would still be in check. In the position, Black can move his General away or he can interpose the Mandarin to escape the check. This second alternative would not be good, since White could reply Cannon (rank 3) takes Elephant, again giving check; the General would be obliged to move as the Mandarin is now pinned, and the Cannon on rank 5 could then capture the Mandarin. Notice that the black Cannon is powerless to intervene in the play.

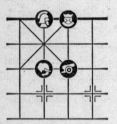

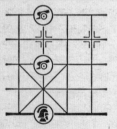

Figure 121

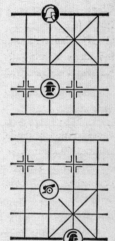

Figure 122

The rules governing check and checkmate are the same as in Chess. If one side checks (attacks the General) the second side must immediately get out of check by capturing the attacking piece, interposing (or sometimes, if the Cannon is the attacking piece, removing) a man, or removing the General. If none of these is possible, it is checkmate.

Generals may not face each other on an unoccupied file. Stalemate is a win for the player giving it, while repeated checks (perpetual check in Chess) as a way to draw are forbidden: the first player must break the repetition.

A few examples will clarify the rules and the moves of the men. In Figure 122, the black King is checkmated. He is attacked by the Cannon and cannot escape this attack by moving forward. The other point open to him is on a file occupied only by the opposing General and is therefore illegal. Without the Soldier the game is drawn, but the General and the Soldier alone can force stalemate.

The shortest possible game – equivalent to Fool's Mate in Chess – is shown (end position) in Figure 123. The play went: 1. B3C3 (i.e., left-hand Cannon one point to the right), F10E9; 2. C3C7* (Cannon takes Soldier), B8C8; 3. C7C10* mate. (An asterisk indicates a capture and a plus sign denotes check.) Black conspired at his own downfall. There are other versions of this mate.

Strategy

Consideration of the board and men illuminates the strategical possibilities. There is no strong diagonal-moving piece, so play tends to concentrate on the files and ranks. This is true from the start, when the untenanted files offer immediate entry for the Chariots and Cannons and at the same time point up the relative weakness of the Soldiers; they are isolated and lack the potential of their chess counterparts.

In Xiangqi the defence is favoured by being able to muster four pieces – the Elephants and Mandarins – that the attack cannot employ. The points to which these pieces have access – only a third of the home territory, you will notice – are naturally easier to defend.

The General, though well guarded by the Mandarins, cannot seek sanctuary elsewhere. His confinement to the fortress simplifies planning for the attacker.

It can be seen that the game is dominated by the three most powerful pieces of which the Chariot is the strongest. It is not easy to put a value on the Cannon. In the early stages of the game when the board is full it is a very strong piece, but as the men diminish, so do the potential screens, and a Cannon in the end game can have a hard time

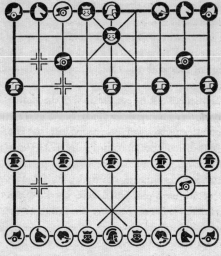

Figure 123

finding targets. The Horse and Cannon can be taken as being of approximately equal value, but few beginners are tempted to give up a Cannon for a Horse.

The game has been extensively analysed. The openings are, understandably, more limited than in our Chess – for one thing, the symmetry of the starting position effectively halves the number of possible openings. The openings can be divided into three main classes: Cannon, Horse and Soldier. Cannon openings are the most favoured, with the move of a Cannon to the central file perhaps the most common of all. The Horse openings are aimed at a secure base and are rather more passive, while an initial move of a Soldier on either the C or G files ('the Immortal points the way') allows the corresponding Horse to enter quickly into the battle. The consecration of individuals in the names of many chess openings is in contrast to the objective opening descriptions to be found in Xiangqi: how about 'Horse through fortress against advanced Soldier and Horses (Chariots not developed)'?

Game endings have been studied for centuries and theory has established the forces necessary to reach a decision. For example, with a Cannon, Elephants and Mandarins on both sides, the addition of a Horse is not enough to win. Yet a Horse alone forces a win by stalemate in conjunction with the General – unlike Chess where a lone Knight cannot mate.

A feel for Xiangqi can be got by playing through this game. The winner was the then champion of China. 1. H3E3, H10G8; 2. H1G3, J10H10; 3. J1H1, C7C6; 4. H1H7, B10C8; 5. B1A3, A7A6; 6. B3D3, H8J8; 7. H7G7*, J8J9; 8. A1B1, A10A8; 9. B1B7, J9G9 (attacking the Chariot); 10. G7F7, F10E9; 11. G4G5, G10E8; 12. G1J3 (defending the Soldier G5 and strengthening the flank), H10H6; 13. F7F9, G9G10; 14. G3F5, C6C5 (a sacrifice to open the rank); 15. C4C5*, C8D6; 16. F5D6*, H6D6*; 17. D1E2, G10H10; 18. D3C3, H10H5; 19. F9G9, H5H7 (with his Horse under attack, Black counter-attacks White's Chariot – check the position in Figure 124); 20. E3E7*, G8E7*; 21. B7E7*, H7H1 +; 22. J3G1, B8C8; 23. E7C7, H1H8; 24. C3H3 (a

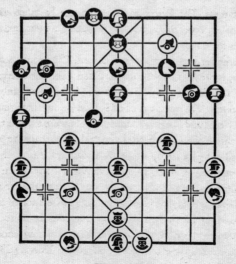

Figure 124

blocking move; Black is now on the defensive), D6E6; 25. G1E3, E6E4⋆; 26. G5G6, E8G6⋆; 27. G9G6⋆, C8E8; 28. C7F7, E9F10 (White threatened 29. G6G10+, E9F10; 30. F7F10⋆ + [or G10F10⋆ +] followed by mate with the other Chariot); 29. G6F6, D10E9; 30. F6F4, E4E5; 31. F7F5, E5E6; 32. F5F6, E6E5 (Black avoids the exchange of Chariots because his position is inferior); 33. C5C6, A8C8; 34. F4C4, C10A8; 35. C6D6, C8D8; 36. C4C7 (note the busy play on the ranks—another feature of Xiangqi), E5D5; 37. D6E6, D5D2; 38. A3C4, D2C2; 39. F6F7, D8D4; 40. C4D6 (the Horse is defended by the Soldier), C2C7⋆; 41. F7C7⋆, E8F8; 42. C7J7⋆, D4A4⋆; 43. J4J5, F8F2; 44. J7J8, H8H9; 45. J8A8⋆, A4G4; 46. D6E8, F2H2 (the black Cannons defend each other); 47. E3G1, G4G1⋆; 48. H3E3, resigns. White threatens 49. A8A10 +, E9D10; 50. Horse gives double check and mate. If 48 ... E10D10; White mates in three by A8A10 + or A8D8 +. (The end position is given in Figure 125.)

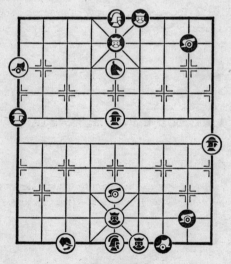

Figure 125

• WHERE TO BUY THE GAMES •

Card games

Special packs can be obtained for each of the games described. But these are luxuries: ordinary packs can easily be adapted.

Traditional games

These can generally be bought in any small town. The exceptions are Fanorona, Hex, Lasca, Mancala, Nine Men's Morris, Shogi, Tablut and Xiangqi, most of which are to be found in any specialist games shop. Pentominoes (Golomb's Game) are currently available as Hexed from Peter Pan Playthings. Finding Go and Reversi outside a city may require a little looking. Remember that Renju is played with a Go set. Xiangqi is available from almost any Chinese supermarket or fancy goods shop, but with the exception of this game and Shogi, traditional games are easily and cheaply made at home.

Proprietary games

Several of the better-known games can be bought almost anywhere but in case of difficulty may be obtained direct from the addresses given below:

Black Box –   Games Centre,
                22 Oxford St,
                London W1A 2LS

Hexagonal Chess –
    Hexagames Ltd,
    Mail Order Dept,
    32 Rosedene Avenue,
    London SW16 2LT

The L Game –
    Double Games Ltd,
    10 Hampstead Gardens,
    London NW11

    Jabo Inc.,
    P.O. Box 595, Decatur,
    Georgia 30031, U.S.A.

Master Mind –
    Invicta Plastics Ltd,
    Oadby,
    Leicester LE2 4LB

Napoleon at Waterloo –
    Simpubs Ltd,
    Oakfield House,
    60 Oakfield Avenue,
    Altrincham,
    Cheshire WA15 8EW

    Simulations Publications Inc.,
    257 Park Avenue South,
    NY 10010, New York, U.S.A.

Scrabble –
    Spear's Games,
    Richard House,
    Enstone Rd,
    Brimsdown,
    Enfield,
    Middlesex EN3 7TB

Skirrid –
    Skirrid International Ltd,
    142 New Walk,
    Leicester LE1 7JL

Brain Games

Star Chess –   Waddingtons Videomaster Ltd,
                      36–44 Tabernacle St,
                      London EC2A 4DT

War in Europe –   As for Napoleon at Waterloo

• BIBLIOGRAPHY •

Below is a short selection of books that cover usefully the next stage for the beginner. A few titles of general interest include the classic reference works.

All the major publishers are represented overseas. The books of one or two of the small publishers are more easily found in specialist games shops.

BACKGAMMON

The Backgammon Book by Oswald Jacoby and John R. Crawford (Macmillan)

Teach Yourself Backgammon by Robin Clay (Hodder and Stoughton)

BLACK BOX

Black Box Game Book by Eric Solomon (Strategy Games)

CARD GAMES

The Pan Book of Card Games by Hubert Philips (Pan)

The Penguin Book of Card Games by David Parlett (Allen Lane)

CHESS

Begin Chess by D. B. Pritchard (Elliot)

Chess by Edward Lasker (Batsford)

The Game of Chess by H. Golombek (Penguin)

Learn Chess by Edward Penn and John Littlewood (Pitman)

DRAUGHTS

Move Over by Derek Oldbury (Nicholas Kaye)

Brain Games

GO

Basic Techniques of Go by Haruyama Isamu and Nagahara Yoshiaki (Ishi Press)

Go: A Guide to the Game by D. B. Pritchard (Faber & Faber)

Go for Beginners by Kaoru Iwamoto (Penguin)

HEXAGONAL CHESS

First Theories of Hexagonal Chess by W. Glinski (Hexagonal Chess Publications)

THE L GAME

The 5-day Course in Thinking by Edward de Bono (Penguin)

MASTER MIND

The Official Mastermind Handbook by Leslie H. Ault (New American Library)

SCRABBLE

The Scrabble Book by Derryn Hinch (Macmillan)

The Complete Book of Scrabble by Gyles Brandreth (Robert Hale)

SHOGI

Shogi: Japan's Game of Strategy by Trevor Leggett (Charles E. Tuttle)

WARGAMING

The Comprehensive Guide to Board Wargaming by Nicholas Palmer (Arthur Barker)

The Best of Board Wargaming by Nicholas Palmer (Arthur Barker)

XIANGQI

Hsiang Ch'i – The Chinese Game of Chess by Terence Donnelly (Wargames Research Group)

GENERAL

Board & Table Games (Vols. I and II) by R. C. Bell (Dover)

Games Ancient and Oriental and How to Play Them by Edward Falkener (Dover)

History of Board Games other than Chess by Prof. H. J. R. Murray (Oxford University Press)

History of Chess by Prof. H. J. R. Murray (Oxford University Press)

The Illustrated Book of Table Games edited by Peter Arnold (Hamlyn)

The Compleat Strategist by J. D. Williams (McGraw-Hill)

More About Penguins
and Pelicans

For further information about books available from Penguins
please write to Dept EP, Penguin Books Ltd,
Harmondsworth, Middlesex UB7 0DA

In the U.S.A.: For a complete list of books available from
Penguins in the United States write to Dept CS, Penguin Books,
625 Madison Avenue, New York, New York 10022.

In Canada: For a complete list of books available from Penguins
in Canada write to Penguin Books Canada Ltd, 2801 John Street,
Markham, Ontario L3R 1B4.

In Australia: For a complete list of books available from Penguins
in Australia write to the Marketing Department, Penguin Books
Australia Ltd, P.O. Box 257, Ringwood, Victoria 3134.

In New Zealand: For a complete list of books available from
Penguins in New Zealand write to the Marketing Department,
Penguin Books (N.Z.) Ltd, P.O. Box 4019, Auckland 10.

Play the game with Penguins!

THE PENGUIN BOOK OF WORD GAMES
David Parlett

Here are over a hundred games – some old, some new, some oral (and even loud), some written. Whether you choose DAFT DEFINITIONS, CHARADES, TWENTY QUESTIONS or UP THE DICTIONARY, WORD PING-PONG and CONSEQUENCES, you are sure to find yourself chortling with mirth, strangling the odd friend or two and even increasing your vocabulary!

THE PENGUIN BOOK OF CARD GAMES
David Parlett

Some 300 card games from Britain and around the world are explained simply but authoritatively in this specially prepared book. The author, a games consultant, inventor and noted writer on card games, believes that everybody would enjoy cards if only they knew how to find the games most likely to appeal to their own idea of enjoyment – which might be Bridge, but could equally well prove to be Bismarck, Black Maria, Belote, Bezique or Bavarian Tarock.

THE PENGUIN ENCYCLOPEDIA OF CHESS
Edited by Harry Golombek

A sumptuous work of reference, with entries covering every aspect of the game, from the theories and players to chess in the cinema and chess in Shakespeare.

'I prophesy that within only a few months chess-playing households throughout the English-speaking world, and indeed beyond it, will be seeking chess information, and settling chess arguments, with a cry of "Where's the Golombek?" '–Bernard Levin in *The Times*

NOTES ON RUBIK'S MAGIC CUBE

David Singmaster

So you've solved the Cube . . . now what? How, exactly, does it work? How do you do the duo twist and the mono swap? What is a Cubist's thumb? Singmaster's unique blue guide is specially for everyone who thought they knew everything about the Cube, it's packed with new information, plus the latest news and results from Cubists all over the world.

'The definitive treatise' – Douglas Hofstadter
'Une veritable bible du "cubiste" ' – *Science et Vie*
'Beyond all understanding' – *New Standard*

GÖDEL, ESCHER, BACH:
An Eternal Golden Braid

Douglas R. Hofstadter

Linking the music of J. S. Bach, the graphic art of Escher and the mathematical theorems of Gödel, as well as ideas drawn from logic, biology, psychology, physics and linguistics, Douglas Hofstadter illuminates one of the greatest mysteries of modern science: the nature of human thought processes.

'Extraordinary, exhilarating . . . this splendid *tour de force* . . . leaves you feeling you have had a first-class workout in the best mental gymnasium in town' – *New Statesman*

THE MAGIC OF LEWIS CARROLL

Edited by John Fisher

Behind the seemingly absurd events in Lewis Carroll's fantasies of Alice and the Snark there lie a mass of mathematical games and puzzles, logical conundrums, word-plays and conjuring tricks. Although his serious work as a mathematician at Oxford was unremarkable, Carroll was able to weave webs of improbability in his 'entertainments' which can confuse even the best brains, and have earned him his place in the history of mathematical and logical thought.

In this thoroughly entertaining collection, John Fisher gathers together both Carroll's own puzzles and other contemporary tricks and games which influenced him.

MS READ-a-thon—
a simple way to start
youngsters reading

Boys and girls between 6 and 14 can join the MS READ-a-thon and help find a cure for Multiple Sclerosis by reading books. And they get two rewards — the enjoyment of reading, and the great feeling that comes from helping others.

Parents and educators: For complete information call your local MS chapter. Or mail the coupon below.

Kids can help, too!

- -

"FAT IS A FEMINIST ISSUE..."

This astonishing and highly sensible new book by a
practicing psychotherapist tells you how to get off
the diet/binge merry-go-round and lose weight by
enjoying your food, your life and yourself!
Illustrated with actual case histories; complete with
special sections on compulsive eating and *anorexia
nervosa* (self-starvation).

A co-founder of the London Women's Therapy
Center, *Susie Orbach* is a specialist in the treatment
of compulsive eating.

FAT
IS A
FEMINIST ISSUE

THE ANTI-DIET GUIDE
TO PERMANENT WEIGHT LOSS

Susie Orbach

BERKLEY BOOKS, NEW YORK

FAT IS A FEMINIST ISSUE

A Berkley Book / published by arrangement with
Paddington Press Ltd.

PRINTING HISTORY
Paddington Press edition published 1978
Berkley edition / April 1979
Seventh printing / June 1981

ISBN: 0-425-05009-2

A BERKLEY BOOK ® TM 757,375
Berkley Books are published by Berkley Publishing Corporation,
200 Madison Avenue, New York, New York 10016.
PRINTED IN THE UNITED STATES OF AMERICA

For
Eleanor Anguti,
Carol Bloom
and
Lela Zaphiropoulos

Contents

Acknowledgments

Thanks are due to many, many people. First to Carol Munter, the original compulsive-eating and self-image group, and all the women with whom I have worked and who have shared their feelings about their bodies with me. Without these people there would be no book and nothing to say. Thanks too to all those people who have generously encouraged, helped and supported me in this work in one way or another over the past six years. They include Dale Bernstein, Patrick Byrne, Warren Cohen, Anne Cooke, Clare Dennis, Luise Eichenbaum, Peggy Eliot, Ian Franklin, Barbara Goldberg, Clara Caleo Green, Rose Heatley, Altheia Jones Lecointe, Eddie Lebar, Bob Lefferts, David McLanahan, Laurence Orbach, Ruth Orbach, Rosie Parker, Jeremy Pikser, Cathy Porter, Ron Radosh, Olly Rosengart, Julie Saj, Steve Sandler, David Skinner, Dee Dee Skinner, Laura Schwartz, Michael Schwartz, Ann Snitow, Jimmy Traub, Redesign, Spare Rib and the Women's Therapy Centre.

Finally, four people have come through with

support in immeasurable ways. Sara Baerwald has provided consistent no-nonsense support from afar. Malinda Coleman miraculously dropped everything to provide crucial help at a critical time. Gillian Slovo cared for me very well in the final stages. Joseph Schwartz came through in unimaginable ways providing love, support, patience, criticism, handholding and chicken soup throughout—my love and deep appreciation cannot express how important this has been to me.

Preface

In March 1970, I went to the Alternate U on Sixth Avenue and 14th Street in New York City to register for a course on compulsive eating and self-image—women only. I walked into a room jammed with forty women of various sizes talking about their bodies and their eating habits. Carol Munter, the course organizer, visibly delighted by the turnout, was suggesting that we break up into four groups. It was the first time since the beginning of the women's liberation movement that women had dared to come forward for discussion groups specifically dealing with body image. The call for the course had

seemed to me almost like a travesty—feminists concerned about how they looked! At the time we were used to rejecting male ideals of how we should look as projected in advertisements and movies. We were ostensibly happy in our blue jeans and work shirts. We were not used to discussing clothes or body size with our female friends; there was, in fact, a widespread feeling of relief that we could relax in our clothes and bodies and not worry about what was especially fashionable, provocative or appealing. We wore the clothes of rebellion and did not care what others thought. Or did we?

Before we divided into groups, Carol Munter mentioned two things. The first was that she knew someone who had lost a lot of weight without dieting; the second, that she had constructed in the closet next door a four-way mirror by pasting long strips of aluminum foil on the walls. Anyone who wanted could go into the closet and look at herself in private from all four sides for as long as she wanted. Carol thought these two things—non-dieting and self-acceptance—might be keys to weight loss. I scarcely paid attention. I was thinking, "What am I doing here? I often look at myself in the mirror, I'm not frightened to do that. . . . I'm slimmer than some, will the other women accept me?"

Our group set a meeting time for the following week and we all dispersed. I was confused, having anticipated a discussion of nutritional standards in the United States and the Third World, or perhaps a look at the food and fashion industries or the incidence of obesity in "rich countries." I was hesitant to explore the topic of compulsive eating outside the context of a political vocabulary—a vocabulary that looked at the relationship between

patriarchy and Western society with the family as
the lynch pin. I was uneasy but held on to the slogan
that the personal is political.

I would not have gone back but for one thing.
Despite my discomfort and need to compare myself
with the other women, I also experienced an
overwhelming relief to be in a group with women,
fat and thin, who were all compulsive eaters. The
problem had been named and perhaps I did not
have to feel quite so ashamed. In the last year or so I
had become quite used to talking about very
personal topics in consciousness-raising groups and
I was suddenly quite excited that Carol was
suggesting we discuss in the same way a subject that
had been so hidden and so private.

Six months later I left the group. I no longer
defined myself as a compulsive eater and I had
stabilized at a weight I found acceptable. It turned
out to be rather higher than my previous Twiggy-
like fantasies. Food no longer terrified me and I
could live in my body. I find this knowledge
continues to amaze me, so painful were those ten
years of dieting, bingeing and self-hatred. So what
had happened in the group that had produced this
transformation? Really a lot!

We had taken the formula of a women's group
and one by one we shared how we felt about our
bodies, being attractive, food, eating, thinness,
fatness and clothes. We detailed our previous diet
histories and traded horror stories of doctors,
psychiatrists, diet organizations, health farms and
fasting. We knew enough to know that all our
previous attempts at getting our bodes the right
weight and shape had not worked. We wondered
why we had wanted them so right, *what* was so

powerful about looking a particular way that we
had all tried and succeeded in losing weight dozens
of times. We did not understand why we could not
keep "it" off; why every time we neared the goal "it"
would creep up, or why we always broke our diets.
Why were we so plagued by our body size and
shape?

We began asking new questions and coming up
with new answers. We were a self-help group at the
time when energy from the women's liberation
movement sparked us all into rethinking many
previously held assumptions. The creativity of the
movement prepared a fertile soil in which feminist
ideas, nurtured and developed in countless
consciousness-raising groups, in mass marches and
demonstrations, in organized political campaigns,
found new applications and usefulness. Compulsive
eating was one such area.

Compulsive eating is a very painful and, on the
surface, self-destructive, activity. But feminism has
taught us to be wary of this label. Feminism has
taught us that activities that appear to be self-
destructive are invariably adaptations, attempts to
cope with the world. In our group, we turned our
strongly held ideas about dieting and thinness
upside down. Carol reminded us of her friend who
lost weight without dieting. Slowly and unsurely we
stopped dieting. Nothing terrible happened. My
world did not collapse. Carol raised the central
question; maybe we did not want to be thin. I
dismissed that out of hand. Of course I wanted to be
thin, I would be. . . . The dots turned out to hold the
answer. Who I would be thin was different from
who *I* was. I decided I did not want to be thin, there
was not much in it. You were more hassled by men,

you became a sex object. No, I definitely did not
want to be thin. . . . I developed a new political
reason for not being thin—I was not going to be like
the fashion magazines wanted me to be; I was a
Jewish beatnik and I would be *zaftig*. I relaxed, ate
what I wanted, and wore clothes that were
expressive of me. I even felt a little smug. I ignored
the diet sheets in the newspapers, I enjoyed the
different food phases I was going through and I
walked down the street feeling increasingly confident. But the dots nagged. Why was I afraid of being
thin? The things I was frightened of came into
vision. I confronted them, always asking myself—
how would it help to be fat in this situation? *What*
would be more troublesome if I were thin? As the
image of my fat and thin personality conflated, I
began to lose weight. I felt a deep satisfaction that I
could be a size that felt good for me and no longer
obsessed with food. I promised myself I would not
be responsible for depriving myself of the food I
liked. I had learned a crucial lesson—that I could be
the same person thin as I was fat. Satisfied, I left the
group. Together we had developed a theory and
practice that made sense. Carol and I went on to
help other women sort through this problem. We
ran groups. We became therapists and worked with
women individually and together for five years.

This book is an attempt to share this work. It is
my view of what we learned in that first group and
then with the subsequent groups and individual
women who shared their compulsive-eating problems with us. As such, this book is necessarily
limited; it does not have enough scope to provide a
comprehensive picture of compulsive eating, but it

does address dimensions that have been missed by other people who work in the field. The observations and insights are drawn from women from the United States, Canada and England. They are all white and range in age from seventeen to sixty-five. They include grandmothers and single women. The women are from working-class backgrounds and middle- and upper-middle-income groups. I very much hope that this book will be useful to a wider audience, particularly black and Latin women, but I recognize that their cultural experience is different from those of the women with whom these ideas were developed and may therefore not address significant themes for them.

Compulsive eating has been studied by many different people, including psychiatrists, psychoanalysts, psychologists, doctors, nutritionists and endocrinologists.[1] By and large, the approach has been either to try to remove the resultant obesity or to treat the underlying cause of distress that has produced compulsive eating. Compulsive eating has never been strictly defined but what it has meant for me and the women I have worked with is:

Eating when you are not physically hungry.

Feeling out of control around food, submerged by either dieting or gorging.

Spending a good deal of time thinking and worrying about foot and fatness.

Scouring the latest diet for vital information.

Feeling awful about yourself as someone who is out of control.

Feeling awful about your body.

Our approach has been to see compulsive eating as *both* a symptom and a problem in itself. It is a symptom in the sense that the compulsive eater does not know how to cope with whatever underlies this behavior and turns to food. On the other hand, the compulsive-eating syndrome is so highly developed and painfully absorbing that it has to be addressed directly as the problem too. Consequently, we address both aspects. We explore and demystify the symptom to find out what is being expressed in the desire to be fat, in the fear of thinness and in the wish to fill and starve ourselves. At the same time we attempt to intervene directly so that the feelings and behavior around food can change. Underlying problems need to be exposed and separated, though not necessarily worked through. The perspective is always to see the social dimensions that have led women to choose compulsive eating as an adaptation to sexist pressure in contemporary society.

We are aware that contemporary preoccupation with thinness is both new and restricted to those Western nations that appear not to have food shortages. The food production in these countries is largely in the hands of multinational corporations.[2] They cover all aspects of the market from "high protein," "vitamin rich" foods and "wholesome, natural" foods, or dietetic candies, jellies, ice creams, milks and sodas. Women, as the most important purchasers of foods, are presented with a seemingly vast choice. They must choose wisely for their families' health and welfare. At the same time every woman is continually confronted with images of slimness and trimness and advice on how to eat sensibly, lose weight and have a happy life. This general concern with thinness affects both women

and men, and people are often driven to reduce their size when they were not previously over large. Thus starts a cycle of food deprivation and compulsive eating. Women are especially susceptible to these demands to lose weight because they are brought up to conform to an image of womanhood that places importance on body size and shape. We are taught that we must both blend in and stand out—a contradictory message indeed.

Men are increasingly being affected by similar pressures and although I have worked with several men, I have not attempted to formulate a theory that describes how sexism affects men's body size.

This book is written as a self-help manual. However, therapists may wish to incorporate this method into their own work with compulsive eaters.[3]

To all women who suffer from the problem of compulsive eating, I hope that the accumulated experience of other women as expressed in this book will speak to you.

Susie Orbach
London, 1978

Introduction

Obesity and overeating have joined sex as central issues in the lives of many women today. In the United States, 50 percent of women are estimated to be overweight. Every women's magazine has a diet column. Diet doctors and clinics flourish. The names of diet foods are now part of our general vocabulary. Physical fitness and beauty are every woman's goals. While this preoccupation with fat and food has become so common that we tend to take it for granted, being fat, feeling fat and the compulsion to overeat are, in fact, serious and painful experiences for the women involved.

3

Being fat isolates and invalidates a woman.
Almost inevitably, the explanations offered for
fatness point a finger at the failure of women
themselves to control their weight, control their
appetites and control their impulses. Women
suffering from the problem of compulsive eating
endure a double anguish: feeling out of step with the
rest of society, and believing that it is all their own
fault.

The number of women who have problems with
weight and compulsive eating is large and growing.
Owing to the emotional distress involved and the
fact that the many varied solutions offered to
women in the past have not worked, a new
psychotherapy to deal with compulsive eating has
had to evolve within the context of the movement
for women's liberation. This new psychotherapy
represents a feminist rethinking of traditional
psychoanalysis.

A psychoanalytic approach has much to offer
toward a solution to compulsive-eating problems. It
provides ways for exploring the roots of such
problems in early experiences. It shows us how we
develop our adult personalities, most importantly
our sexual identity—how a female baby becomes a
girl and then a woman, and how a male baby
becomes a boy and then a man. Psychoanalytic
insight helps us to understand what getting fat and
overeating mean to individual women—by explaining their conscious or unconscious acts.

An approach based exclusively on classical
psychoanalysis, without a feminist perspective is,
however, inadequate. Since the Second World War,
psychiatry has, by and large, told unhappy women
that their discontent represents an inability to

resolve the "Oedipal constellation." Female fatness has been diagnosed as an obsessive-compulsive symptom related to separation-individuation, narcissism and insufficient ego development.[1] Being overweight is seen as a deviance and anti-men. Overeating and obesity have been reduced to character defects, rather than perceived as the expression of painful and conflicting experiences. Furthermore, rather than attempting to uncover and confront women's bad feelings about their bodies or toward food, professionals concerned themselves with the problem of how to get the women thin. So, after the psychiatrists, analysts and clinical psychologists proved unsuccessful, experimental workers looked for biological and even genetic reasons for obesity. None of these approaches has had convincing, lasting results. None of them has addressed the central issues of compulsive eating which are rooted in the social inequality of women.

A feminist perspective to the problem of women's compulsive eating is essential if we are to move on from the ineffective blame-the-victim approach[2] and the unsatisfactory adjustment model of treatment. While psychoanalysis gives us useful tools to discover the deepest sources of emotional distress, feminism insists that those painful personal experiences derive from the social context into which female babies are born, and within which they develop to become adult women. The fact that compulsive eating is overwhelmingly a woman's problem suggests that it has something to do with the experience of being female in our society. Feminism argues that being fat represents an attempt to break free of society's sex stereotypes.

Getting fat can thus be understood as a definite and purposeful act; it is a directed, conscious or unconscious, challenge to sex-role stereotyping and culturally defined experience of womanhood.

Fat is a social disease, and fat is a feminist issue. Fat is *not* about lack of self-control or lack of will power. Fat *is* about protection, sex, nurturance, strength, boundaries, mothering, substance, assertion and rage. It is a response to the inequality of the sexes. Fat expresses experiences of women today in ways that are seldom examined and even more seldom treated. While becoming fat does not alter the roots of sexual oppression, an examination of the underlying causes or unconscious motivation that lead women to compulsive eating suggests new treatment possibilities. Unlike most weight-reducing schemes, our new therapeutic approach does not reinforce the oppressive social roles that lead women into compulsive eating in the first place. What is it about the social position of women that leads them to respond to it by getting fat?

The current ideological justification for inequality of the sexes has been built on the concept of the innate differences between women and men. Women alone can give birth to and breast-feed their infants and, as a result, a primary dependency relationship develops between mother and child. While this biological capacity is the only known genetic difference between men and women,[3] it is used as the basis on which to divide unequally women and men's labor, power, roles and expectations. The division of labor has become institutionalized. Woman's capacity to reproduce and provide nourishment has relegated her to the care and socialization of children.

The relegation of women to the social roles of wife and mother has several significant consequences that contribute to the problem of fat. First, in order to become a wife and mother, a woman has to have a man. Getting a man is presented as an almost unattainable and yet essential goal. To get a man, a woman has to learn to regard herself as an item, a commodity, a sex object. Much of her experience and identity depends on how she and others see her. As John Berger says in *Ways of Seeing*:

Men *act* and women *appear*. Men look at women. Women watch themselves being looked at. This determines not only most relations between men and women, but also the relation of women to themselves.[4]

This emphasis on presentation as the central aspect of a woman's existence makes her extremely self-conscious. It demands that she occupy herself with a self-image that others will find pleasing and attractive—an image that will immediately convey what kind of woman she is. She must observe and evaluate herself, scrutinizing every detail of herself as though she were an outside judge. She attempts to make herself in the image of womanhood presented by billboards, newspapers, magazines and television. The media present women either in a sexual context or within the family, reflecting a woman's two prescribed roles, first as a sex object, and then as a mother. She is brought up to marry by "catching" a man with her good looks and pleasing manner. To do this she must look appealing, earthy, sensual, sexual, virginal, innocent, reliable, daring, mysterious, coquettish and thin. In other words, she offers her self-image on the marriage marketplace. As a married woman, her sexuality will be

sanctioned and her economic needs will be looked after. She will have achieved the first step of womanhood.

Since women are taught to see themselves from the outside as candidates for men, they become prey to the huge fashion and diet industries that first set up the ideal images and then exhort women to meet them. The message is loud and clear—the woman's body is not her own. The woman's body is not satisfactory as it is. It must be thin, free of "unwanted hair," deodorized, perfumed and clothed. It must conform to an ideal physical type. Family and school socialization teaches girls to groom themselves properly. Furthermore, the job is never-ending, for the image changes from year to year. In the early 1960s, the only way to feel acceptable was to be skinny and flat chested with long straight hair. The first of these was achieved by near starvation, the second, by binding one's breasts with an ace bandage and the third, by ironing one's hair. Then in the early 1970s, the look was curly hair and full breasts. Just as styles in clothes change seasonally, so women's bodies are expected to change to fit these fashions. Long and skinny one year, petite and demure the next, women are continually manipulated by images of proper womanhood, which are extremely powerful because they are presented as the only reality. To ignore them means to risk being an outcast. Women are urged to conform, to help out the economy by continuous consumption of goods and clothing that are quickly made unwearable by the next season's fashion styles in clothes and body shapes. In the background, a ten billion dollar industry waits to remold bodies to the latest fashion. In this way,

women are caught in an attempt to conform to a standard that is *externally* defined and constantly changing. But these models of femininity are experienced by women as unreal, frightening and unattainable. They produce a picture that is far removed from the reality of women's day-to-day lives.

The one constant in these images is that a woman must be thin. For many women, compulsive eating and being fat have become one way to avoid being marketed or seen as the ideal woman: "My fat says 'screw you' to all who want me to be the perfect mom, sweetheart, maid and whore. Take me for who *I* am, not for who I'm supposed to be. If you are really interested in *me*, you can wade through the layers and find out who I am." In this way, fat expresses a rebellion against the powerlessness of the woman, against the pressure to look and act in a certain way and against being evaluated on her ability to create an image of herself.

Becoming fat is, thus, a woman's response to the first step in the process of fulfilling a prescribed social role which requires her to shape herself to an externally imposed image in order to catch a man. But a second stage in this process takes place after she achieves that goal, after she has become a wife and mother.

For a mother, everyone else's needs come first. Mothers are the unpaid managers of small, essential, complex and demanding organizations. They may not control the financial arrangements of this minicorporation or the major decisions on location or capital expenditure, but they do generally control the day-to-day operations. For her keep, the mother works an estimated ten hours a

day (eighteen, if she has a second job outside the home) making sure that the food is purchased and prepared, the children's clothes, toys and books are in place, and that the father's effects are at the ready. She makes the house habitable, clean and comfy; she does the social secretarial work of arranging for the family to spend time with relatives and friends; she provides a baby-sitting and chauffeur-escort service for her children. As babies and children, we are all cared for. As adults, however, women are expected to feed and clean not only their babies but also their husbands, and only then, themselves.

In this role women experience particular pressure over food and eating. After the birth of each baby, breasts or bottle becomes a major issue. The mother is often made to feel insecure about her adequacy to perform her fundamental job. In the hospital the baby is weighed after each feed to see if the mother's breasts have enough milk. Pediatricians and baby-care books bombard the new mother with authoritative but conflicting advice about, for example, scheduled versus demand feeding, composition of the formula or the introduction of solid foods. As her children grow older, a woman continues to be reminded that her feeding skills are inadequate. To the tune of billions of dollars a year, the food industry counsels her on how, when and what she should feed her charges. The advertisements cajole her into providing nutritious breakfasts, munchy snacks, and wholesome dinners. Media preoccupation with good housekeeping and, particularly, with good food and good feeding, serves as a yardstick by which to measure the mother's ever-failing performance. This preoccupation colonizes food preparation so

that the housewife is presented with a list of "do's" and "don'ts" so contradictory that it is a wonder that anything gets produced in the kitchen at all. It is not surprising that a woman quickly learns not to trust her own impulses, either in feeding her family or in listening to her own needs when she feeds herself.

During the period in her life which is devoted to child rearing, the woman is constantly making sure that others' lives run smoothly. She does this without thinking seriously that she is working at a full-time job. Her own experience of everyday life is as midwife to others' activities. While she is preparing her children to become future workers, and enabling her husband to be a more "effective" producer, her role is to produce and reproduce workers. In this capacity she is constantly giving out without receiving the credit that would validate her social worth.

In a capitalist society everyone is defined by their job. A higher status is given to businessmen, academics and professionals than to production and service workers. Women's work in the home falls into the service and production category. Although often described as menial, deemed creative, dismissed as easy, or revered as god-given, women's work is seen as existing outside the production process and therefore devalued. Women as a group are allowed less expression than the men in their social class. However oppressed men are by a class society, they hold more power than women. Every man has to watch out for his boss. Every woman has to watch out lest her man not approve. The standards and views of the day are male. Women are seen as different from normal people

(who are men), they are seen as "other."[5] They are not accepted as equal human beings with men. Their full identity is not supported by the society in which they grow up. This leads to confusion for women. Women are trapped in the role of an alien, yet delegated responsibility for making sure that others' lives are productive.

Since women are not accepted as equal human beings but are nevertheless expected to devote enormous energy to the lives of others, the distinctions between their own lives and the lives of those close to them may become blurred. Merging with others, feeding others, not knowing how to make space for themselves are frequent themes for women. Mothers are constantly giving out and feeding the world; everyone else's needs are primary. That they feel confusion about their own bodily needs is not surprising and there may be few ways of noting their personal concerns. A form of giving to and replenishing oneself is through food. "I eat a lot because I'm always stoking myself up for the days's encounters. I look after my family, my mother and any number of people who pass in and out of my day. I feel empty with all this giving so I eat to fill up the spaces and give me sustenance to go on giving to the world." The resulting fat has the function of making the space for which women crave. It is an attempt to answer the question, "If I am constantly giving myself to everyone, where do I begin and end?" We want to look and be substantial. We want to be bigger than society will let us. We want to take up as much space as the other sex. "If I get bigger like a man then maybe I'll get taken seriously as is a man."

What happens to the woman who does not fit the

social role? Although the image of ideal sexual object and all-competent mother is socially pervasive, it is not only limiting and unattainable, but it also fails to correspond to the reality of many, many women's lives today. Most women today do still marry and have children. But many also continue to work outside the home after marriage, either to meet economic needs or in an attempt to break the limits of their social role. Women continually juggle with the many different aspects of their personalities which are developed and expressed at great cost against this unfriendly background. In this context, just as many women first become fat in an attempt to avoid being made into sexual objects at the beginning of their adult lives, so many women remain fat as a way of neutralizing their sexual identity in the eyes of others who are important to them as their life progresses. In this way, they can hope to be taken seriously in their working lives outside the home. It is unusual for women to be accepted for their competence in this sphere. When they lose weight, that is, begin to look like a perfect female, they find themselves being treated frivolously by their male colleagues. When women are thin, they *are* treated frivolously: thin-sexy-incompetent worker. But if a woman loses weight, she herself may not yet be able to separate thinness from the packaged sexuality around her which simultaneously defines her as incompetent. It is difficult to conform to one image that society would have you fit (thin) without also being the other image (sexy female). "When I'm fat, I feel I can hold my own. Whenever I get thin I feel I'm being treated like a little doll who doesn't know which end is up."

We have seen how fat is a symbolic rejection of

the limitations of women's role, an adaptation that many women use in the burdensome attempt to pursue their individual lives within the proscriptions of their social function. But in order to understand more about the way that overweight and, in particular, overeating, function in the lives of individual women, we must examine the process by which they are initially taught their social role. It is a complex and ironic process, for women are prepared for this life of inequality by other women who themselves suffer its limitations—their mothers. The feminist perspective reveals that compulsive eating is, in fact, an expression of the complex relationships between mothers and daughters.

If a woman's social role is to become a mother, nurturing—feeding the family in the widest possible sense—is the mother's central job. By and large, it is only within the family that a woman has any social power. Her competence as a mother and her ability to be an emotional support for her family defines her and provides her with a recognized context within which to exist. For a mother, a crucial part of the maternal role is to help her daughter, as her mother did before her, to make a smooth transition into the female social role. From her mother, the young girl learns who she herself is and can be. The mother provides her with a model of feminine behavior, and directs the daughter's behavior in particular ways.

But the world the mother must present to her daughter is one of unequal relationships, between parent and child, authority and powerlessness, man and woman. The child is exposed to the world of power relationships by a unit that itself produces and reproduces perhaps the most fundamental of

these inequalities. Within the family, an inferior sense of self is instilled into little girls.[6] While it is obvious that the growing-up process for girls and boys is vastly different, what may be less apparent is that to prepare her daughter for a life of inequality, the mother tries to hold back her child's desires to be a powerful, autonomous, self-directed, energetic and productive human being. From an early age, the young girl is encouraged to accept this rupture in her development and is guided to cope with this loss by putting her energy into taking care of others. Her own needs for emotional support and growth will be satisfied if she can convert them into giving to others.

Meanwhile, little boys are taught to accept emotional support without learning how to give this kind of nurturing and loving in return. Therefore, when a young woman finally achieves the social reward of marriage, she finds that it rarely provides either the nurture she still needs, or an opportunity for independence and self-development. To be a woman is to live with the tension of giving and not getting; and the mother and daughter involved in the process leading to this conclusion are inevitably bound up in ambivalence, difficulty and conflict.

If we look at it from the mother's point of view, the process of leading her daughter to adult womanhood is ambivalent for several reasons. The first is the question of independence. The mother, who has been prepared for a life of giving, finds her feeding, nurturing and child-rearing capacity—so integral to her success in her social role—satisfied. She needs to be needed and has indeed fulfilled herself as a "good mother" by attentively feeding her child. Thus, mothers do and do not want their

daughters to leave them. They do because the maternal role also requires them to prepare their daughters for eventual independence: to fail at this is to fail at motherhood. On the other hand, to succeed at this signals the end of motherhood. We have seen that of the limited roles that have been available to women in this century, motherhood is the only one in which women have legitimate power. Therefore, their personal success at being mothers results in their loss of power. Their personal success is a dead end; it does not lead on to the creation of a new, equally powerful role.

The mother's ambivalence is, however, even more painful in that mothers do and do not want their daughters to be like them. For a daughter to be like her mother is a way, at least partially, to validate the mother's life. But, the mother's life remains an invalidated life and the daughter's act of reproducing her mother's lifestyle can be no more than a perpetuation of powerlessness. In her love for her daughter, the mother must inevitably want a different life for her.

Nevertheless, mothers may feel ambivalent about the changing opportunities available to their daughters which were not available to them. They may be jealous of these opportunities, and fearful of their daughters' welfare in a world they know to be hostile to women, at the same time as they acquire some indirect satisfaction at their daughters' ambition and success. While a mother must be a mother, a daughter can be ambitious and engaged in the world.

Let us now look at these conflicts from the daughter's point of view. Daughters do and do not want to leave their mothers. For a daughter to leave

is for her to become independent, part of the world, to signal her emergence as a female adult. However, this autonomy itself causes problems. As we have seen, independence in the world is not yet an option for female adults. Daughters feel ambivalent about their opportunities in the world; they are ill-prepared to take them up, as they have learned both from the culture at large and from their own mothers.

Daughters identify with the powerlessness of their mothers as women in a patriarchal society. They have been brought up to be like their mothers. But daughters both do and do not want to be like their mothers. While they identify with their mothers as women, as givers, as caretakers, they may nevertheless desire a different experience of womanhood. In leaving, in moving outside the prescribed female role, the daughter may feel she is betraying her mother or is showing her up by doing "better." She may also feel nervous about being on shaky, untested ground. Furthermore, if a daughter identifies with her mother's powerlessness, she may see her role as that of taking care of her mother—to provide her mother with the love, care and interest she never received. She becomes her mother's mother? Leaving becomes even more of a betrayal.

How do these ambivalences and conflicts in the mother-daughter relationship come to express themselves in fat, food and feeding? How is each adult woman who suffers from compulsive eating expressing what happened to her with her mother. It is obvious that feeding plays a crucial part in the relationship of mother and child, whatever the child's sex. Within the whole spectrum of nurturing activities expected of mothers, physical feeding is

the most fundamental—indeed, instinctive. A mother's breasts provide food for her children, virtually without any conscious act on her own part, whereas all other nurturing activities, including the vital provision of emotional support, must be learned.

Because of her ambivalence toward her daughter, a mother's willingness to provide her with sensitive nurturing, both physically and emotionally, can be undermined. Both female and male babies experience their first love relationships with the mother, but early on the mother must withhold a certain degree of support and sustenance from her daughter, in order to teach her the ways of womanhood. This has specific consequences. In *Little Girls,*[7] Elena Gianini Belotti cites a study of mothers' attitudes and actions when feeding their babies. In a sample of babies of both sexes, 99 percent of boys were breast-fed, while only 66 percent of girls were. Girls were weaned significantly earlier than boys and spent 50 percent less time feeding (in the case of breast- and bottle-feeds this meant much smaller feeds than the boys'). Thus, daughters are often fed less well, less attentively and less sensitively than they need. Inappropriate and insensitive physical feeding is subsequently paralleled unconsciously by inadequate emotional feeding.

While unconsciously the mother may not be nurturing her daughter well, she gives up feeding her daughter only reluctantly. In the absence of an alternative role, the distinction between herself and her child now outside the womb may become blurred. The mother may see her child as a product, a possession or an extension of herself. Thus, the

mother has an interest in retaining control over how much, what, when and how her child eats. She needs to encourage this initial dependency for her own social survival.

There may be great ambivalence about feeding and nurturing. A mother must make sure her daughter is not overfed in case she becomes greedy and overweight—a terrible fate for a girl. She must make sure the child looks healthy—this is normally associated with a certain roundness—and she needs the child to depend on her; for who else is she, if she is not seen as mother? Yet she may also dislike this dependency, which ties her down, drains her and prevents her from directing her energies elsewhere. Finally, she must prepare her daughter to become the future nurturer and feeder of someone else—her daughter's future child, lover, husband or parents. She must teach her daughter to be concerned with feeding and nourishing others at the cost of not fully developing herself.

Meanwhile, on the daughter's side, as she develops from child to woman, the daughter's feeding of herself can become a symbolic response to both the physical and emotional deprivation she suffered as a child, an expression of her fraught intimacy with her mother. As the child gets more adept, she begins to feed herself and select her own foods, producing a developing sense of independence of the mother. But this break causes conflict for the daughter. On the one hand, the daughter wants to move away and learn to take care of herself; on the other hand, this ability to nurture herself suggests a rejection of the mother. This rejection takes on a deep significance because of the social limitation of the woman's role in patriarchal

society. If the mother is not needed as mother, who will she be? The daughter feels guilty about destroying her mother's only role. As she seeks emotional sustenance through other social relationships, the adult daughter may continue to suffer deprivation, as her own partner has, very often, not learned to give. She turns to eating in the search for love, comfort, warmth and support—for that indefinable something that seems never to be there.

Compulsive eating becomes a way of expressing either side of this conflict. In overfeeding herself, the daughter may be trying to reject her mother's role while at the same time reproaching the mother for inadequate nurturing; or she may be attempting to retain a sense of identity with her mother. Popular culture abounds with evidence of the symbolic value that food and fat hold between mothers and daughters. In *Lady Oracle,*[8] for example, Margaret Atwood shows how the daughter's fat becomes a weapon in her battle with her mother. When her mother gives Joan a clothing allowance as an incentive to reduce, Joan deliberately buys clothes that flaunt her size and finally, with the purchase of a lime-green carcoat, succeeds in reducing her mother to tears:

My mother had never cried where I could see her and I was dismayed, but elated too at this evidence of my power, my only power. I had defeated her; I wouldn't ever let her make me over in her image, thin and beautiful.

Similarly, in the movie, *Summer Wishes, Winter Dreams,* when the mother criticizes her daughter's size, the latter blasts back that her fat is her own, that it is something for which she alone is

responsible, that it is something her mother cannot take away too.

Women engaged in exploring their compulsive eating in relation to their mothers have come to the following varied realizations:

My fat says to my mother: "I'm substantial. I can protect myself. I can go out into the world."

My fat says to my mother: "Look at me. I'm a mess; I don't know how to take care of myself. You can still be my mother."

My fat says to my mother: "I'm going out in the world. I can't take you with me but I can take a part of you that's connected to me. My body is from yours. My fat is connected to you. This way I can still have you with me."

My fat says to my mother: "I'm leaving you but I still need you. My fat lets you know I'm not really able to take care of myself."

For the compulsive eater, fat has much symbolic meaning which makes sense within a feminist context. Fat is a response to the many oppressive manifestations of a sexist culture. Fat is a way of saying "no" to powerlessness and self-denial, to a limiting sexual expression which demands that females look and act a certain way, and to an image of womanhood that defines a specific social role. Fat offends Western ideals of female beauty and, as such, every "overweight" woman creates a crack in the popular culture's ability to make us mere products. Fat also expresses the tension in the mother-daughter relationship, the relationship which has been allocated the feminization of the female. This relationship is bound to be difficult in a patriarchal society because it demands that the

already oppressed mothers become the teachers, preparers and enforcers of the oppression that society will visit on their daughters.

While fat serves the symbolic function of rejecting the way by which society distorts women and their relationships with others, particularly in the critical relationship between mothers and daughters, getting fat remains an unhappy and unsatisfactory attempt to resolve these conflicts. It is a painful price to pay, whether a woman is trying to conform to society's expectations or attempting to forge a new identity.

When something is "amiss" in this way, we can expect a psychological imbalance and reaction. Few things could be more "amiss" than the attempt of a patriarchal culture to inhibit a young girl's desires to be creative and expressive, to push her almost exclusively into restrictive gender-linked activities, thoughts and feelings. A woman's psychological development is structured in such a way as to prepare her for a life of inequality, but this straitjacket is not accepted lightly and invariably causes a "reaction." Psychological disturbance often distorts a person's physiological capacity: ability to eat, sleep, talk or enjoy sexual activity. I suggest that one of the reasons we find so many women suffering from eating disorders is because the social relationship between feeder and fed, between mother and daughter, fraught as it is with ambivalence and hostility, becomes a suitable mechanism for distortion and rebellion.

An examination of the symbolic meanings of fat provides insight into individual woman's experience in patriarchal culture. Fat is an adaptation to the oppression of women and, as such, it may be an

unsatisfying personal solution and an ineffectual political attack. It is to this problem that our compulsive-eating therapy speaks, and it is within a feminist context that this is developed in the following chapters.

What is fat about for the compulsive eater?

Many people who are compulsive eaters underestimate the connection between their eating and body size. The compulsive eater often experiences her eating as chaotic, out of control, self-destructive and an example of her lack of will power. At the same time, however, she may say that really she just likes to eat a lot and is too greedy for her own good and that if it were not for the pounds and inches all this eating put on, she would be quite content. Some women say that if only there was a magic pill that allowed them to eat and eat incessantly while remaining at their ideal size, they would be quite

happy. Indeed, women have had bypass surgery to achieve this state. So it is clear that people do see a connection between overeating and obesity and they attempt, through various deprivation schemes, to keep their overeating to a minimum so that they are not too fat.

What is crucial about this connection from the point of view of breaking the cycle of compulsive eating/dieting, however, is something often overlooked or misunderstood, both by compulsive eaters themselves and by those who try to help them. This is the idea that compulsive eating is linked to a desire to get fat. Now this point is not very obvious and can be difficult to understand. However, it is vital that we address it when trying to understand the immovability of the compulsive eater's seemingly bizarre relationship with food.

If one recognizes that compulsive-eating habits express an interest in being large, many things fall into place and the possibility of breaking the addiction to food is there.

Compulsive eating is a very, very painful activity. Behind the self-deprecating jokes is a person who suffers enormously. Much of her life is centered on food, what she can and cannot eat, what she will or will not eat, what she has or has not eaten and when she will or will not eat next. Typically, she cannot leave one mouthful of food on her plate and finds herself eating both at mealtimes and all through the day, evening or night. Much of her eating is done in secret or with eating friends, while at public meals she is the professional dieter and much admired for her abstinence. If she wants to eat cake she will go to the bakery and pretend that the cheesecake she buys is for her daughter or a friend, she will have it

wrapped and only dare to eat it out in the open when she thinks no one will spot her. Alternatively she will buy some candy and hide it in her pocket, stealthily putting it into her mouth while she walks or drives along the street. The obsession with food carries with it an enormous amount of self-disgust, loathing and shame. These feelings arise from the experience of being out of control around food and compulsive eaters try numerous ways to discipline themselves. Many think that if they do not have access to food they will be alright. Therefore, if a compulsive eater lives alone her kitchen closets and refrigerator will probably contain only the most meager range of foods. The kitchen will seem almost medicinal with its skim milk, ice milk, cottage cheese, dietetic sodas and jellies that masquerade as real food.

Alison, a twenty-nine-year-old zoologist, explained the pitfalls in her system of banning enjoyable foods from her apartment. She woke up in the middle of the night and felt driven to eat. She had been bingeing all evening so there was virtually nothing except dry cereal in the apartment left to eat. For the last two weeks she had had in mind a batch of homemade chocolate-chip cookies she had baked for Greg, her upstairs neighbor. Greg had gone away on vacation and Alison knew that there were still some cookies left because, while watering his plants, she noticed the cookie tin sitting on the kitchen counter. She got out of bed and took the keys to get into his apartment, found the cookies and stood there eating them all. She felt she could not just have one or two because that would not be enough, and if she ate a substantial number, when he returned, Greg would realize some were missing.

Alison's solution was to stand in his freezing cold apartment and eat the lot hoping that when he returned he would not remember that he had left any cookies at all.

If the compulsive eater lives with others, the kitchen is more likely to be full of appetizing foods that she denies herself or feels she must deny herself. Helen, a fifty-year-old mother of two who has been watching her weight for the last thirty years, is so petrified of the food in her house that she has arranged with her husband that he lock the kitchen door at night. She has a coffee percolator by her bed and celery and carrots on ice and she is banned from the kitchen on all occasions except when preparing family meals and eating her dietetic version of them. Her situation is just an extreme example of what many compulsive eaters go through in their attempts to stay away from food.

Helen brought her husband in on her problem but for Alison it was of paramount importance that nobody else knew that she was eating in that way. Many women with compulsive-eating problems find it excruciatingly painful that others should think that they themselves are large because of the amount they eat. They cannot bear other people making the connection between food intake and body size. This explains, in part, the public side of the compulsive eater who eats sparingly. Other women feel differently. A new and highly publicized method for weight control is a procedure of wiring the jaws together. The women involved in this treatment have been extremely large—well over 250 pounds. While their teeth are braced and wired they subsist on a liquid diet. The braces are loosened once a week so that the teeth can be brushed.

These various ways of coping with the situation, although particularly extreme, capture the desperation that many compulsive eaters experience, and illustrate how compulsive eating is both a very painful activity and one which is enormously hard to give up. When people repeatedly act in a way that causes them a lot of pain we look to the possible reasons that are involved. Labeling such behavior simply as self-destructive, for example, does not increase one's understanding of the forces behind compulsive eating. Instead, it judges the activity negatively and this provides yet another reason for the compulsive eater to adopt a self-deprecating attitude which is relieved only by a binge or yet another timetable to lose the weight. It is our experience that before an habitual activity—in this instance, eating compulsively—can be given up, the reasons for it need to be explored. As I argued earlier, getting fat is a very definite and purposeful act connected to women's social position. Before giving up compulsive eating the meanings of the fat for the individual woman need to be explored. In giving up compulsive eating she is almost certainly going to stabilize at a lower weight. In order to feel at home with this new constant weight, and, more importantly, her smaller size, the compulsive eater needs to understand what her previous interest has been in being overweight and in being preoccupied with food intake. If she can understand how her fat has served her she can begin to give it up.

In this chapter, I shall describe six important steps we take in the groups:

1. To demonstrate that the compulsive eater has an interest in being fat.

2. To show that this interest is largely unconscious.
3. Specific exercises are done to bring this theme to a woman's consciousness.
4. Once this interest in being fat is recognized, the meanings for each individual woman can be explored.
5. Then we ask whether the fat does what it is supposed to do.
6. We help each woman reclaim aspects of herself that she has previously attributed solely to the fat.

Because fatness has such negative connotations in our culture it may be hard to imagine that anyone could have an interest in getting fat.

To be fat means to get into the subway and worry about whether you can fit into the allotted space.

To be fat means to compare yourself to every other woman, looking for the ones whose own fat can make you relax.

To be fat means to be outgoing and jovial to make up for what you think are your deficiencies.

To be fat means to refuse invitations to go to the beach or dancing.

To be fat means to be excluded from contemporary mass culture, from fashion, sports and the outdoor life.

To be fat is to be a constant embarrassment to yourself and your friends.

To be fat is to worry every time a camera is in view.

To be fat means to feel ashamed for existing.

To be fat means having to wait until you are thin to live.

To be fat means to have no needs.

To be fat means to be constantly trying to lose weight.

To be fat means to take care of others' needs.

To be fat means never saying "no."

To be fat means to have an excuse for failure.

To be fat means to be a little different.

To be fat means to wait for the man who will love you despite the fat—the man who will fight through the layers.

To be fat, nowadays, means to be told by women friends that "Men aren't where it's at," even before you have had a chance to know.

Above all, the fat woman wants to hide. Paradoxically, her lot in life is to be perpetually noticed.

These popular conceptions of fatness, while accurate, present an incomplete picture of the compulsive eater's experience. There is also something positive to be gained from being fat that we must explore. I am not suggesting that the desire to be fat is a conscious one. Indeed, I would argue that people are largely unaware of it, and it is not at all easy to discuss this in the abstract. In the groups we do the following exercise to provide us with insight into some of the ways in which fat serves us. I

suggest you close your eyes for ten minutes and have someone read you the following fantasy exercise:

Imagine yourself in a social situation... this could be at work, at home, at a party, whatever... notice what you are wearing... whether you are sitting or standing... whom you are talking to, or having something to do with.... Now imagine yourself getting fatter, in the same social situation... you are now quite large.... What does it feel like?... Notice what you are wearing... whether you are sitting or standing.... Notice all the details in this situation... how are you getting on with the people around you?... Are you an active participant or do you feel excluded?... Are you having to make more or less of an effort?... Now see if you can detect any messages that this very fat you has to say to the world.... Is there any way in which you can see it serving you?... Are there any benefits you see from being this fat in this situation?...

When we do this exercise in the groups we get a variety of responses and many are what one might expect. They include feeling like a freak, an outsider, or a blob or assuming that whomever one had contact with was doing so out of pity or was also a freak. But more significantly, people were able to see a new meaning in the fat. For some, the fantasy sparked feelings of confidence and substance as though the fat represented concrete strength. For others, being fat felt very safe as though it were an excuse for failure and that in worrying about body size the women did not have to think about any other possible problems in their lives. Some women felt that being fat protected them insofar as it

allowed them to contain their feelings; other women talked of feeling comfortable in their bigness and warmth and having plenty of love to give to others. However, the most common benefits that women saw in being large had to do with a sexual protection. In seeing herself as fat, a woman is often able to desexualize herself; the fat prevents her from considering herself as sexual. Having done the exercise, so many women report feeling relaxed at a party, not feeling they were on show or had to compete but were comfortably talking to female friends. Others felt the fat separated them from the kind of women they had ambivalent feelings about—the ones whom they perceived as self-involved, trivial and vain. Others felt that it meant they could hold their own and keep unwanted intruders away. Many women felt a relief at not having to conceive of themselves as sexual. Fatness took them out of the category of woman and put them in the androgynous state of "big girl."

As people in the groups are slowly able to incorporate these positive aspects and benefits into their views of fatness, they begin to develop a different self-image. The image of fatness then is no longer one-sidedly negative, inextricably tied up with an ugly vision. Instead of regarding themselves as hopeless, helpless or willfully destructive, they can see that their compulsive eating has had some purpose, that it has had a function. As this function becomes more apparent it is possible to be more generous to yourself, to regard the compulsive eating and the attempt to get fat as a way in which you have handled particularly difficult situations. The compulsive eating can then be looked on as an attempt to adapt to a set of circumstances rather

than as irrational, "crazy" behavior.

I would now like to explore just why these images of largeness are comforting. What is it that women are saying they feel more capable of when they are fat?

Many women experience the social expectations placed on them as unattainable, unrealistic, undesirable, burdensome and oppressive. Central among these expectations is the feeling that women should be, on the one hand, decorative, attractive and an embellishment to the surroundings and on the other hand, that they should do the hard concrete work of raising the children, running households, while at the same time maintaining jobs outside the home. For many women the physical model of the shy, retiring flower, demurely smiling beneath lowered eyelashes, is too frail and insubstantial to accomplish the daily tasks of living that are their responsibility. As such, to these women the fat represents substance and strength. Harriet, a thirty-five-year-old community worker who lives with her husband and two children, put it this way: "I had the feeling that my fat gives me substance and physical presence in the world. It allows me to do all the things I have to do. In the fantasy I saw myself in my office sitting at my desk and taking up an enormous amount of space. I felt the capacity to do anything I needed to do—challenge my boss and fight more effectively for the community group that I'm there to serve. I felt my strength in this exaggeration of my size. Then in my fantasy I went home, and with the realization of the extra bulk it struck me that I walked into an antagonistic situation with my fat as my armor. As I walk into the house I am reminded of all the tasks that have to

be done there that I either execute personally or direct others to do. I feel quite angry about all this, both about feeling so bossy but, of course, also because the terrain of the household is mine—and not by choice. So I see the fat in the situation as making me feel like a sergeant major—big and authoritative. When I go through this fantasy seeing myself thin, what immediately strikes me is just how fragile and little I feel, almost as though I might disappear or be blown away."

Barbara, a twenty-seven-year-old book-jacket designer, talked about the annoying expectations of many of her male colleagues. She felt that her bulk and substance was an expression of her need to be noticed as a productive human being rather than a decorative accompaniment to the environment. She felt that whenever she looked the slightest bit sexy—and this corresponded to the way she looked when she was thin—her colleagues only reacted to the sexual aspect of her. She experienced this as both a frightening demand and also a deflection from her work. As it is for so many women, taking her work seriously was quite a struggle for Barbara. She had grown up with the idea that she would work for a couple of years after school and then get married and have children. But ideas had changed and by the time she left college she wanted to work to have a career rather than for a stop-gap measure. This decision was not trivial; she felt she had a lot of support for her change of mind because all her friends were also pursuing work as a central part of their lives. But Barbara was in conflict about her capacity to be a good worker, not because her art work was erratic, second-rate or inadequate but because she was battling with an unconscious idea

that taking herself seriously in her work life was
inappropriate. In the group we were able to expose
this conflict and Barbara saw how difficult it was for
her to be thin/sexual on the job because she and the
men there collaborated in trivializing her. She felt
the only way she could hold on to that aspect of
herself that was involved in a career was by having
an extra layer covering her femaleness. As she said,
"The fat made me one of the boys."

In the group we also worked to expose the
conflict that Barbara felt about the different models
of adult female behavior; the one she grew up with
which was modeled not only on her mother's life but
also on a popular conception of femininity in the
1950s and early 1960s; and a model that she and her
contemporaries were struggling to articulate, a view
of womanhood that was less limiting and struck at
the very roots of women's oppression within the
family. This conflict is, in my experience, a difficult
and painful one for many women and not one that
will be resolved by a sudden flash of insight. In the
groups it is important to realize that the goal is not
necessarily to resolve this or any other conflict
which may lie at the root of the compulsive eating.
What is important, however, is that the conflict be
brought to light, that the woman should understand
that it exists and that eating compulsively is not
going to make it go away—it may cover it. The fat
may provide for something less threatening to
worry about. But the critical issue is to make the
woman acknowledge the conflict so that it need not
be expressed indirectly and hidden from the person
who is experiencing it. This acknowledgment then
becomes a powerful weapon in the fight against
compulsive eating. It is very reassuring to discover

that there are substantial reasons for why one is eating in such a seemingly inexplicable way. It provides one with the tools; thus when Barbara, for instance, noticed that she was bingeing, she could ask herself what was really troubling her. If she did not come up with any spontaneous answer she could review her day or events leading up to the binge and see if there were any incidents that particularly encapsulated her conflict about who she could be as a woman in the world. In this way she could decode her own behavior. This then gave her a chance to intervene on her own behalf and she could move on to ask herself whether being fat in that particular situation was really going to help her out.

So one meaning of the fat is the woman's need for recognition in a work setting. But another theme that frequently comes up is almost diametrically opposed to this. It is often the case that people's fat fantasies are widely different and that even within the same person the fat may express many different meanings. Barbara, for example, could see the use of the fat in her attempt to be taken seriously at work, but at the same time we discovered her fat also symbolized her fear of being successful both in work and courtship. Her fear of success, of course, stems largely from the social position of a young woman of today growing up with contradictory messages about what she can accomplish. Stepping outside what has been laid out for one is frightening. A useful, protective device is to make the assumption that one will fail; in Barbara's view the excess weight provided her with an excuse should she not succeed in love and work. She found out that she could not bear the idea that her work life or love life would not be satisfying, once she had committed

herself to trying to have both. She felt sure that if there were failure on either score, it would be attributable to a character weakness on her part. This idea, in turn, was so painful that she focused instead on her weight as an excuse in the case of potential failure. As long as she was overweight, and love and career did not quite work out as she hoped, she could imagine that if she were thin, everything would be just fine. Thus, this fantasy allowed her to exert some control over her circumstances as though in an inspired weight loss she would be able to sort out social attitudes to women at work and love relationships with men.

In Barbara's case the fat served two distinct purposes, albeit somewhat contradictory ones. Firstly, it provided her with a way to express competence on the job; secondly, if she did not succeed at work or in her love life she could blame her excess weight. As these two themes emerged in the course of her therapy, Barbara was able to see that getting fat was a personal adaptation she had made in trying to cope with a very difficult situation. In addition to being able to expose the conflict, she was able to see the dilemma of a young career woman today and how she felt she had to deny or solve the difficulties facing her entirely on her own. Other women in the group identified with what Barbara was going through and, as they began to share their difficulties, they broke their individual isolation and feelings of impotence which had in part led to the weight gain.

Failure and success are powerful concepts within our world. Very early on we absorb the idea that a limit has been set on what is available and we learn to compete for what is around. If we are successful

we are rewarded, and if we are unsuccessful our lot is to suffer. When we are very young it is hard to see quite how the odds are stacked or in whose favor, and the competition seems fair—with failure or success being the individual's fault or triumph. As we get older, we may question the basic assumptions behind the scramble or even how the pie is divided up, whether it is the number of possible "A"s in a class or the division of labor itself. But ideas absorbed and structured into the personality die hard, and feel almost impenetrably lodged. While we may reject the notion of competition because of the devastating effects it has wrought in relationships between people as well as in world politics, we may nevertheless find ourselves unwittingly competitive. Competitive feelings get triggered in a situation of scarcity where there is not enough to go round, or where only a certain number of people can be rewarded. The apprehension of possible exclusion or denial can foster either a desire to compete individually for some of the scarce resource or to sort out cooperatively a way to deal with the shortage. Another alternative is to opt out of the competition. But by and large, as we grow up we are encouraged to compete against others. In school this is expressed through grades or which team you make or your position in class. But girls and boys, women and men, are trained to cope with scarcity and competition in different ways. The cliché of "let the boy win at tennis" expresses an aspect of the competition between women and men. We learn that if there is a game between the sexes in which one side has to lose, we had better make sure we are the losers. In general, men are taught to compete against other men for jobs and status. They gain

prestige in the world of work by being better than other men, and they measure their success by comparing it with that of others. Although women also exist in the world of work, men are rarely encouraged to compete against women because they do not tend to take women's presence in traditional male preserves very seriously. Similarly, women are strongly discouraged from competing with men or each other at work. Woman are forced to compete with each other for the man who will help the winner secure her social position. A woman's success in the world continues largely to be regarded as a reflection of her husband's status. In this battle for social survival, women are essentially competing on the basis of their sexual appeal while other aspects of their personality are viewed as attributes to be paraded in the attempt to secure a man.

Women's liberation is challenging this value system for both women and men. However, those of us in our twenties and upward have grown up with these values and ideas and, although they are being shaken up, they nevertheless continue to play a significant part in our personalities. Often we do not realize how much a part of us they are. When we do notice these competitive feelings, we find them distasteful and inappropriate in a changing world and try to suppress, hide or ignore them.

The acknowledgment of a whole range of competitive feelings is difficult for many women and often we attempt to cover these feelings by getting fat. The fat has several functions in this regard.

1. It provides space and protection for the feelings. Without the fat a woman might worry

unconsciously that her feelings will be exposed. There would be no difficulty in getting thin if the competitive feelings could find no place to hide and just disappeared. But problems like that never do just disappear; they either get actively repressed and reappear in another form; or they become exaggerated and completely exposed; or they get acknowledged with the potential for being worked through.

2. The feeling of being fat-outsize—larger than life, removes the possibility of competing since everyone knows that "fat women can't win and, in fact, aren't even in the same game."

3. In the very act of compulsive eating—the most frequent route to getting fat—one may be attempting to blot out competitive feelings that may have been stirred up. Again, we see the dual function of compulsive eating—to dull the feeling that is difficult to cope with and to provide a way for the energy behind the worry (in this case feeling competitive) to be harnessed to a more familiar concern about body size.

Compulsive eating also helps out in other circumstances when women are frightened to show certain emotions. These are feelings such as anger, that women are afraid to show because they are considered inappropriate for women, many of whom have been hurt when they expressed them.

A preparation for a life of inequality inevitably leads to many of these turbulent and hence socially unacceptable feelings in women. In addition to difficulties with competition in which women are expected to lose on all fronts except the sexual one where she must succeed in getting her man in order to move toward adulthood, other feelings engen-

dered by social situations can be swallowed up by the fat.

Anger is a particularly difficult emotion for women to accept in themselves. Jennifer is a forty-eight-year-old teacher in London. She is married and has two sons, aged eighteen and twenty. Professionally competent and well recognized for her work in inner-city education, she has had a history of compulsive eating since she got married. Jennifer was an orphan, brought up by many different foster parents. She never felt safe or loved in any of the homes in which she stayed and at eighteen she received a scholarship to college and left her last foster parents permanently. At that point she was truly on her own with no pretense that anyone around her was taking care of her. She felt quite strong and able to cope, and remembers feeling particularly relieved that she did not have to pretend to be grateful for every ounce of attention paid to her. She roomed with other young women and felt quite envious of their family life. When she was twenty-five she got married to Doug, a draughtsman, and for the first time found herself in a stable family environment. Jennifer decided to work for a couple of years so that they would feel more secure financially. It was at that time Jennifer noticed that she was becoming preoccupied with her food intake, and her weight began to fluctuate wildly. Jennifer knew that psychological issues often got expressed in weight gain or loss but just could not pinpoint what was going on because she felt that for the first time her life was making some kind of sense and she felt a security that she had not thought possible before. Both of her pregnancies proceeded relatively comfortably. Jennifer took

four years off from her work as a teacher and then went for further training before resuming a full-time job. The family stayed in the same neighborhood for twenty years and Jennifer developed some solid friendships and, as she put it, "a real feeling of community." Yet she continued to eat in a way she found quite disagreeable, alternately picking and shoveling. The only way she could understand this behavior was by seeing it as an expression of how inadequate she felt her own parenting had been. She saw herself continuing the previous pattern of erratic caring of herself. This insight provided her with some relief but the eating problem still continued. In the course of her therapy, we did a fantasy of Jennifer fat and thin with her foster parents in the same room. In a response to a question about what the fat was saying to her many foster parents, Jennifer was suddenly overcome by enormous feelings of rage. She experienced the fat as all the poisonous, venomous feelings she had stored up through the many years of being shuffled about. She felt that if the fat itself had a mouth it would shriek hateful and angry thoughts to all those people who had supposedly cared for her. Her fat was a way to keep quiet about all those feelings but she also experienced it as an indictment of the inadequate parenting she had had. As we discussed it more, she said that without it nobody would know that she had suffered and people would take it for granted that she could just float through life quite easily, that she was like everyone else. Once she had felt these feelings of rage much of her compulsive eating made sense. She began to notice that whenever she felt angry, with her kids, at school or with Doug, she rushed to eat to swallow the feelings.

To feel the anger was to put herself in jeopardy—she felt a tape going through her head every time she got angry, it said: "Nice girls don't. Be grateful or you'll be thrown out." These sentences were those that were taught to her very early on indeed. To express anger or disappointment in a foster home was unacceptable and carried with it not only this exclusion from the female sex but also the fear of abandonment and rejection. If she got angry at her foster parents she would be sent back. The discovery of the roots of the compulsive eating eased the situation for Jennifer. She began to allow herself to experience anger directly and risk the consequences instead of eating it away. She also became aware of her anxiety about levels of insecurity she felt within her own family as though if she expressed displeasure at something she would be turfed out. On most levels she felt quite safe with Doug and it was, in fact, this safety that had allowed that historic anger and rage to emerge—albeit indirectly—in the first place. Jennifer was caught in a changing situation. As a youngster she had to put up and shut up. She could show no anger or rebellion. When she was able to leave these unsatisfactory homes and start her own family she felt more secure and in charge of the situation but she understandably carried past insecurities with her. The part of her that felt securely established with Doug, her career and the kids provided enough space for her to reject the dreadful past she had had but she was not quite able to do that openly and expressed that rejection by eating compulsively.

In Jennifer's case, her fat was a delayed response to a series of extremely precarious and deprived home circumstances. It was not until she had set up

her own home that she found herself eating
erratically and yoyo-ing on the scales. This pattern—becoming obsessively involved with food
after the troublesome events have passed—is quite
common. There seems to be a psychological
mechanism that works in the following way for
some people; a girl grows up in a difficult
environment, but needs to survive it as much intact
as possible in order to get out. Any expression of
breakdown or weakness would only prolong the
imprisonment and make escape more difficult. All
her resources are harnessed so that she can endure
the horrible circumstances and prepare for an exit.
She finally leaves this setting and puts herself in a
safer place. As she begins to relax in her new-found
safety and lets her defenses down all the wretched
feelings from the past have a chance to come up. It is
not as though in leaving the situation she has left the
feelings behind. The safety and security of the new
situation provides for a detoxification process. But
these feelings are very powerful and very often
extremely painful and the human organism may
respond by trying to continue to ward them off. In
the case of someone who starts compulsive eating at
this point, what is happening is that the feelings are
coming up but are experienced as too dangerous to
confront. The woman turns to compulsive eating to
anesthetize the feelings and cover them with a layer
of fat. The feelings do not get expressed and
cleansed; instead they get transformed into a
symptom which then has to be demystified before it
can be made to go away.

I should now like to discuss why the expression
of anger is so difficult for women. In Jennifer's case,
there was an explicit threat of expulsion should she

express anger at her treatment but in general, women are actively discouraged from expressing anger, rage, resentment and hostility. We are raised to be demure and accept what we are given with no complaints. We all learn how little girls are made of sugar and spice and all things nice. So we try hard not to show our anger or even feel it ourselves. When we rebel and show dissatisfaction we learn we are nasty and greedy. Whether we realize it or not we are being taught to accept silently a second-class citizenship. Secondary status is further compounded by having our anger denied us. Anger provides a way for people to challenge injustices at whatever level—be it a child's anger in response to a punitive parent or the collective anger of others fighting to have their day-care centers restored.

But there are few models of righteously angry women for us to follow. Indeed, I think most of us are pretty frightened around an angry woman—so unfamiliar is the sight. Anger, as a legitimate emotion for many women, has no cultural validation. Little girls are encouraged to cry if they do not get what they are wanting instead of angrily protesting; "There, there, dear." In Edward Albee's play *Who's Afraid of Virginia Woolf*, Martha, the angry wife who protests against the life of a helpmate, is portrayed as a bitch and a harridan. Much of popular culture attests to the negative value we place on women's rage. It is not surprising, therefore, to find that for many women, the unconscious motivation behind the weight gain is a flight from anger. In this case, the symbolic meaning of the fat is a "Fuck you!"

Behind the suppression of anger lies one of the

most important themes for women today. Gaining weight to express anger, to be able to say, "Fuck you," is only a part of a larger problem. Expressing anger is an assertive act. Assertion for women is difficult. Consider these typical situations:

Ann is extremely tired after a long day at work. She plans to spend the evening alone just resting, watching television and reading. Her neighbor Jack calls up and asks if she would not mind helping out by baby-sitting for his children for an hour while he and his wife go to the store. Ann feels she must be cooperative but knows from past experience that the hour is rarely such and the whole evening will be gone. Reluctantly, she goes next door. At 11:30 p.m. Jack and Penny return. They have been to the store and the movies. Ann is at this point angry but blames herself for having agreed to baby-sit without conditions in the first place. She goes home muttering to herself and eats.

Bill and Roz planned to go to the movies together. Bill calls Roz up from work to check that it will be alright for him to bring some friends home to dinner. Roz, who had already started cooking, takes his decision as a *fait accompli* and reluctantly agrees, feeling she has no right to refuse. She goes into the kitchen and starts banging around fixing dinner and feeling very moody. She assumes that Bill has forgotten about their movie date and she feels rejected. She feels put upon as she is cooking but also feels guilty for being so ungenerous and unspontaneous. She noshes her way through the cooking and when Bill and his friends sit down for supper she shovels the food into her mouth, at this

point angry about her inability to assert herself in the first place.

In both situations Ann and Roz feel unentitled to demand what they actually want. Ann is afraid to set limits on her own altruism and Roz does not stand up for herself and the movie date. Both women blame themselves for not having asserted themselves and also for feeling selfish enough even to conceive of their own wants in the first place. They both eat away the bad feelings and focus the negative feelings on the food rather than addressing the difficult issue of assertion. *They feel safer using their mouths to feed themselves than using them to talk and be assertive. They imagine that their fat is making the statement for them while the suffering prevents the words from coming out.* None of this is conscious, the seeds for this behavior have been planted in the mother-daughter relationship in which the mother encourages the girl child to adopt a pleasing manner. The mother prepares her daughter for a life in which major decisions are made for her rather than by her. *The girl will be taught to accept that her needs come second and that keeping quiet is safer than assertion.* Consequently, women are confused and afraid to act on their own behalf. To do so often makes one appear aggressive and *that* has such negative connotations for women that it feels less dangerous to adopt an acquiescent stance. So for women, there is great confusion between unassertive, assertive and aggressive behavior. The recent rush of courses and self-help assertion-training books is witness to the magnitude of this problem. And there have been unfortunate consequences for women who have

risked stepping out of line in the past. *Women have been condemned as castrating or domineering when they have attempted to assert their rights.*

There are, in addition, other consequences about being unassertive that add to the problem. If one is not trained to be assertive it is quite hard to define how much you will or will not give to others. By and large, women are taught to nurture the world. As one psychoanalyst, Mercy Heatley, put it, women are the "sewage treatment plants" for the family and, as such, are always giving emotionally to others. In discussing what their fat and food symbolized to them many women have described it as being a kind of "fuel for the furnace," a private storehouse they can draw on when they need to be replenished in order to go on feeding others. For some women, however, the fat in this case represents a rejection of just this kind of service to others. In the woman's mind the excess weight is a message to others to keep away and not make any demands, almost a "Can't you see I've got enough on my hands without worrying about anyone else." For others, it is a statement which embodies both these feelings—the fat expresses a shapeless capacity to both absorb and repel outside demands. So the fat expresses both an attempt to be separate from others while, at the same time, a woman's sheer size encompasses everything around her. It is as though the woman can take on everyone else's needs without them actually penetrating her—the weight acts as a shock absorber for others and as a cushion against her becoming too affected.

As I have said in discussing responses to the fat fantasy, the most frequently stated advantage women saw in being fat had to do with sexual

protection. It is almost as though through the protective aspects of the fat, women are saying they must deny their own sexuality in order to be seen as a person. *To expose their sexuality means that others will deny them their personhood.* In adolescence, girls are supposed to magically transfer their friendship interest in boys to a sexual one—they learn a ritual called dating. This sudden transition can be quite formidable and difficult to cope with. As Mary, a twenty-seven-year-old doctor, put it, "When I was about six or seven years old, girls and boys used to play together. Then we were separated out and, until the age of eleven, contact with boys was fairly limited, particularly as I went to an all-girls school during that period. Then at twelve I went to a coed junior high school and looked forward to playing with the boys again. Their games seemed more exciting and I really missed the adventures they got up to. However, something weird seemed to be happening; instead of fooling around together we were supposed to fix ourselves up real pretty and accumulate dates. This was a way for us to continue to hang out with the guys. But along with this went a whole series of rules and regulations about kissing and touching—it seemed to me as if in order to play with the fellows I had to put out. This was quite disconcerting, not because I didn't like kissing, which I did, but because it seemed that all of a sudden girls and boys were really different and had to relate to each other within a rigid set-up. It was really quite confusing for all of us and everything seemed downhill from there on. Sports were divided and we had the great job of cheering the boys on. I kept feeling that if this is going to be what being grown up is all about I'll

keep my puppy fat on and try and avoid this whole dating trip."

So Mary spent the next fifteen years, as she put it, "slightly overweight." She noticed during the course of her therapy that her eating binges occurred almost uniformly when she was in any kind of potentially sexual situation. She would gorge away before going to a party, for instance, and convince herself that she was too big to be considered sexual. This allowed her a kind of ease to relate to people at the party—women and men—on her terms rather than on the exchange value of her body. The example of Mary shows quite clearly how the fat is conceived as providing a means of removal from the sexualizing and hence, also competitive aspects of relationships for women.

This sexual division has wide-ranging conse-quences. Many women have shared the feeling that being fat was a way to stand out in a crowd, to be noticeable, to be different without having to invest as much as they assume thin, attractive women do.

Several women have mentioned that their sex was a disappointment to their parents. Rita remembers eating energetically in order to get big, to prove her existence. Quite strikingly, she stopped bingeing for the first time when she got pregnant. When she had life inside her she felt this was ample evidence of her right to exist. If Rita could reproduce, she had a real role, as a mother, even if she had felt unwanted as a child.

These varied explanations of the meanings behind the fat, from eating as protection to eating as an expression of anger, will not necessarily provide they key for everyone who feels they have this problem. Because the syndrome of compulsive

eating, compulsive dieting, weight loss and weight gain is so highly developed and, in a sense, so absorbing a preoccupation in itself, it may be hard to get outside it enough to realize just what it is doing for you. In a sense, compulsive eating provides a beautiful, insulated world: obsessing about how terrible you are for overeating leads to feelings of self-disgust; these feelings have no outlet and are quickly covered up or numbed by the intake of food or banished by the fantasy of reincarnation after the plan for the new diet has been made. All negative feelings get harnessed to complaints and self-loathing about body size and eating habits and the fat provides a less threatening issue to worry about than other possible problems. It may also be true that while the fat has one meaning for you today, it has had quite another when it originally developed. In other words, the historic reasons and driving force behind the impulse to get fat in the first place may be quite different from its current significance, so it often proves useful to look back and see how getting fat has helped people at certain times in their lives. In order to tap this information in the groups we do weight histories to reveal when the "problem" first started. I should like to illustrate this point by drawing on some case histories of women I have worked with. Some of the historic reasons that I will outline will be of clearly feminist content and others will be less explicitly so, though in each example it will be obvious what feminine personality-development has meant to each of the women whose lives I am describing.

Rea was an only child. Her parents had high expectations for her which included academic

excellence, sociability and beauty. She felt pressed by these demands to be the perfect, happy child and felt that she did not have much space in which to develop her own independence. She became quite overweight in adolescence and it was to this period that we returned to examine when she came into therapy in her early thirties. Her fat began to make sense set against the background of intense parental concern that she be successful. Rea did not see herself in the same light as did her parents. She felt inadequate. She felt that she was a selfish, ungrateful and bad person. She felt that she could not cope with her parents' demands and that she would be increasingly incompetent. Her fat expressed both the resentment at having to be so perfect and the need to hide and contain the bad person she felt she was inside. She feared being thin because she felt she would then be everything her parents wanted; she would be in their image and without a self.

Jane, a fifty-five-year-old legal secretary, put on weight after her mother's death. Up to the age of twenty-five, Jane had been quite thin and fairly relaxed about her body image. She was an only child, her father died when she was a teenager and she was very close to her mother. She married when she was twenty-two but shortly afterward her husband Tom was sent overseas to fight in World War II. When her baby girl Carol was eighteen months old Tom returned from the war. About a year later Jane's mother died of cancer. For the preceding year and a half she had been losing a lot of weight and looked very thin and ill. When Jane officially stopped mourning she began to put on

weight. By the time she was twenty-seven she was 25 to 30 pounds heavier than she had ever been before, except during her pregnancy. She was quite staggered by the increase in her size and at first she put it down to lack of exercise after Carol's birth. Friends suggested that maybe she had enjoyed pregnancy so much that her excess weight was a desire to look continually pregnant. But this explanation made little sense to Jane because her pregnancy had not been the easiest time for her. A psychiatrist friend at the time expounded that she wanted to look pregnant so she could get the attention and praise from Tom he assumed she had missed at the time of her genuine pregnancy. The weight stayed on and eventually, as standards in fashion and health demanded slimness, Jane started the round of diets and diet doctors. Outwardly Jane had a fairly contented home life—she and Tom really liked each other and Carol, their only child, kept up continued contact with them after she had grown up and left home. However, Tom reported that almost every night Jane cried out in her sleep for *her* mother. In the course of therapy this piece of information from Tom was discussed in detail. Jane came to understand that the weight gain had much to do with the loss of her mother, as she said, "My mother died tragically of cancer. She became very thin before her death. I've had a need to feel big ever since then and worried, I suppose, that if I get thin I might disappear or die like her." Facing her mother's death and her own fears about dying if she became thin allowed Jane to determine a size for herself that was both physically and psychologically comfortable. As it turned out, Jane felt that she no longer wished to be as svelte as she imagined she

might and her weight stabilized at about fifteen pounds lower than it had been.

Death has been a factor in the fat for other women with whom I have worked. Sheila, a twenty-eight-year-old graduate student, had lost her older brother Ivan when he was twelve and she was ten. She gained weight from that time on and in the group we discovered that the origin of becoming fat had had two distinct symbolic meanings. Sheila felt the oversized body allowed her to carry her brother with her. She remembered that she had really enjoyed being with him and played with him a lot. Ivan had been the pride and joy of the family, first born and male it was anticipated that he would fulfill his parents' ambitions. About two years after his death they had another child, Maureen. Sheila felt a great deal of responsibility for being both a little mother to Maureen and a son to her parents. To her, what a son meant was quite distinct from what being a daughter had meant. It demanded that she be very good at sports, achieve scholastically and plan for a successful career of which her parents could be proud. In being a daughter she was expected to do decently at school but a career was to come second to a successful love life. In her adolescence, Sheila's father took her to ball games. She enjoyed being one of the boys and having a much more developed relationship with her father than she had had before she became a teenager. In the therapy, what emerged was a guilt for feeling good that she could have so much of her father. She imagined that if her brother had lived, this would not have been the case. Symbolically, she felt the second meaning of her fat was to round out her curves—to make her less feminine so she could look

more the part of a son. When she had lost weight over the years she took with her the same desire to look boyish and she was always annoyed that she still had hips and breasts and could not achieve the androgynous body she wanted.

Sheila had been trying to cope with the problem of how to be the teenage son and the little mother. This latter aspect is one showed by many girls at even earlier ages than Sheila. Often a seven-year-old daughter will be expected to be mother's little helper or substitute in looking after the babies that follow her.

Melinda, the eldest girl in a family of seven, recalls a blissful early childhood when she and her older brother would play together. When she was seven years old her mother had another baby. It seemed to Melinda that her childhood was over; not only did she have to share her mother with yet another child but she was expected to, and indeed did, carry out many grown-up tasks. As more and more babies came, Melinda became a second mommy to them so that at eighteen when she left home she felt well trained to start her own family. She became large instead, however, explaining that if she looked like a big earth mother no one would assume she was at all available. She had had her lot for the moment!

This mothering learned so early on leads many women to teach their daughters to deprive and deny themselves. Florence and her daughter Laura both had compulsive eating problems. Florence's ideology was that eating goodies was an indulgence— and a disgusting one at that. She felt it was indecent

to give into oneself with almost any form of pleasure, but particularly bodily pleasures. Food and sex were inviting and exciting but one must stay away from them. Florence ate sparingly all year round. On vacation when she overate she felt guilty and on her return would immediately put herself on the Mayo Clinic Diet to lose the excess. She was iron-willed and very self controlled but terribly afraid of food. Her husband hid his candies in the glove compartment of his car and she considered his love of dessert a sign of his character weakness. Laura rebelled against this code of self-denial. She despised her mother's meanness with herself and characterized her as compulsively thin. She felt her mother never gave herself pleasure with food or sex. Laura chose the opposite route and tried to get pleasure from both activities. However, since the food and sex were both experienced behind closed doors with one ear open for her mother's intrusions, Laura could not be as much in control as she wanted and her eating expressed these tensions. In the group, she learned to eat just for herself and her own pleasure without having to get so big as though to prove her mother was right. She did not have to be ostracized by her size in order to give to herself.

Because of the prevailing position of women in the family, mothers also deny themselves in situations where there just is not enough to go round. They make sure that in a situation of shortage their husbands and children have as much as possible. If a mother fails to provide enough food on the table she feels herself a failure. When prices soar, a mother with a fixed income has less and less to spend on the family shopping and even though

she experiences this along with all other house-keepers, it is she alone who must face the family and the complaints and disappointment if the food is not up to scratch. In the depression of the 1930s this was particularly acute; money was very scarce and there was never enough food on the table. Mothers talking about this period say they held back so there would be enough for the rest of the family—they could always make do, *they* were not at school using their brains or out on the streets looking for work everyday, so they felt it was only right that they should suffer.

Carolyn, one of the daughters of that time who subsequently became fat, said, "When I was young it was depression time. My mother would go hungry and try to be sure to provide enough food for us kids, which there wasn't. When I got married I had enough food for the first time in my life and I feel like I'm eating to protect myself against those terrible feelings of hunger I had as a child."

Rose, Carolyn's daughter, born at the end of the Second World War, remembers battles she had with her mother who worried lest she not eat enough—she recalled all the spoonfuls she ate for the poor starving children in Europe, never understanding how eating extra would help them.

Rose remained quite slender until the age of seventeen when she left home to travel round Europe. When she returned, her parents greeted her with approval about her gain in weight. She, however, was quite unhappy being that big—she felt it made her too like them. She got involved with the diet-binge syndrome for the next twelve years. The following themes were explored in her therapy. When she had lived at home, a way to rebel against

her parents had been to be thin. Not only were both her parents overweight but they also constantly encouraged her to eat. When she left home, she gained weight as an expression of her conflict about giving up her parents. The fat was a way to take with her a part of her home life—her parents. One of the most critical parts of her therapy was the termination process. Rose had at this point lost about twenty-five pounds and stabilized at a weight she felt fitted her frame. The anticipated separation from the therapist and from the fat brought forth issues related to Rose's childhood struggles to separate herself from her mother. For Rose, these battles about food symbolized her attempts to strike out on her own, to define herself and develop some independence from her mother. As the conflict was brought to light—that is, both Rose's interest in developing a separate identity and her fear of it because of the social and psychological dangers she perceived if she were separate from her mother—she could feel a safety for the first time in determining her own food intake. Her body for her then expressed this surer feeling of independence; it was defined and self-contained and not "all fat, stuck like a mayonnaisey glue to my mother."

Body size means different things to different women. In Rose's case being large was being stuck, capitulating, it meant accepting all those extra spoonfuls of food she had not wanted; in Barbara's case it was an attempt to desexualize herself in the face of her work colleagues; for Harriet it represented strength and substance; for Jane, her anger, and so on. Not only will fat have different meanings for different women but at different times the meanings will take on more, or less, significance.

At the beginning of a compulsive-eating group a woman may only be able to see the fat as a graphic symbol of everything she dislikes in herself. She may describe it as the ghastly manifestation of the ugliness and horridness she feels inside. The fat both covers and exposes her perceived terribleness. As the group goes on in time and other women share their stories, this same woman may well be able to separate that fat from a definition of ugliness and explore some of the ways her fat has served her in the past. She will be able to see that the fat was an attempt to take care of herself under a difficult set of circumstances. As she moves toward a conscious acceptance of this aspect of the fat she can utilize the self-protective impulse in a different way. As she is able to understand that she became fat as a response—to mother, to society, to various situations—she can begin to remove the judgment that it was good or it was bad. *It just was.* It is extremely painful and difficult, if not impossible, to change if one has a negative self-image. An understanding of the dynamics behind getting fat can help remove the judgment. When the judgment is given up and you can accept that the fat just was, you can go on to the question of, "Is it serving me well now?"

It is necessary for those who work in the area of the unconscious to explain about the existence of an unconscious life which has its own force and symbols. These symbols then need to be translated into the language of everyday experience so that we can explore them. Then, as conscious people, we need to intervene to question the rational and seemingly irrational fears and fantasies that rise from the land of dreams and motives. I find myself in a situation where I have asked the reader to

consider that compulsive eating is linked to an unconscious desire to get fat. I have further argued that in order to give up the fat this motivation must be exposed. I will now propose, however, that the protective function the fat is meant to serve is one step away from the truth—that the fat itself does not actually do the job it is meant to do. By attrituting to the fat a powerful protective role, a woman sets herself up for a situation in which a life without the fat would be a defenseless one. This is a frightening proposition indeed. We aim to offer the compulsive eater another option, that of seeing that the qualities she feels are in the weight are, instead, characteristics that she herself possesses but has assigned to the fat. In drawing on various aspects of the histories of women with whom I have worked, I have suggested that the discovery of the meaning of the fat has subsequently led to a reappraisal of whether it is the fat *itself* which actually keeps people away, desexualizes one, helps contain the angry, (hurt, disappointed) feelings or provides substance. If, indeed, it is not the fat itself that has done all these things but rather the individual, two questions arise:

1. How and why has the individual woman withheld this power from herself and attributed it solely to the fat?
2. How can she reappropriate this power so that she feels it to be more a part of her essential self—who she is? This is so that when she gives up the weight she is not giving up the main methods in which she has dealt with the world.

The first question speaks to an issue of crucial importance that arises from the socialization of

women. Women are systematically discouraged
from taking responsibility for various activities,
actions, even thoughts. Men both act for them and
describe their experience. While women's experience is exceedingly rich, it is rarely described or
heard. Only in literature have women consistently
had a voice and a wide audience. In the areas in
which women, almost without exception, have
taken enormous responsibility—in child-rearing,
nurturing and housekeeping—their actions are not
seen as defined and delineated because they are
described as natural and inevitable. If it is natural
you must do it. If it is natural it does not count.
Hence it is devalued. Now the paradox lies in the
fact that so many of the women described in this
chapter have, in fact, defied this stereotype of
femininity. They have purposefully gone out into
the world and taken on responsibilities that fall
outside the scope of their role expectations. But they
are caught in a sense of self which denies their power
and this self-devaluation seems inexplicable unless
it is considered as a consequence of living in a
culture that has withheld social power from women
and demonstrates this by denying and punishing
those who violate prescribed social roles. It is not
hard to see how a woman might adopt a self-image
that is in tune with the idea that women are
powerless. In doing so she accustoms herself to the
idea that it is not *her* who has direct power but her
"unowned" fat. If it is *her* who can keep people away
and not simply her fat then she becomes more in
charge of herself. If she is more in charge of herself
and acts more for herself in a determined way, will
what she wants be attainable? Or will she be
punished and rejected by others for daring to define

herself rather than fitting in with others' expectations of herself? A further paradox is encapsulated in the compulsive eater whose imagined sense of herself thin is as the powerfully attractive sexual woman. As she subscribes to the image of the thin, sexual woman—a view offered to her consistently by the mass media—she reaches for the elusive power that this image promises but does not deliver. It is precisely this non-recognition of the person in the thin sexual image that causes her unconsciously to reject this thinness. For many women, "thin= sexy=powerful" is an experience that lasts no more than the fleeting moment when she makes her entrance, her initial impact. After that, her image is appropriated by others and translates into "thin= sexy=powerless" and at the same time she may find no way to handle being thin, sexy and in charge. It is this critical question of how women can define and manage their own sexuality that is being grappled with so often in the fat/thin dilemma. And it is the lack of support for a redefinition that compounds the woman's relinquishing her *own* power to her fat. This, then, is an explanation both for the occurrence of a symptom and its tenacity. Giving up a symptom and owning the power assigned to it means you are taking yourself seriously. Taking themselves seriously has been a risky business for women. It is helpful to remember here that in both the attempt to conform to appropriate female behavior and the attempt to reject it, women pay heavily. The issue that confronts us is whether we will risk being punished for rebelling or accept being punished for following feminine roles. As many women have pointed out, the very words "mother" and "wife" conjure up self-denial while the alternative images

of women—career woman, single parent, lesbian—
provoke hostility and ostracization.

Having described the conventions by which
women have been forced to exist I think it clarifies
why we might choose something else—the fat—to
act for us. Reappropriation of your power (temporarily given to the fat) involves a reevaluation of
yourself. This very reevaluation produces a change
in consciousness and with the awareness of what has
been given away, we can slowly incorporate into our
new self-image what belongs to us. In owning the
power of the fat we can give it up.

What is thin about for the compulsive eater?

We know that every woman wants to be thin. Our images of womanhood are almost synonymous with thinness. If we are thin we shall feel healthier, lighter and less restricted. Our sex lives will be easier and more satisfying. We shall have more energy and vigor. We shall be able to buy nice clothes and decorate our bodies, winning approval from our lovers, families and friends. We shall be the woman in the advertisements who lives the good life; we shall be able to project a variety of images—athletic, sexy or elegant. We shall set a good example to our children. No doctors will ever again yell at us to take

off the excess weight. We shall be admired. We shall be beautiful. We shall never have to be ashamed about our bodies, at the beach, in a store trying to buy clothes or in a tightly packed automobile. We shall be light enough to sit on someone's knee and lithe enough to dance. If we stand out in a crowd it will be because we are lovely, not "repulsive." We shall sit down in any position comfortably, not worrying where the flab shows. We shall sweat less and smell nicer. We shall feel good going to parties. We shall be able to eat in public without courting disfavor. We shall not have to make excuses for liking food.

These images and desires bombard our consciousness daily. In seeing ourselves thin, we can all find something positive with which to identify. When we are fat we crave thinness as we crave the food, searching within it for the solution to our varied problems.

But the fact is that while many of us want to be thin many millions of women are overweight or concerned with body size. One of the theses of this book is not obvious. Women fear being thin; fat has its purposes and advantages. Our experience shows that many women are positively afraid of being thin. Woman's conscious experience is of wanting to be thin, but her body size can belie this intention suggesting that in the same way that fat plays an active role in our lives, so thinness is the other side of the coin. Being fat serves the compulsive eater in a protective way; being thin is a fearful state—the woman is exposed to the very things she attempted to get away from when she got fat in the first place.

In trying to absorb this idea, I suggest you close your eyes for two minutes and think about a social

situation that you were involved in today. This might have been an incident at work, at the shops or in the home.

Now carefully go over what happened in that particular situation.... Notice what you were wearing ... whether you were standing or sitting and how you were getting on with the people around you.... Were you an active participant or did you feel excluded?... Be aware of as many details as possible....

Now imagine yourself thin in exactly the same situation.... Notice particularly what you are wearing and how you feel in your body. Are you sitting or standing?... How are you getting on with the people around you?... Notice particularly if there is a difference in the way you are getting on with others now.... Do you feel more or less included?... Are people wanting different things from you?...

When you have become familiar with the details of the situation, see if you are aware of any negative feelings that being thin engenders in you. Is there anything frightening about being thin in this place?

When women in the groups I work with try this fantasy exercise they are often very surprised at the kinds of things they find out about themselves. After an initial joyful experience of seeing themselves thin they contact feelings and ideas associated with thinness that sound like the following:

1. They feel cold and ungiving.
2. They feel angular, almost too defined, and self-involved.
3. They feel admired to the point of having expectations laid on them. They feel they will not be

able to keep people at bay—particularly those with a sexual interest.

4. They do not know how to cope with their own sexual desires; they feel free to be sexual now but unsure of the implications.

5. They feel they command too much power.

6. They do not know how to define the boundaries around themselves and feel invaded by others' attention because they will not know how to fend it off. They are worried about where they exist in this new admiration.

7. They feel uncomfortable amongst other women who throw competitive glances.

8. They are worried by the need to have everything worked out—to have their lives fit together. They feel there are no longer any excuses for the difficulties they face in their lives. They feel they must give up all the pain that their fat has expressed. They are particularly concerned that when they are thin they will have no room to feel blue, and that no one will see their neediness. It is very important to realize that concern about body size, as reflected by these themes, is a constant preoccupation for women because these images are the only socially acceptable models of feminine behavior.

I should like to take each of these feelings in turn and show why they are such common fears when women do that fantasy exercise.

1. The fear that being thin means to be emotionally cold is a familiar one. We know how very deeply our identities are formed around the model of the woman as a giving, caring person. Experiencing oneself as cold and ungiving is in direct conflict with

this very basic notion we learn as little girls. How many of us can comfortably accept that there are aspects of ourselves that reject this giving, nurturing woman? We fear being cold so much because we rarely allow ourselves to show this side of our personalities.

Annie, a fifty-eight-year-old teacher and expectant grandmother, said, "All my life I've striven to create a warm and loving place around me. If I imagine myself thin now, I feel icy and frozen, like an emaciated version of myself. I feel I wouldn't fit into my life. It would be as if I'd stopped being lively, warm and giving which is how I see myself now." Just as we think one candy means we eat the whole roll, so we worry that showing any coldness means we shall be cold people. We are expected to be caring and giving and, furthermore, we expect this from ourselves. So many of our daily relationships center on our capacity to nurture others. To be cold, even temporarily, is virtually to deny our own sexual identity.

2. Being angular and too defined causes problems because we are so used to having our personalities defined for us. By this I mean that we tune our antennae to adjust to others' expectations of us because our social position has discouraged us from forging our own identities.

We are defined to fit the traditional female stereotypes. When we struggle for self-definition, we are met with curiosity, lack of support and even hostility. Diane, a Canadian psychiatrist in therapy for compulsive eating, expressed a common fear. She worried that if she were thin, people would think that she was really only interested in herself

and not in others. If she looked thin and beautiful
(in her mind, the two go together), that would mean
she was vain and self-involved since thinness was
something she had to work hard to attain. Diane felt
her fatness covered her feelings of self-importance;
if she were thin, these feelings would be apparent.
Since Diane's work was to help others, the idea that
she might be so involved with herself horrified her.
Her discomfort was of a kind familiar to many
women. We grow up to be concerned with others
and often feel guilty when we notice that we have
our own needs, desires and concerns which really
come first. For Diane, the dilemma was particularly
acute and she noticed that she stuffed several
cookies down her mouth just before sessions with
her patients. By doing this, she felt she was
accomplishing two things: she ensured that she
remained big—which to her meant being stable and
reliable; and she was preventing herself betraying
her feelings of self-involvement when she was
working with someone. Stuffing down the cookies
she stuffed her feelings.

3. Being admired is also not without its difficulties.
If we are admired when we are thin we often feel that
it is only our bodies that are being appreciated. A
woman's body has been her primary asset; how she
sees it measuring up against the bodies of other
women is an important factor determining how she
feels. How she looks will partly determine her
choice of lovers and husband. It is important that
she makes a good impression with her looks to a
much greater extent than her male counterpart.
This, of course, is a preposterous position—to be
valued on the basis of current fashions of sexual

attractiveness. What about the active, thinking part of us? Thus being thin carries with it worries about whether we shall be regarded as a complete person, rather than simply as a sexual one.

4. The desire to be sexual is double-edged. On the one hand, many women associate thinness with sexual desirability, and they feel more in control of their choice of partners. As thin people they feel it is legitimate to select those in whom they are interested; as overweight people they feel they must wait for the man or woman who will fight through the layers to find the person. On the other hand, many women fear the new-found sexuality that being thin promises. Many feel that they will act on it in ways that are different from their current sexual behavior. One of the worries that comes up time and time again in groups is, "If I become thin and very attractive maybe I'll be turned on to other men apart from my husband and I don't want to jeopardize our relationship." We have so little say over the determination of our sexuality and consequently it is often hard for us to feel, let alone act on, what we want sexually.

One woman I worked with spelled it out this way: "If there is less of me, people will see more of me, I shall be exposed. What will be exposed is my sexuality. Fat, I hide it in cheerfulness and pretend I'm not sexual myself. Thin, I reveal a sexuality that is unformed and feels unfettered because I'm thin so rarely that I don't get used to feeling comfortable with my own sexuality."

Images of female sexuality radiate from billboards, the television and the cinema. Advertisements for cars and tractors often show women

draped over the goods. Female sexuality becomes a commodity in the eyes of both men and women.

The significance of this last point produces a further complication. Men's sexual objects are women. However, women's sexual objects are also women for sexuality is normally presented in female images. Therefore women become confused if they do not fit the image that has been set up for them. If a woman does not look like the sexually vital woman in the advertisement or on the fashion page, how dare she be sexual?

But why should thinness prove to be a problem of sexuality? For many, the answer lies in the fact that weight has been experienced as a way to avoid sexuality. While avoiding sexuality is a very painful way to cope, it may, nevertheless, be a safer option for women who fear that thinness is equated with sexual desirability. As with all the fantasies attached to thin, in the groups we work on new ways of saying "no" and "yes" to sexuality so that we can be whatever weight and at the same time still struggle to define our sexual needs. Thus, if fat has been a way of saying "no" to sex we must learn to use our mouths to speak to assert the "no" rather than hoping that the world will magically understand that the food we just put in our mouths was an attempt to say "no." Mouths have two important functions—to allow us to speak and to ingest food. Sometimes compulsive eaters worry that they do not know how to use their mouths in the first of these ways.

5. There are, as well, deeper levels of resistance to being thin. One of the fears many women discover

they associate with being thin is that of feeling too powerful. In our culture, girls from a very early age are taught that their role in life is to be one of helpmate to a potent man. Their own sense of identity will develop from their husbands' positions; they will be the wife and loving mother, and the power behind the man. Girls are consistently discouraged from having power in their own right outside the mothering role. The meaning of being thin for many women is that they will be doing *too* well and will have exceeded their social place.

Power presents women with three interrelated problems: the first stems from cultural images of powerful women; the second from the way little girls are brought up; and the third, from the imagined or real consequences of being powerful. The few well-known examples we have of powerful women have either been equated with destruction, like Helen of Troy or Cleopatra, or they have been coupled with images of emasculated men, like Maggie of *Maggie and Jiggs*.

The all-powerful mother is only powerful *as mother*. Once father reenters the home, he reappropriates his authority from *his wife*. Thus, a little girl learns about power in a very confused way; her mother's power, the female power, is negated by that of her father but her father's power, male power, is generally equated with ruthlessness and competition.

In growing up, the young girl learns how to cope with second-class citizenship. Her mother teaches her to yield to others (as she herself does to her husband) and to expect others to define the shape of her world. Concepts of femininity exclude thinking

of oneself as powerful and effective because to a woman, "powerful" means "selfish"—acting for oneself means depriving others.

Women risk social isolation if they become too powerful. If a woman is powerful and can take care of herself, she may worry that she will not need anyone else and that she will become too self-contained and alone. This fear is fostered by the reactions of others. Men frequently react against a woman's attempt to be powerful in her own right—"What she needs is a man."

Women are frequently no more encouraging to those women who try to act on their own behalf. They may feel threatened, jealous or betrayed. Thus if we exceed our social place by first conceiving of ourselves as powerful and then acting as powerful people, we may feel ourselves to be in jeopardy.

Work on this problem is an integral part of the groups. We explore why women have been taught to accept this secondary role and examine the power structure of individual families or school networks.

6. A very complicated fear which women almost invariably experience centers on the question of female boundaries. Psychoanalytic literature is full of references to the problem women have with boundary definition. What is meant by boundaries is the amount of space one takes up in the world—where one begins and where one ends. The reason why boundary issues are so difficult for women has social roots in the development of a feminine psychology. We know that the female role requires the woman to be a nurturing, caring person who gives emotional sustenance to the people around her. She is required to merge her interests

with those of others and seek her fulfillment in
adjusting her needs and desires to others—mainly
lovers and children with whom she is centrally
involved. She is actively dissuaded from developing
her autonomy economically and emotionally. Being
fat expresses an attempt both to merge with others
and, paradoxically, to provide an impenetrable wall
around herself. Similarly, many women associate
thinness with boundary issues. If the fat has been a
way to express her separateness and her space,
without it the woman will feel quite vulnerable and
defenseless. Maggie, a thirty-eight-year-old clerk,
put it this way: "If I don't have all this weight *on me,*
people will get in real close and I won't have any
control or protection." Drawings perhaps describe
how these themes are experienced.

In figure A the woman is fat and experiences her
true self as existing somewhere inside the fat. The fat
provides physical protection against her believed

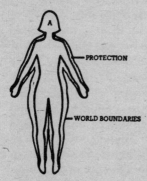

vulnerability. She imagines that if she loses the
weight she will be losing a protective coating against
the world.

The loss of fixed boundaries of the self produces another of the terrifying states women have associated with loss of weight. This terror a woman may feel is the fear of people invading her. The fat may have allowed her to keep a certain distance from people. She imagines that it all has to do with the fat, that people themselves do not approach her and that she has little right to approach them. Thus, a woman will worry that while thin, people will encroach on her space in an active way and penetrate her. Once again, we see that the body states of fat and thin have been the way that compulsive eaters deal with the difficulties in their social relationships.

7. An issue of enormous difficulty for women is that of competition. They have been forced to compete with each other in order to get the man who will supposedly take care of them and, in particular, to legitimize their sexuality. This competition between women is extremely fierce and painful even if only acted out on an unconscious level. It makes us assess each other so we can feel comfortable or uncomfortable when we engage with others. We walk into parties and unwittingly rank ourselves by our own attractiveness compared with the other women. This is so much a part of our culture that it is even institutionalized. Perhaps its most degraded form is the Miss World Contest in which women compete on the basis of their beauty and personality. Many women attempt to avoid these painful competitive feelings by getting fat. Contemplating a return to thinness exposes tbe competitive impulses. Many women are not sure how they will cope with

either their own competitive desires or the animosity that they imagine they will rouse in other women.

8. Finally, another of the most frequently expressed fears associated with being thin is crystallized by the statement made by Penny, a twenty-four-year-old teacher. She felt that there were great chunks of her life that had not fallen into place even though she enjoyed her work, friendships and love relationships. She had anticipated that if she could lose ten pounds everything in her life would run smoothly. The reason for this, she felt, was the excess weight. As we probed further together, we discovered that her image of thinness expressed competence and confidence. It allowed no space for anything to go wrong in her life—if she were thin what could possibly be a problem? If she were thin she would not know how to express her pain and sadness if she felt it. She realized that the extra weight provided her with a reason for why everything did not fit into place. Without that reason she worried about her capacity to be in charge of her life in the way that the absorbed media messages promised. As she put it: "If I'm as thin as I really think I want to be I'll just have to get it together!"

Before moving on to detail the actual experience that compulsive eaters have had on the occasions when they have lost weight, it is important to point out that both the images and experiences of thinness contain contradictory messages. The same women attribute divergent worries to fatness and thinness. One might say, "If I'm thin I'll feel weak and almost

disappear." Her fat self imagines that the weight gives her strength and substance. We may also discover, however, that for this same woman, thin also connotes a wiry kind of strength and fat its very opposite, a flabby indefinable quality—a blob.

Contradictory images are familiar to all of us in many of our daily activities. It is less commonly understood that the compulsive eater has contradictory feelings about body sizes. Nutritionists, psychologists, doctors and the diet and beauty columns of women's magazines rarely raise the issues that we have found so central in breaking the fat-thin, diet-binge cycle.

It is often the case that compulsive eaters' previous experiences of losing weight and becoming thin have been very difficult. There are many reasons for this which will be explored below but first, some preliminary remarks to provide a context for understanding the varied reasons.

The negative images associated with thinness are largely unconscious. This means that they are not readily accessible to people in their waking lives. The fantasy exercises in this book help to provide clues to finding out more about ideas we hold that we are not generally aware of. Unconscious ideas are as much a force in people's daily existence as the conscious desires, thoughts and actions we put into practice. The unconscious is an active part of all of us and when we attempt to change our behavior or our feelings and it does not work, we look into the varied reasons that stand in our way. Social factors are critical determinants here and must never be underestimated, but our unconscious intent—formed by the repression of socially unacceptable

desires—is a persuasive intervener and one that needs to be reckoned with. In addressing the issues of body size and self-image in the groups, we aim to help each other do the emotional work necessary so that this time being thin will be understood in all its ramifications and the anticipated dangers will be minimized. This means that we will be working to:

(1) Explore the ideas that women hold on a conscious and unconscious level about thinness and fatness.
(2) Detach these ideas from body states so that the various qualities an individual ties up with her size will be attributed to her directly and not to her thin self or her fat self. This will allow her to express different aspects of herself without regard to size.
(3) Provide women with alternative ways, apart from eating, by which they can protect, assert and define themselves.

The fears of thinness that compulsive eaters hold based on previous experiences of losing weight center on a number of themes. But the one feeling shared by nearly all compulsive eaters, whatever their own individual psychology, focuses on the effects of losing weight through a diet. Generally, the only way the compulsive eater has found to lose weight has been through a severe restriction of her food intake. Because her body size is such a crucial subject for her, in turning to a diet she invests it with the power to do wondrous things for her. In fact, many women report that once having decided to diet the amount of psychic energy required to actually mobilize, to drastically regulate them-selves—is so enormous that they feel marvelous,

pure, uncriticizable, almost high. Nothing disturbs them till they break it and the recriminations set in. Having deified dieting, the breaking of it signals a return to the tortuous state of compulsive eating.

For a woman the experience of depriving herself while on a diet operates on two levels. The one which produces the high allows her to continue the diet feeling self-righteous and contemptuous of her previous eating behavior. But on another level, eating by rules and regulations is a constant reminder to the compulsive eater that she cannot be trusted. Thus, when she loses the weight, her experience of being normal sized and like everyone else is achieved only at the expense of her remaining in the prison of compulsive dieting, vigilantly fighting off the monster of compulsive eating, and keeping it at bay.

This battle to banish the bingeing puts the woman in an extremely precarious state. She is as worried as ever about what can and cannot go into her mouth and rarely does she feel confident that this particular diet will end her eating problem. Her days and nights are no less filled with worries of food intake and body size. If life for the compulsive eater is felt to be a process of continuous eating, then dieting exists outside life and is felt to be unreal. The addiction continues with all its concomitant obsessions: "Will I be able to resist those French fries and desserts?" "Will I be able to eat what Joyce is serving for dinner or will it be too fattening?" This tension adds to the feeling of distrust about her capacity to maintain the diet once the weight has been lost. The specter of hugeness is always round the corner. The compulsive eater does

not develop a confidence that she will remain thin.
She has become a thin woman, someone who looks
different and acts in different ways from her fat self,
but a new woman whom she does not know very
well. She is someone she is not sure she can trust or
really get to know because she is unsure of how long
she is going to be thin. If she is habitually thin for
two months every year having dieted for one month,
and fat for the remaining nine, then she is bound to
be more familiar with her fat self. She really does
not believe that her thin self is going to be around
that long so she develops a suspicious relationship
with it. Thus, her thin life has a precarious quality
which is not conducive to self-confidence.

There is, in addition to all this, a new body to
contend with, a smaller version of herself. (We tend
to feel so small in our effect on the world,
particularly as women, that reducing our physical
presence feels almost bizarre.) Connected to this
unfamiliarity with her body, is a drastic change in
the woman's self-image. Many women report that
they wore clothes that were quite unusual for
themselves, not simply in the size that the label read,
but also in the style that they had selected. Losing
weight had held out the promise of fulfilling those
aspects of dress they had denied themselves fat.
This, for example, may have meant dressing
attractively, a taboo idea for most overweight
women. "If I am fat, I must be horrible and don't
deserve to have nice clothes."

Having dressed in a different way when thin,
these women acted differently with others but
discovered that they were ill-equipped to deal with
the reactions they stirred up. Kate, an anthropology

graduate student, discovered that once, when thin, she had been to a party in tight blue jeans and a cheesecloth shirt (in place of her usual cover-up dress over pants) and her women friends, while initially complimentary and supportive, seemed to hover around when their husbands and lovers approached her. Kate was nervous that the other women felt jealous and would dislike her, but she did not know how to keep their husbands away. In the group, we discussed the various meanings of this new clothing. In the end, she was determined that the next time she lost weight, she would risk feeling good and sensual in her clothes without threatening her friends. She decided to share her new and fragile acceptance of her body with her friends and she reassured them that she was not interested in their lovers. This also helped her clear up her own confusion about dressing sensually and sexually.

Body image and protection are very important. In the groups we try to address these two problems in the following ways: group members are encouraged to accept the physical aspects of being fat. Self-acceptance is the key task in the group; without it weight loss and breaking the addiction can only be temporary. We aim for a situation in which women can actually experience the ownership of their fat and the diverse meanings they have attributed to it. When they lose weight they can take its significance with them as necessary. They will not feel that they are losing a protective covering, they grow into their bodies and then they will feel that they have their whole bodies which they then can afford to compress. These diagrams help to show the process we aim for in the groups.

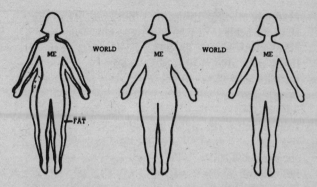

To help in the very difficult task of self-acceptance and the preparation for a new slim body and new self-image we employ the following strategies. Bear in mind that you first have to own something before you can lose it. You must first accept your body in its largeness before you can give it up. A full-length undistorted mirror is the first place to start. Group members set aside time each day—maybe just a couple of minutes at the outset—to observe their bodies. Most compulsive eaters are very aware of how their faces look but not in relation to the rest of their bodies. What we try to do in this exercise is to observe our bodies. We are using the mirror to see ourselves without judging the image it holds. This is both a frightening and difficult project for many women because one is so used to making a grimace and judgment on the few occasions we do see our whole bodies. We are so familiar with avoiding possibly unacceptable visions, keeping our heads down as we walk past shop windows lest we cast a glance at ourselves unaware and trigger negative feelings. So, in doing the

exercise, a woman is asked initially to look at the reflected image of herself as she would a work of art, for example, a sculpture, getting to know its dimensions and texture. She is looking to find out where it begins and ends; where it curves or bumps in and out; what color changes there are. The woman tries this in several different positions starting first by standing, then sitting—without having to hide half of her body—and finally, standing sideways. Some people have a greater ease doing this exercise dressed; others find it more manageable nude. So we start with what feels most comfortable and stay with that until the woman can have the experience of looking in the mirror and not flashing to feelings of disgust.

The second step in the mirror exercise is aimed to help you experience yourself existing throughout your body. Many women experience their fat as something that surrounds them with their true selves inside or, alternatively, that their fat trails them, taking up more room than it really does. So when a woman is standing in front of the mirror the emphasis in this part of the exercise is to feel herself *throughout* her body. She follows her breath on its course from her lungs through her body. The large thighs she may wish to reject are as much a part of her body as the wrist that seems so much more acceptable. Try to see the various parts of your body as connected. Start with your toes and remind yourself of how your toes are connected to your feet and your feet are connected to your ankles and your ankles are connected to your lower leg, and so on. It will provide you with a holistic view of your body. You will begin to experience yourself as existing through the fat.

This new approach has another function. If you can experience yourself as existing throughout the fat, then when you lose weight, you will not feel you have lost a protective covering; you will feel you have become compressed. This is because if you feel yourself all through the fat then what is all of you is part of you. In giving up the size you are making an exchange—you swap the fat for your own body, and that is power.

The drawings are worth repeating here because these will help toward an understanding of what we are trying to achieve in reducing the discrepancy between the fat self and the small interior physical self. We are aiming for a situation where the sequence, me:fat:world, is replaced by me:world.

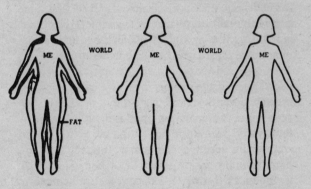

As I mentioned above, women report that when they have lost weight they have allowed themselves to wear very different clothes from those they wore when they considered their bodies as unacceptably large. A compulsive eater may have at least three wardrobes. These generally consist of one or two smocky-type items that will cover her at her absolute maximum weight; nondescript clothes for

a medium weight; and clothes for when she was or will be thin which tend to be more stylish and varied and allow for a greater range of expression. The clothes in the larger sizes will almost undoubtedly be circumscribed by what is available in the shops and by what a compulsive eater thinks is permissible to wear. When you look at the clothing racks in sizes 18, 20 and up there is much less variety and styling than in the 10s and 12s. The taboos in people's minds against bright colors, horizontal strips and good design for fat people correspond to what is available in the stores. By and large, cheap, stylish clothing is not available over size 14. It is therefore not surprising that when a woman loses weight she can experiment with projecting different images through her dressing, because for the first time alternative clothing is readily available. However, it is also true that as long as she feels her body size is unacceptable, she will be using her clothing to hide her body and avoid drawing attention to it. The initial goal of the groups is to give each woman a greater acceptance of her body. Without such acceptance we maintain that weight loss will be temporary because it will continue to trigger off frightening feelings. To avoid this state we do preparatory work in the area of body size, body image and dressing. We encourage the women to throw out or pack away or trade with other group members, all the clothes in their closets that do not currently fit them. This means that every morning, instead of confronting three sets of clothes (indeed, three different people in their closets) and torturing themselves about the "thin" clothes that continually await and attack them, they will be looking at the clothes that do fit. Much of the compulsive eater's negative self-image gets expressed in the way she

dresses and carries herself. This then produces a spiralling of self-hate. One woman I worked with said, "I feel ashamed of my body and I just cover it as efficiently as possible in a big smock. Then I realize I don't like my clothes either, so I end up doubly hating myself." Almost inevitably, these self-rejecting feelings lead the compulsive eater to cram food into her mouth to assuage the feelings and then, of course, come renewed recriminations and resolutions to start yet another diet.

Having bared one's wardrobe, we are ready to move to step two. This involves experimenting with various images of yourself and dressing to express those now, not waiting until you are thin to wear the kinds of clothes in which you imagine yourself thin. It is not a criminal act to tuck in your blouse, shirt or sweater when overweight. It rarely makes you look larger to be more defined. This latter idea is one of the misconceptions we carry around supposing that loose clothing makes us look less big than fitted clothing. It may attract more attention. If so, that gives you the opportunity to work on reactions to one of the imagined consequences of being thin. Better to test it out and see how it feels while you still have the safety of the fat. It is important to test out your ideas of the images you want to express to find out what really feels good and what feels scary. In the groups, women can get some feedback for the images they are projecting; they can discuss whether there is a discrepancy between what they wish to project and are indeed projecting. Group members can also help each other go shopping for clothes or material to make garments[1] and help each other through a day of real or imagined critical sales staff and fellow shoppers.

Mirror work and dressing for now are thus two

of the basic techniques used in the group to help women both accept their current body size and prepare for a smaller one. In addition, we encourage group members to adopt a self-image close to the one they imagine they will have when thin. This has its physical aspects as well as emotional ones, and an aim of the group is to work on the different levels simultaneously.

Another of the preparatory exercises employed is to imagine not only what you intend to project when thin through your clothing but also through body position and stance as well. Many women report that when they were thin before, they sat, stood and danced quite differently, generally adopting more open postures. These different stances produced a variety of effects, some of which they were comfortable with and others with which they were not. The difficult ones mainly had to do with others' responses and the women found that they did not know how to deal with people's reactions. Putting on weight again had been their only option. An illustration from my work with Janet describes well her actual experience of becoming thin in the past.

Janet is a twenty-six-year-old social worker in a drug-addiction agency. She grew up in Brooklyn, the eldest of three children in a middle-class Jewish family. She was of average weight until she was thirteen. Her mother was slightly overweight and from time to time was preoccupied with dieting. At the dinner table her mother would often be eating a modified version of the family meal—no potatoes or desserts. When Janet's body started to develop into that of a woman she put on about fifteen pounds. She felt quie uncomfortable with the changes going on in her body and she sought advice

from the adolescent girls' magazines on how to cope with this new shape and the distressing feelings that accompanied puberty. She gravitated toward articles entitled, "How to Look Like a Happy Teenager; What to do about the changes going on in your body." Under cosy headlines these articles contained a ghastly message. Janet learned there was something decidedly wrong about her shape and was told that the answer lay in weight control. Thus started thirteen years of dieting and bingeing. Janet's initial experience of terror and anxiety about her body changes found no outlet except in these magazines. She had no other place to explore the revulsion, excitement and fear that she was feeling about periods, bras and pubic hair. Indeed, her introduction to her menstrual periods itself was quite confusing. Although prepared for the event so that she was not initially frightened when the blood began, she had no real way to understand the response from her mother. On telling her, she was slapped on the cheek[2] and offered congratulations. Subsequently, she overheard her mother telephoning family friends to announce with pride that Janet was a woman. Thus, an introduction to womanhood was accompanied by an act of violence. It was hard for Janet to put together the slap and the congratulations. The idea that she had done something wrong, or indeed was all wrong, provided the basis for her to latch on to those articles and advertisements which promised solutions to one's failures through attaining the correct body size. The very first diet she went on made her feel wonderful. She experienced it as an act of independence from her family. She would decide what to eat rather than eat whatever was put on the

table. The diet had a double edged function. She could try and transform her body and she could establish her separateness from the family. She performed adequately academically and went away to college and graduate school. When I first met Janet she had been working for two years, she had a large circle of friends which included some close women friends, and had been living with Alan, an architect, for over two years. With one exception, she felt quite pleased with the way her life was going, feeling herself to be quite active, social and competent on the job. The one exception was her obsession with weight, dieting and body size. She was 5 feet 2 inches and felt overweight at 130 pounds. She had successfully dieted many times to 112 pounds but had never maintained the weight loss for more than a few months. Her current weight was not far off the maximum she had ever been. In the course of the therapy we traced the different times when her weight had increased and decreased. As I have sketched out above we discussed in detail the original feelings that had propelled her toward the diet-binge syndrome. Two important discoveries were made. The first was that many times Janet had geared up to diet and, having lost the weight, felt herself attractive enough to get sexually involved with men. These relationships varied in length but almost inevitably her eating went through three phases when she was sexually involved. The first phase, which lasted a week or so, was characterized by a startling lack of interest in food. These were the only times since she was thirteen that Janet can remember actually not being preoccupied with her food intake. She ate quite little and was not particularly aware of how it tasted. The

length of the second phase varied. With Alan she kept quite close to her diet for about three months, with no significant weight variation but with a considerable preoccupation and worry about food with days defined as "good" or "bad"—depending on her intake. After three months they went on vacation together and Janet relaxed the proscription on her consumption of food although her obsession was just as great. Privately, she judged, worried or praised herself according to what passed between her lips. She resolved to diet when she got back from their vacation. Meanwhile, she ate a wide range of foods, particularly the kind of which she deprived herself during the previous months. When she and Alan returned to New York she had put on enough weight to convince herself that she must diet yet again. For the next fifteen months she yoyoed but became increasingly bored and unconvinced by the whole approach.

So one pattern was: weight loss to sexual involvement to weight gain. The other instances when she lost weight corresponded to big changes in her life—entry into high school, leaving home to go to college, leaving college and taking summer jobs, the beginning of the year she worked between college and graduate school and the return to New York City to work in the drug-addiction agency. Each one of these occasions represented Janet's growing independence and autonomy. She met them with confidence and a slim body and was quite perplexed as to why the impulse to eat compulsively returned shortly after she had settled in new surroundings.

In the course of the therapy, Janet described her experiences in sexual relationships and with new

places, jobs and school challenges. What began to emerge was that the issues of separation and sexuality were more difficult for her than she had been aware of. In her sexual relationships she was able to see that she believed her acceptance was based on her looking a particular way and being thin. She received plenty of sexual attention which, although she enjoyed, threatened her—she did not know how to turn people away. She also did not know if she was as sexual inside as she projected outside because, in her periods of weight gain, she did not feel at all sexual and had not met with much sexual interest from others. In addition, she worried that she might become uncontrollably promiscuous if she were thin all the time. Her mother's attitude toward her was painful and confusing. Whereas her mother had previously encouraged dieting, she now passed comments on how Janet was looking pale and as if she might disappear. Janet had not become the thin, beautiful daughter her mother had wanted, and she was hurt by her mother's ambivalence toward her newfound self-acceptance. She was also confused by the reactions of men; she could not seem to please both her mother and men at the same time.

As we replayed her feelings frame by frame, Janet sensed the vulnerability she experienced in herself as a thin woman. She felt that she had become what everyone had encouraged her to be and was met by disapproval from her mother on the one hand, and abundant sexual interest from men on the other. She realized that she felt quite unable to handle these two kinds of attention. The disapproval from her mother made no sense to her and Janet felt angry as though she were being

betrayed. She felt quite inadequate to handle all the sexual attention and felt that she had no way to say "yes" or "no" in a way which corresponded to her own desires. She felt she had no tools by which to select whomever she was interested in but, perhaps more confusing, she felt that now she had a beautiful body she was required to project the sexuality she had hidden in her overweight periods.

In dealing with the theme of separation, Janet realized that as she had taken on the new challenges at school, college, and in her job, she had, indeed, been quite worried about what was expected of her. She had coped with her anxieties by attempting to take a hold of herself—putting herself on a stringent diet. When she started college she projected an image, and attempted to believe in that image of herself—one that expressed independence, competence, interest and general enthusiasm. Underneath this construct, and into the diet, were placed her fears of inadequacy, loneliness, boredom and lack of security. She rarely allowed herself to have those feelings for more than an instant and set herself the task of living up to her idealized self-image as a thin person.

As she realized how ungenerous she had been to herself in her thin times, so it emerged how much of an investment she had made in being thin whenever she put on weight. To be thin was a state that allowed no pain, no mistakes and represented independence and sexuality.

In the therapy we worked toward Janet's acknowledgment of just how scary her past experiences of being thin were. Having seen this, Janet looked to aspects of herself that she left behind in the fat. She began to incorporate those

into an idea of herself thin. She learned how to be
assertive so that she could say "yes" or "no" in
sexual and other situations rather than being the
victim of her body size. She looked at the feelings
that seemed unacceptable while she was thin and
began to articulate them directly rather than hiding
them within the fat so that when she lost the weight
again she was sure she could express them directly
then and did not worry that she had no place to hide
them. She allowed herself the possibility that she
could be thin and have conflicts; that whatever
conflicts she had with her mother, with her own
sexuality, with her anger or whatever, they could all
exist as part of her when thin. This did not mean
resolving all the difficulties but acknowledging and
accepting them. It meant giving up the idea that
being thin meant that her life had to work out right
all the time.

The actual progress of Janet's therapy was, of
course, not a straightforward march with one theme
unfolding after the other in the orderly fashion I
described above. Insights and realizations come
suddenly, fade away and come back again. Only
through fantasy work, slow loss of weight, intermit-
tent bingeing, and the hard work necessary to try
out the insights in fearful situations, does such a
complete picture emerge. Janet's therapy lasted
fourteen months after which she had completely
broken the compulsion and had lost weight. She
stabilized at about 112–114 pounds. Follow-up
sessions verified that the understanding Janet had
reached about her own experience of eating had
permitted her to remain permanently at the weight
she desired. She had found more direct and assertive
ways for dealing with the problems of sexuality and
womanhood than body size.

For Janet then, work on the meanings of fat and thin provided her with the opportunity to change her self-image. She closed the gap between her fantasies of who she would be thin and who she was in reality. This exploration and then abandonment of the thin fantasies allowed her to give up unrealistic expectations of personality change.

As we have seen, women unconsciously fear being thin. If one is thin then one is expected to fit the norm. If one is thin others will equate comforming in body size with conforming with stereotyped female behavior. If one is thin, how can one be self-defining? It is precisely these confusions that have kept many women away from permanent thinness, and it is these underlying issues that need to be confronted so that a woman can experience the choice of being thin *and* herself.

It takes quite a bit of unraveling to separate the threads that push women to lose weight one week and gain it the next. In clarifying the tensions, I have tried to identify the varied reasons why thinness may be feared. A major question that needs to be confronted individually is, "How will I be who I wish to be if I look as I am supposed to look?" Consideration of this question is essential and goes a long way toward providing solutions to being a thin woman in this culture.

The experience of
hunger for the
compulsive eater

The women I see have already tried many different ways to lose weight including hypnosis, Weight Watchers Inc., diet doctors, cellulose fillers, appetite suppressants and diuretics, Overeaters Anonymous and magic. All these methods are external schemes. Food intake is limited and particular foods—such as ice cream, cake and bread—are banned. This is all based on the principle that if you reduce your caloric intake (or carbohydrate intake) you will lose weight. Diets range from Stillman's Water Diet to Atkin's and the Mayo Clinic Diet, from the Banana Diet to the Drinking Person's

Diet. A million diets and a million dieters. Millions of dollars too: ten billion dollars is spent annually by the American public to get thin and stay thin.[1]

All these diets and weight-reduction schemes have two things in common. First, there is a devastatingly high rate of recidivism. Dieters lose weight by the ton but their success in keeping their weight down is less formidable.[2] Statistics are scarce but the maintenance rates are rumored to be scandalously low. The second feature these schemes share is a stress on reinforcing the compulsive activity and an emphasis on cultural stereotypes of thinness and fatness.

None of these plans addresses the central issues behind compulsive eating. Two of these issues are the experience of hunger and the need to break food addiction. "Fat people" are not as aware of the actual mechanism of hunger as "normal weight" non-compulsive eaters.[3] This means that compulsive eaters do not use their gurgling stomachs to tell them when to eat. Eating becomes so loaded with other meanings that a straightforward reaction to a hungry stomach is unusual. Indeed one of the features of compulsive eating is eating in such a way that physical hunger is never felt. The social stigma attached to being overweight accentuates this problem. Fat people in our culture feel the stigma in this way; "Fat is bad, I should always be trying to lose weight and I definitely should not enjoy food." In general, compulsive eaters divide food into categories of "good foods" and "bad foods." All the diets work on the principle that food is dangerous. Only through rigorous deprivation can the compulsive eater redeem herself, lose weight and begin to enjoy life. So the mechanism of hunger on which

"normal" eaters rely is distorted. Years of guilty eating and mammoth deprivation schemes mean that the compulsive eater is very out of touch with the experience of hunger and the ability to satisfy it.

Distortions of the eating process cause confusion for the compulsive eater while the myriad of weight-reduction schemes infantilize her and reduce her control over her own eating to a minimum. As anyone who has ever dieted knows, the structure of a diet is rigid. Diets become moral straitjackets which confine the compulsive eater. *In turning to dieting, all the compulsiveness evident in overeating is now channeled into a new obsession—to staying on the diet.* Follow these rules, eat what the authorities tell you. Above all, do what women are so good at—deprive yourself. Even the so-called liberal diets ("Eat fat and grow slim," "Enjoy as much food and vegetables as you like") rely on a structure that disenfranchizes the woman from her own body. "Eat bananas seven times a day; weigh four ounces of fish and three ounces of grated cheese; drink one glass of pulp-free orange juice a day and unlimited cups of black coffee or tea; use one bowl only and eat with chopsticks; always eat in the same place or at the same time; always eat a big breakfast; eat starch, cut out fat; cut out fat but eat high protein; lose weight and *get/hold your man*." But never, never let yourself go or find out what you like to eat, when or how.

In the main, the compulsive eater knows two realities: compulsive eating (out of control) or compulsive dieting (imprisonment). To be a compulsive eater means to be a food junkie. Compulsive eaters crave their food as badly as a junkie craves heroin or an alcoholic thirsts for liquor. They spend

much of their energy battling against their addiction. They are always going "cold turkey"—dieting or fasting—or trying their methadone substitute—cottage cheese. While a drug addict or alcoholic is not continually struggling against the heroin or liquor, the compulsive eater is caught in an antagonistic relationship with the food she so wants. While the junkie may spend hours hustling the money and connection for the next fix, the compulsive eater will devote the same kind of psychic energy working out what to eat or not. In the end, as the heroin "fixes" the drug addict and the liquor "stuporizes" the alcoholic, so the binge "narcotizes" the compulsive eater.

A curious aspect in the compulsive eater's addiction is that from a look at her kitchen or her public eating one might get the impression that certain foods are illegal. The presence of particular foods is so rare, and ingestion so clandestine, that one might be forgiven for assuming that criminal penalties are given for the possession and consumption of certain foods. It is as though foods are classified, with ice-cream sundaes and French fries as felonies; bananas and cream as misdemeanors and food in general as a violation. In fact, one well-known slimming organization characterizes food in just this way. Some foods are legal and can be eaten incessantly and in unlimited quantities, others are illegal and are to be eaten only in a restricted way. Thus the compulsive eater is encouraged to create her own jail sentence and in doing so she faces the world very much as does the junkie or alcoholic. This tension converts food into an enemy or an evil to be warded off constantly while at the same time it provides, however shortlived, a treat and comfort.

Unlike other addicts, however, the compulsive eater can find temporary relief in not eating. Not eating means she is being "good" and conjures up immediate images of the rewards to come from thinness. Contrary to popular images of greed, the compulsive eater is quite frightened of food and what it can do to her. Short spells of withdrawal remove her from the responsibility of what she is putting in her mouth. The food is a drug, it is magical, it is poison, it is to keep one alive, it is suffocating, it is tantalizing, but only very rarely is it seen as an essential enjoyable aspect of life. It is from this fear of food that the compulsive eater's large appetite springs. The compulsive eater can eat a lot of food. Often she does not taste the three boxes of cookies, ten celery stalks, four packets of potato chips and frozen pizza that she can consume at one sitting. The food is so guiltily eaten that enjoyment is limited. The feeling of insatiability is very strong and the compulsive eater will cram seemingly unappetizing foods, like dry cereal, into her mouth during a binge. The food must be eaten quickly so that it is no longer dangerous. Once consumed, the crisis has passed and the compulsive eater is left with the familiar bad feelings following a binge.

Compulsive eating means eating without regard to the physiological cues which signal hunger. People who have never had difficulty distinguishing hunger pangs take it for granted that their bodies are wanting food then. They may be quite astonished by the extent to which this mechanism is so underutilized by the compulsive eater. For a compulsive eater it is an equally astonishing idea that people who do not have difficulty with food rely on their stomachs to tell them what, how much

and when to eat. For the compulsive eater, food has taken on such additional significance that it has long since lost its obvious biological connection.

The word "hunger" usually connotes the desire to eat. The body is depleted and needs nourishment. In its extreme form hunger becomes starvation. In its current Western setting the satisfaction of hunger is a social experience. While there is controversy about what exactly constitutes hunger, and what controls appetite and satisfaction, it is strikingly clear that the compulsive eater very rarely eats in response to the stomach cues which signal hunger.[4] Indeed, when we introduce this possibility as an important way out of the whole syndrome, people are eager to be reintroduced to aspects of their bodies they have ignored for so long. While one is rejecting one's body, an enormous alienation exists between it and oneself. This estrangement makes it hard to be receptive to signals from the body. If you have never felt your body was alright or acceptable but was cumbersome, unattractive or not pleasing in some way, it is quite a leap to trust what it has to say, as if an enemy territory were commanding. To listen to a body that has constantly been an unseemly colony is to own that body. To own your own body means to take its needs seriously and disregard many of the external values and measures to which you have attempted to mold it. This distortion of the hunger mechanism does not have a clear origin and it may begin very early on in life. What is clear is that many young women begin to tamper with this mechanism in an effort to transform their bodies at the time of puberty. An analogy may make this distortion process more graphic for those who have considerable difficulty

envisaging hunger and an appropriate response. Take, for example, a tickle in the throat. This feeling is satisfied by a cough. A sneeze is preceded by a slight irritation in the nostrils. These reactions are virtually involuntary and few people suffer from the continual need to deny a cough or a sneeze, on the odd occasion it may be polite to stifle the sneeze or cough but not on a continuing basis.

Another example in which one acts less automatically is when one's bladder is full and there is a need to release the pressure. Again, most people will grow up with a confidence about knowing how to follow the signals that they need to urinate and the amount will vary considerably. Sometimes there will be a great deal of pressure on the bladder, sometimes less, but the information that one needs relief will become available quite obviously. These three physical activities are all under self-regulation and depend for satisfaction on recognition of the cues. This is true for the hunger mechanism too. The infant has the capacity to develop a harmonious relationship with its various bodily needs. It can learn to identify hunger cues and feel contented when satisfactorily fed. The confidence that there will be satisfaction is shaped by positive interaction with the environment. When a child cries from hunger and is fed, and cries for affection and gets held, then her cues will have been responded to appropriately and as the child develops she will be able to trust that she can both recognize and fulfill her needs.

Many women who have compulsive-eating problems do not feel confident that they can recognize their signs of hunger and then eat to fulfill them. Not only has the hunger process been abused

through years of dieting and bingeing but pre-puberty eating is often remembered as tortured, interrupted and conflicted. In tracing back, we surmise that such a woman's very early signs of bodily needs were misinterpreted by her mother so that there is confusion over a variety of physical sensations. For example, it every time a child cries it is answered with food, then the food takes on the role of comforter. However, if a baby's diaper needs changing or a baby wants some kind of physical contact, providing food will give neither satisfaction or comfort, nor will it allow the infant to develop trust in its own body. Feeding in response to other bodily needs alienates a child from its body and interferes with the individual's ability to recognize both hunger and satisfaction. This early distortion may well be a contributing factor to many women's discomfort with their own bodies; a discomfort which is then readily available to manipulation by how society says one *should* look and what one *should* eat. Outside cues become powerful sources on which to rely in the absence of confidence that one can take care of one's own needs. Diet sheets and bakeries are equal contenders when a woman is seeking information about how to care for herself. Often compulsive eaters will describe their current eating in a way that confirms our impression that early satisfaction was interfered with. Daphne, a thirty-two-year-old librarian, described much of her eating as a search for something that is missing. "When I go to the refrigerator I'm quite aware that it is not food I am actually after but it's as though I'm looking for a missing piece." The missing piece turns out to be a general unease and unsureness about

whether she can provide adequately for her own needs.

This discourse on hunger and the distortion of the mechanism is not meant to put the blame on mothers for misinterpreting their children's body signals. It is true that in their role as primary caretakers, they often do misinterpret their infants' needs, but an explanation that stops there misses crucial issues that affect all women. The question is more *why* mothers give their children food when that is not what they may be wanting. Why is it that food is always at the ready to be offered when the child expresses discomfort? What are the social forces that produce this kind of mothering? We look for the answer in the social position of women. It is in her role as mother that a woman is unequivocally accepted. It is in her role as mother that she is counseled to be attentive and nurturing to her child. Nearly all of us will have grown up at a time when child care was seen to be the province of mothers. They were seen as the only ones who could adequately care for their children and establish the emotional bonding considered crucial for "healthy" development. However, while considered the essential figure in the infant's daily life, the mother is not considered expert on child rearing. Instead, she will be encouraged to draw on the expertise of a wide range of specialists—pediatricians, child psychologists, analysts, nutritionists—who will tell her how, when and what she should or should not feed her child. Most "experts" contradict each other as the fashion in child rearing changes and the different disciplines rush to fit their theories into prevailing ideologies.

Thus the mother is acclaimed on the one hand as *the* only suitable primary caretaker but on the other, is considered to be inadequately prepared to cope with this job and must rely on conflicting "expert" opinions. If is in this situation that the woman comes to motherhood and the care of her child, and it is not surprising that she then distrusts her own reactions to her child's signals. Alternately deified and devalued, it is hard for her to feel secure about her own responses. One can well imagine how this insecurity is readily reinforced by other consequences of an enforced maternal role. As a mother, this is the chance in life to have an impact on shaping an aspect of one's world (through the child). This may set off in the mother feelings of delight, inadequacy, fear, insecurity, resentment or enthusiasm which are then expressed through her contact with the child. A mother's fears of inadequacy may cause her to overfeed her child by feeding it automatically every time it cries, just as her resentment at being its sole nurse may make her neglect it. But another factor may be involved: when a child cries and expresses its distress and, as the mother imagines, helplessness, she may see herself as the parent who must respond but also, find her own painful feelings of early deprivation reevoked. If *we* are "inadequate mothers," we are also daughters of "inadequate mothers" who were themselves daughters. If the early distortion in the feeding relationship is attributable to the social forces present in the mother-daughter relationship, then this will be as true for our mothers as daughters, and our mother's mothers as daughters. As long as a patriarchal culture demands that

women bring up their daughters to accept an inferior social position, the mother's job will be fraught with tension and confusion which are often made manifest in the way mothers and daughters interact over the subject of food.

The experience of hunger, then, will not be the compulsive eater's motive for eating. She will not experience her eating as self-regulatory but as a kind of outside force tempting, pleasing and betraying her. Once overweight she will most probably adopt an attitude that says she is not entitled to eat, as though fatness can only be excused, or as if fat people only have a right to exist if they do not eat. Fat people move into a category quite apart from the rest of the population. While advertisers court us to eat more and more, slimming columns, doctors, fashion magazines and friends counsel those overweight to curtail their food intake. But to tell a compulsive eater to control something she feels is out of her control has the effect of making her feel powerless and guilty; powerless for being so apparently ineffectual and guilty for whatever food she does eat. This guilt further distances her from discovering what it is she would *like* to eat because she has become preoccupied with what she *should* or *should not* eat. Food is something to be feared, and to eat feels like committing a sin, for one feels so undeserving and unentitled. Eating takes place quickly and frequently furtively.

A compulsive eater would describe this experience in one of several ways:

1. FOOD AS SOCIAL: "I'm never hungry at suppertime but I like everyone to eat together because it *feels*

like we are a happy family if we eat together. Mealtimes are significant not for the food but for the appearance of family closeness."

2. MOUTH HUNGER: "I really need to put some food in my mouth although I don't feel hungry in my stomach."

3. EATING PROPHYLACTICALLY: "I'm not hungry at the moment but I might be hungry in a couple of hours and I won't be able to get anything then, so I'd better have some food now."

4. DESERVED FOOD: "I had a ghastly day. I think I'll cheer myself up with a nice nosh."

5. GUARANTEED PLEASURE: "Eating goodies is the only way to give myself a real treat. It's the one pleasure that I know how to give myself."

6. NERVOUS EATING: "I just have to have something. What can I cram into my mouth?"

7. CELEBRATORY EATING: "I had such a great day, one packet of Fritos can't possibly hurt me."

8. EATING OUT OF BOREDOM: "I'm not in the mood to do anything at the moment... I'll fix myself a club sandwich."

With compulsive dieting there is *also* no response to physiological hunger. The dieter is eating out of a prescribed set of rules saying what foods are allowed or forbidden; she is eating at specified mealtimes with little regard for what her body wants and when it wants it.

We work on the premise that compulsive eaters

*do not really allow themselves to eat, and conse-
quently are either stuffing their mouths or depriving
themselves. Every time a compulsive eater goes on a
diet she is telling herself that there is something
wrong with her so she must deprive herself.* She
defines her current self as reprehensible, so she
decides to punish herself through denial. In this
way, the compulsive eater rarely allows herself the
direct pleasure that food can bring. A vicious circle
ensues. While she may eat everything in sight when
she is not dieting for fear of imminent deprivation,
she is nevertheless not enjoying the food. "I ate
twenty cookies in ten minutes today. Tomorrow I'm
going to put myself on a diet during which I won't be
able to have any cookies, so I had to get all my
cookie eating in today before I have to be good." At
the same time the twenty cookies are also a rebellion
against the non-entitlement and deprivation.

This diet-binge syndrome can be broken by the
compulsive eater when she begins to see herself as a
"normal" person, with fat being nothing more than
a descriptive word, without connoting good or bad.
If the compulsive eater can begin to experience
herself as "normal" then she can begin to eat like a
"normal" person. This means learning to recognize
the difference between real hunger and psychological hunger, and eating accordingly. It means eating
enough to satisfy one's hunger and eating whatever
food satisfies that particular hunger (be it donuts or
steak). After all, people without a compulsive-
eating problem do not deprive themselves of food
by choice. In observing the eating behavior of
people who do not suffer over food, it is interesting
to note just what a wide range of foods they do eat
and how much at variance with conceptions of

"healthy diet" their daily intake may be. It is also important to realize that they occasionally overeat for pleasure. As this eating is not a substitute for other needs it does not have other connotations. It is the driving compulsion to stuff or starve that we are trying to dissolve rather than dictating "correct" amounts of food intake.

To find out what, when and how much you might like to eat is not as simple as it seems. In addition, the pressure of the diet and fashion industry, which spends incalculable amounts of money making sure that women do not themselves decide what they would like to eat and wear, reinforces the idea that the compulsive eater is irresponsible, out of control, negligent and hateful.

On the psychological level the experience of hunger pangs can be quite scary. Some of the fear comes from an anxiety about one's ability to satisfy bodily hunger: "If I'm not stuffing my face or starving myself, what should I do? How will I know how much to eat? Maybe I'll never want to stop."

Another frightening factor is related to a challenge of the "female-as-child" concept. For if you can respond to the hunger cues that your body does indeed transmit, this places you in a situation where you might actually satisfy yourself and begin to be in harmony with your body. This idea of being able to take care of yourself allows you to see the female as an adult with the rights and privileges that other adults (male adults) have. This means taking your own needs seriously and attempting to satisfy them for yourself. A woman is brought up to be attuned to and satisfy others' needs. The struggle to know what you want or need to eat changes the way you respond to others' needs. As you begin to trust

the capacity to feed yourself you find a basis for being more explicit in relation to other needs. "If I can take care of myself with food and say 'yes' and 'no' to what I am wanting or not wanting, then I can spell out for myself, *and* to others, desires in other areas and feel more in charge of other aspects of my life." Being able to act on one's own needs is a novel experience and one overwhelmingly denied to women in this culture.

When the compulsive eater imagines herself as a thin female adult, when everything else in her life is supposed to hang together better, she has to conform to an image of womanhood rather than be confident with who she is. While this idea is fantasy, it is nevertheless a powerful and scary one: "If I am thin, and look like a 'real' woman, then I must be productive, energetic, together and loving." The struggle to be female and self-defined is hard, with few supports for an expression of true female personhood.

In our work we spend a great deal of time uncovering and demystifying the various fantasies associated with fat and thin. At the same time we work together on the technical side, learning new ways to approach food and hunger. The steps that I outline here start with the idea that we are not going to judge whatever it is that we eat. Rather, we are going to observe the ways in which we eat. Learning not to judge one's food intake is not very easy. Years of attempting to follow the rules do not quickly fade away. To observe an aspect of the self which has been rejected time and time again requires a good deal of self-acceptance. Turning off one's judges— mothers, women's magazines, husbands, lovers, friends, diet doctors and nutritionists—requires

trust in one's self. Being in a group with other women going through the same process can be of great assistance and support.

The first step is to learn about your eating patterns. This means pinpointing those times when you feel particularly vulnerable to attack by the food and to notice any occasions when you feel more at ease with it. By noting your food intake for a short period you will both gather data and develop a sense of yourself as an observer. As an observer you can begin to see that there is a part of you that eats and another part that does other things, including being an observer. Then you have broken away from the idea of yourself as being someone who is obsessed with food. You are ready to move on to becoming a "normal" person who eats like "normal" people.

Now the second step is taken. We move from observation to action. First, we begin to identify the difference between mouth hunger and stomach hunger. Risk going without food for a couple of waking hours until you experience some hunger sensations in your body. Most probably you will feel it in your stomach, though some people feel it in the chest or throat. When you feel the difference between the two types of hunger, see how it feels for a minute or so. Is it reassuring or scary? Do you associate pleasant or unpleasant memories with it? Often the first realized feelings of stomach hunger may produce painful associations which you will want to examine with your group or on your own. Mimi, a woman we worked with, discovered that when she allowed herself to experience hunger pangs, she got in touch with a whole other range of body emotions that she had successfully been trying

to hide from herself. She felt sexual. These sexual feelings made her quite uncomfortable because she had come to think of sexuality as sinful, or not appropriate for herself. In talking about what this meant she was able to separate hunger pangs from guilt-producing sexuality. Another woman, Betty, remembered being hungry as a child when there was not enough food on the table. And Martha, whose family urged her to eat, discovered for herself that hungry feelings expressed capitulation to the family feeding situation. The process of working through these particular situations was enriched by a feminist understanding of the particular problems they each expressed. For instance, in examining Mimi's response to her sexual feelings we explored why and how she learned that sex was sinful for her, for women. In exploring Betty's hunger as a child we brought into focus the painful lot of mothers who hold back when there is not enough food and encourage the children to eat. Betty discovered that she actually denied herself more than necessary in an identification with her mother at the family table. To be a woman meant to be self-denying. Martha's giving in at the table reflected for her an ambivalence in separating from her family, a difficulty particularly acute for women where separation has traditionally occurred only at marriage. Looking at these associations in these ways can provide useful clues to the roots of your own particular history with food. Ultimately, when you have learned to give your body exactly what it wants you will be able to look forward to those hunger pangs because it is a message that your body is wanting something delicious.

The next step is to eat out of stomach hunger

only as much as possible. Do not worry too much about this at first, because anyone with a history of compulsive eating is bound occasionally to eat from mouth hunger. But try to begin to see your body as a finely tuned instrument that likes to be lovingly cared for. When it is very hungry it might want quite a bit of nourishment; when it is only mildly hungry, quite a little less. In line with this, having learned about stomach hunger, try to locate precisely what food or liquid your body is hungry for. That is, once having experienced hunger pangs, work out what particular food or foods will satisfy that particular hunger. Sometimes this will be very easy and you will know right away what it is you are wanting, but often, particularly because of the years of "shoulds" and regimens, you might not know and in this case you might find a two-minute fantasy exercise helpful. Close your eyes and ask yourself "What kind of physical sensation do I have and how can I best satisfy it? Do I want something crunchy, salty, chewy, moist, sweet? Okay, I want some potato chips. Let me imagine myself eating some. No, that's not it. How about some plain chocolate . . . ?"

In this way before you eat the food you will have already imagined how it is most likely going to feel going down. Taste the soup traveling down your throat, bite on the nuts, smell the fresh bread in your fantasy. Find the foods that fit the mood and then eat. Eat as much as your body is wanting. Really taste each mouthful. Enjoy yourself.

Quite frequently, no food will clearly present itself and this can mean one of two things. You are hungry but cannot find exactly what would make sense. Have a little of a food you enjoy and wait till you get a clear message. You may have let the

hunger go on too long so that your stomach is jumping up and down and does not know how to be soothed. Alternatively you may not be hungry for food and it will be important for you to "feed" yourself more appropriately with a hug, a cry, a bath, a telephone conversation or a run. If it *is* something else you are wanting, food will not satisfy the original desire. At the very most, it can provide a temporary relief from feelings that creep up. What is more disturbing is that eating at these times serves to mask other urges and distances you further from the capacity to take care of yourself. Sort out what emotional need you are asking the food to carry for you and ask yourself whether indeed it works. As you discover how unsatisfactory this way of operating is, consider alternative ways to cope with your needs. If you are accustomed to eating compulsively during especially upsetting times, it will be reassuring to know you can feed yourself according to hunger and leave space to feel the distress. As Carol Bloom puts it in her training manual,[5] "Most compulsive eaters increase their non-nurturing eating during stress which usually makes them feel a lot worse. To not eat during those times (when you don't want to) is once again reinforcing a message to yourself, 'I can take care of myself, I can give myself the support I need.' 'It's a way not to desert yourself when things get tough.'"

For many people particular foods have special significance and correlate with particular moods and memories. Some like the calming effects of soup when they are feeling tense, carrots when they are angry or juice when they are feeling energetic. While I am not suggesting that you bite away your anger into a carrot and do not express it elsewhere,

nevertheless food can be expressive. The main point is to pamper yourself with food—to allow every eating experience to be a pleasurable one—to see your stomach hunger as a signal for you to enjoy. Do not worry about regulation mealtimes or balanced meals. We do not believe in good foods or bad foods. *We believe that our bodies can tell us what to eat, how to have a nutritionally balanced food intake and how to lose weight*. The body is a self-regulatory system if allowed to operate. We are not concerned with caloric or carbohydrate value. Take a multivitamin pill every day until you feel that your body is as self-regulating as we propose it can be.

Now these suggestions—eat when you are hungry, eating as much as you want—may sound like a new set of rules that you are supposed to follow. In a sense they are. But we see them rather as helpful guidelines designed to let you trust your own bodily processes and as such, will not be experienced as "shoulds" but as guides until you experience total trust. In a sense, the steps outlined above are no more than a frame-by-frame description of what goes on for "normal" eaters.

Attention to the details of eating is a first step toward having a "normal" relationship with food. As you can say "yes" to a particular food so the possibility is there for you to say "no" to particular foods at particular times. Saying "no" is a great tool in self-definition but it is predicated on the ability to be able to say "yes" in a wholesome, guilt-free way.

A few more tips in demystifying food may be helpful. Try leaving a mouthful of every kind of food and drink you are ingesting on your plate, cup

or glass. This will have two functions. On the one hand, it will begin to put the food at your control and reduce the feeling of insatiability; on the other, it will allow you to reject food. As you get more comfortable you will be able to define precisely how much food you are wanting. This exercise helped Elizabeth, a thirty-eight-year-old mother of three, who was brought up in England during the Second World War. It broke through a pattern she had established years back in trying to leave food on her plate. She had an image of her mother standing over her telling her she must not leave a crumb because soldiers had risked their lives getting the food to her. Food was rationed and goodies infrequent and Elizabeth felt she did not know when she would eat again.

Try loading up your house with "bad foods" that you feel attracted to and scared of. One woman we worked with was persuaded to keep enough ingredients for seventy-five ice-cream sundaes with all the trimmings. When it was first suggested that she fill the refrigerator with ice cream, sauce, nuts and cream she exclaimed, "But I'll eat it all!" The idea seemed so sinful to her. It was pointed out that if she had enough supplies for a minor army and could prove to herself that she did not want to consume it all at once, she would feel much more powerful and more in control of her food. She learned to love the ice cream and treat it as a friend to be called on when she wanted it rather than as an enemy to be conquered. She also took special care always to have plenty of her favorite brand or flavor. If you are really wanting to have coffee ice cream, the chocolate fudge in your refrigerator is a

mediocre substitute. *It is worth going out to buy exactly what you want rather than just eating anything that is around.*

The only restrictions on this scheme are economic. It is unfortunate to have a yearning for fine smoked salmon when your pocketbook can only afford something cheaper. But really think about it. How much money did you used to spend on diet foods, diet books and binges?

In the groups we play a game to help focus on particular foods, and to destroy the idea that it is dangerous to have delicious foods in the house. We imagine that we have a special room filled with all of our favorite foods, and we see what it would be like to be surrounded with all of these wonderful taste possibilities. In the fantasy we see how it feels. Is it reassuring or scary to have all this goodness at one's fingertips? For most people it turns out that the initial flash makes them nervous. "I'll never get out the door! I'll always be eating!" But then, sitting with the fantasy for a minute or two, we find that people feel safe and protected with all the food around. They even find they have other things to do apart from preparing and eating food. If the food is there, if they know that they are never again going to deprive themselves by their own hands, then they can begin to get on with the business of living, and to start to eat in order to live rather than living in order to eat.

All the work you do on locating your hunger and learning how to satisfy it can be accompanied by an examination of the psychological issues that interfere with your ability to satisfy your food needs. For example, if you experience difficulty in allowing yourself to feel hunger, pay attention to both the

physical sensations in the body as well as the psychological factors that prevent you from hearing what your body might be wanting. The psychological issues might range from doubts about your ability to nurture yourself and what it would mean to nurture yourself, to whose power you might be jeopardizing if you were to give to yourself. One woman discovered that, as she began to take her own needs seriously and specifically, she called into question her role in her family which was to take care of everybody else's needs while ignoring her own. Putting herself first in the food department was initially problematic for her. She felt she would be deserting her children. She found out subsequently that as she allowed herself to eat what she wanted, the whole family became more autonomous in that area. Mealtimes became much less tense affairs. Each member of the family chipped in to make something they wanted, and although there was some chaos while everyone was experimenting and messing up the kitchen, in the end each family member determined more of her or his own food intake and, as it turned out, took more responsibility in other areas of household labor.

Some people will find that as they begin to feel less addicted to food in general, certain foods will continue to have "magical" qualities. One woman I was seeing inexplicably ate candy periodically during the day while she was at work. We discovered that the intake of sweets had to do with the attempt to sweeten herself, to make herself "nice" when indeed she was feeling quite angry but felt that, "Women shouldn't get mad; it's not nice. I'd better make myself like sweet and spice." It turned out that she felt angry every time her boss

treated her in a way that was particularly demeaning. Although she was paid to do research she was also expected to "serve." She was expected to prepare the coffee and entertain the various male clients that came to her office. These expectations were examples of the sexual inequality that so often operates in offices, and she, like many other women, experienced conflict and rage when "feminized" in such a way. In the group we role-played ways for her to be more assertive with her boss and to discuss with him other options for the preparation of coffee. When a more equitable work situation was arrived at she found less need to cram her mouth furtively with candies. That is not to say that all her anger disappeared. There are bound to be frictions as long as there are bosses, but the anger was acknowledged and validated by the group for what it was and became separated from her eating activity.

In all that I have said it is important to remember that our goal is not primarily weight loss. *The goal is for the compulsive eater to break her addictive relationship toward food.* While weight loss is generally an important sign that the addiction is broken, our primary concern is that you begin to feel more comfortable about food. This cannot be stressed too strongly. *The problem that we seek to solve is addiction to food.* Continued obsession with weight loss or gain hinders the process of learning to love food and eating what your body is wanting. While this process is not a magical shortcut, its philosophy provides a basis for a more natural and relaxed relationship toward food, and our bodies.

Self-help

If you see yourself as a compulsive eater the chances are that you know other women in the same position. Indeed, it is likely that you have dieted, fasted or gorged with friends even though the compulsive eating may be experienced as a solitary and even masturbatory activity. Women with a compulsive-eating problem tend to seek out others who will be sympathetic and understanding and it is largely true that the only people who can be really so are those who suffer from the same problem. If you do not feel close to anyone who shares this problem you can put up a notice in your college, community

center or women's center, in order to contact others who might be interested in a self-help group. If you feel reluctant to work in a group, the exercises discussed can easily be done on your own. I do, however, suggest that you consider working in a group for the reasons I detail below.

There are several reasons for working on this issue in a group. Some are practical and others are related to the nature of the problem itself. On the practical level there are not enough people doing this work to satisfy the demand and interest for individual therapy dealing with compulsive eating. As more people who have had the problem and gone through it, train and initiate work with others there will be more options for those people who prefer one-to-one settings. But for now I should like to outline the advantages of group work and suggest a model for a self-help group.

For those who have not had friendships solidified on the basis of sharing eating obsessions, coming together with others who have the same problem can be an enormous relief. To be able to meet and talk with other women about this issue can help relieve those terrible feelings of being an isolated freak and a failure. Even for women who have talked endlessly about food obsessions with friends, the previous chats may have been circumscribed by the strictures of talking about diets or diet foods. Grouping with other women to explore explicitly one's relationship to fat and thin can provide a comforting and safe experience. *For some women it is like coming out of the closet. This may be particularly the case for those women who have managed to keep their weight within the cultural norm so that nobody else is aware of their*

problem. For others, it is the relief of a supportive environment in which there is space for the grief and pain associated with a life centered on food to come out. They do not have to make excuses for being large or obsessed with food, they have a chance to be honest about the painful calculations they make every time food passes through their mouths, and the terror they face every morning wondering whether it is going to be a "good day" or a "bad day." They do not have to pretend they eat like a bird. They get a chance, possibly, for the first time ever, to discuss their eating openly and to explore the complicated feelings they may have about their bodies. For everyone in the group, it is possibly the first place they have been in which they feel they do not have to apologize for existing in the first place. Above all, the group offers help in getting through a problem that may seem insoluble on your own.

Beyond breaking the isolation there are, in addition, several other ways in which the group method can be beneficial. Within the group everyone has the same problem and so, although the compulsive eating is the reason which draws everyone together, in that assembling, the group can provide a means for a shift in the self-definition for individual members. What I mean by this is that by being in a group that accepts the part of one that is a compulsive eater—one can move beyond this limited concept of the self as a compulsive eater. As one can begin to see other compulsive eaters or fat women as having other attributes apart from the fat and can begin to see that fat has nothing to do with other values such as beauty, creativity, energy or caring, one can begin to see these attributes in oneself.

For example, when group member Joy can see another member, Mary, as a kind, quick and tough woman then Joy can look beyond her own self-definition as a fat person and see that she has additional qualities too. She can then begin to extend her view of fat so that it does not automatically trigger a response of repulsion or rejection. Fat can then be seen as one of a number of adjectives that can be coupled up with other adjectives—beautiful, gracious, horrid, awful, polite, nice or generous. The fat is seen as just a part of oneself, not the singular most defining characteristic. People are more than any of their parts or even the sum of their parts. If you have a big stomach on which you focus, you are nevertheless more than just a big stomach. However, if you have been defined by others or have defined yourself solely as someone of a particular size—and this definition has had negative connotations, as is the case with the adjective "fat"—then it is hard for that part of yourself not to seem overwhelming. Expanding your definition of self to include other qualities in addition to the fat is crucial. This is so because at the point of giving up the fat you are then not throwing out all of yourself (a common fear) because you are more than the fat. Joan felt that her fat was the only thing she had in life that was all hers. She held on to her extra weight tenaciously, fearing that if she lost it, if she were to give up her fat, there would be no essential Joan left. The group was extremely important to her because she was forced to look at herself through others' eyes—others who accepted her size and sought additional characteristics in defining her. She recognized the uniqueness of others in the group, the particular configuration of

their personalities which made them the people they
were. She could see how they retained these
characteristics at varying weights during the course
of the group, and she was thus able to see her own
essential uniqueness and individuality, not predicated on her fat.

In addition, the group serves other important
functions. The fat conveys messages to the outside
world. For example, many women say when
discussing self-assertion that they do not know how
to say "yes" or "no" directly. They have the fantasy
that their fat is doing it for them. In the context of
the group, where everyone's fat means something
different, it is starkly demonstrated that having the
fat speak for you does not necessarily get the
message across. Of course, in the case of unassertive
behavior outside the group, the fat rarely succeeds
in the job it is meant to do either, but the fantasy can
cling. Within the group, not only *can* one begin to
express oneself more directly but one *has* to.
Without specific articulation the magical meaning
of the individual's fat will never come through.
Group members can support each other in their
attempts to make the exchange—you have a forum
for trying to use your mouth to speak and say what
you are wanting, feeling or thinking instead of
continuing to hope that the fat is doing it for you.
Taking risks of this nature is often easier in groups.
Group members who experience themselves as
particularly unassertive can use the group to try out
ways of asserting themselves. Group members can
provide accurate feedback and encouragement. In a
one-to-one situation the feedback is, of necessity,
more limited.

When talking about images of thinness, some

women have expressed the fantasy that "When I am thin I will be competent, attractive, together, in good relationships ... perfect." Group members can help each other challenge such unreal expectations—they can demonstrate from their own past histories of times when they were thin that life was not wonderful and easy all the time. This can then aid others in giving up such notions of perfection which rely on a race against oneself in which one is bound to lose. But perhaps more instrumentally, it is likely that group members will be of varying sizes and that there will be one or two women who represent the ideal weight of others in the group. These women, the compulsive thins, so to speak, have kept the problem within physical bounds and are as thin as the culture demands its women to be. Despite this, they have not found that in thinness everything in their life runs smoothly, and this can be an enormously helpful lesson to those who imagine that being thin means that everything will be fine. Losing weight then can be seen as just that, rather than heralding a whole transformation of one's life.

As well as helping women redefine themselves, the group is also valuable in providing a direct way of dealing with compulsive eating itself. Within a compulsive-eating group the focus of attention is always on what is the fat or thin expressing in one's life at the moment, or in one's past or in the here and now of the group. It is as though the protective functions of the fat, by being discussed and explored in the group, lose their power within that group and members have to search for new ways to protect themselves without relying on the weight. This then provides a learning experience in which group

members can see that they have other protective
mechanisms apart from the fat. This makes giving
up the fat much less scary.

Inevitably, during the life of a group, people are
at different sizes at different times. It can thus be
noted that one can lose weight and nothing
necessarily terrible happens. For example—Jill and
Margot, who were different sizes, both feared their
own "promiscuity" if they were to lose weight. In
both their cases their thin periods were times of
intense sexual activity. In the course of the group
both realized how scary these thin/sexual experiences had been and knew that before losing weight
again they would have to promise themselves that
hectic sexual activity did not automatically accom-
pany being thin. Margot lost a good deal of weight
first. She continued to reassure herself that she
could be thin and not express her sexuality as long
as she was scared. Meanwhile, Jill began to
incorporate sexuality into her life, so that she gave
up the idea of leaving sex only for thin times and
then scaring herself with her sexual interest when
slim. As Jill noticed Margot's new-found sexual
selectivity she was very encouraged. She could see
that sex was no longer bound up with weight in a
deprivation/binge model of "too fat to fuck" or
"thin and promiscuous." For Jill and Margot then,
each other's actions spelled important lessons. Jill
saw that someone with whom she strongly identified
could achieve something that had previously
seemed so impossible—Margot had lost weight
without becoming promiscuous. Similarly, Margot
learned from Jill that it was possible to be sexual at
any weight. This was particularly comforting
because Margot wished to get pregnant and had

connected many of her fears of pregnancy and
motherhood with the idea that she would not be
able to have sex if pregnant because she would be so
large that she would be sexually undesirable. Jill's
ability to be sexually involved at a higher weight
than either had thought possible helped Margot
recast her ideas about sexuality and size. She could
see that Jill's size did not indeed preclude her from
being sexual and attractive and she was heartened
by this.

There are other important aids that emerge from
working in a group setting which will become
obvious as I detail a self-help model. At this point,
though, I should like to spell out a few suggestions
to help a group start.

It is my experience that the number of people in a
group should not be too small. An optimum group
would have between five and eight members. Since
it seems to take a while for a group to stabilize its
membership—a few people always tend to drop out
or move away—initially it is a good idea to form
with slightly more than the number you desire. Age,
size or cultural background seem to make little
difference to the outcome of the group. Of course
the similarity or difference in these factors will get
expressed in the flavor and feeling of any particular
group.

It is important to have a set length to the group
session, one that does not vary from week to week.
About 2½ hours makes sense for an eight-person
group, or 1½ hours for a five-person group. A
prescribed time is important for a couple of reasons.
First, as in any therapy group, it designates those
particular hours during which the group will
purposefully focus on the psychological issue at

hand. The session time should not be vague because
the issue of definition—beginning and end—is a
particularly critical one for compulsive eaters in all
respects. Second, if the time is clearly defined then
each member is likely to attempt to get her needs
met from the group in a systematic way. This will cut
into the feelings of insatiability and dissatisfaction
that many compulsive eaters experience. These
sessions then take on the additional significance,
since an allotted time out of the daily routine of
things is devoted to them. They become the time in
the week that is guaranteed for reflection and
exploration.

It is likely that everyone will come to the group
with the expectation and desire that participation
will produce dramatic and instant weight loss.
While it is hard to banish such thoughts, it must be
emphasized that weight loss is not the immediate
goal. The aim of the group is to break the addictive
relationship toward food, and the guidelines that
follow point to that end. In achieving this goal the
group will find it helpful to approach the problem
on two levels simultaneously. One level is the
exploration of the symbolic meanings of fatness and
thinness for the individuals in the group. On the
second level we work on new ways to approach food
and hunger. But before moving into the specifics of
the first few meetings, an important aside on what I
understand about psychological processes.

Any symptom such as compulsive eating has
occurred for a good reason. We do not produce
symptoms unless we have no other routes to express
distress. It is not wise to attempt to remove
symptoms without providing insight into their
origin and purposes. In addition, unless alternative

strategies are developed for dealing with the conflicts that the symptoms were protecting an individual could feel quite helpless. This could lead to a hazardous situation in which, in an extreme case, the individual develops a new symptom. If we just remove a symptom, like compulsive eating, we are then not only devaluing it, in effect, saying it was just a bit of craziness that needed surgical removal, we are also risking—precisely because of its importance—a "symptom switch." It is not particularly helpful to give up compulsive eating one week to be hit by a new symptom (such as insomnia or anxiety) some time later. What I am suggesting here is that anxiety may occur if a woman begins to do all sorts of things she imagined she would do when thin without having sorted out what it is that worries her in those situations. Without the weight to rely on she may feel undefended and scared. If she is no longer eating to assuage these feelings and cannot contain them, she may well convert them into anxiety. I am using anxiety here to express a severe state of unease and helplessness, in which an individual is seemingly incapable of intervening on her own behalf.

Anxiety is a reaction to a feeling that is unacceptable, frightening or overwhelming. The individual finds the anxiety, however troublesome, safer than the tolerance of the trigger emotion or event. For example, Sara was extremely frightened by her angry feelings, imagining that they could kill her. She worried that if she allowed herself to come into contact with her anger for more than a split second, her rage would overpower her family and friends and wipe them out. This fantasy is quite common among women and is largely due to the

taboo against the open expression of female fury. Sara then got frightened by her own anger and instead of being able to sit with the fantasy she became anxious. The diagram below may help to explain this process.

When Sara could accept that exploring her fantasy did not mean that she would carry it out—just because she felt like attacking all and sundry it did not mean she would—she no longer became anxious. She sat with her anger, it came and went and she felt in charge of it.

This digression about anxiety helps to explain how a rapid rejection of the compulsive eating can

UNACCEPTABLE
ANGRY FEELING
CREEPS INTO
SARA   FANTASIES
                    OF ACTIVE
                    RAGE TO
                    OTHERS   SARA GETS
                                FRIGHTENED
                                AT HER RAGE

                                        SARA HAS A
                                        REACTION   SARA IS
                                        TO THE   ANXIOUS
                                        FRIGHT. NO AND IS
                                        LONGER   DISTANCED
                                        FEELS THE   FROM HER
                                        ANGER   TRUE
                                                    FEELING

produce the same alienated symptom elsewhere unless sufficiently explored and incorporated. So I am concerned here to stress a few points:

1. Giving up the fat is a gradual process with emotional work being done at the same time.

2. The scary aspects of giving up the fat need to be faced.
3. Alternative ways of coping must be instituted.
4. Conflicts related to the eating and weight must be exposed.

These cautions are not, however, meant to suggest that it is necessary to restructure the whole personality before a symptom—such as compulsive eating—can be dissolved. It is our experience that, following the above lines, compulsive eating can be given up and that in learning to take care of oneself in the area of food an enormous self-confidence ensues.

When starting self-help groups we adopt the following structure for the initial meeting. The time is divided into two parts with the first half devoted to a preliminary exploration into the symbolic meanings of fat and thin for individual women. The second part is devoted to a discussion about food. Since you will presumably be doing this without a group leader it may be helpful for one group member to tape in advance the fantasy exercise that follows so that all members can participate during group time. If you do decide to tape it, leave good pauses where the dots are. The whole exercise should take around 15 minutes to read. Group members are asked to hold all the images in their heads during this time after which they will share their experiences with each other.

Get as comfortable as you can.... Close your eyes ... and imagine yourself at a party.... You are getting fatter ... you are now quite large.... What

does it feel like?... Take a note of your surroundings.... How do you feel about them?... What kind of party is it?... What kinds of activities are going on?... Notice whether you are sitting or standing, or moving about.... What are you wearing and how do you feel about your clothes?... What are they expressing?... Observe all the details in this situation.... How are you interacting with the other people at the party?... Are you on your own or talking, dancing, eating with others?... Do you feel like an active participant or do you feel excluded?... Are you making the moves to have contact with others or are the other people at the party seeking you out?... Now see what this "fat" you is saying to the people at the party.... Does it have any specific messages?... Does it help you out in any way to be fat in this situation?... See if you can go beyond the feelings of revulsion you might have to locate any benefits you see from being this size at the party.... Now imagine all the fat peeling and melting away and in the fantasy you are as thin as you might ever like to be... you are at the same party.... What are you wearing now?... What do these clothes convey about you?... How do you feel in your body?... How are you getting on with the other people at the party?... Do you feel more or less included now?... Are people approaching you or are you making the first moves?... What is the quality of your contact with others?... See if you can locate anything scary about being thin at the party... see if you can get beyond how great it feels and notice any difficulties you might be having with being this thin.... Now go back to being fat at the party... now thin again.... Go back and forth

between the two images and particularly notice the differences.... When you are ready, open your eyes....

Now go around the room and share your fantasy. You will find that describing it in the present tense helps make the experience more vivid. For example, "In my fantasy I'm at a beach party, it's a very hot day and I'm wearing a terry-toweling robe over my swimsuit, trying not to draw attention to myself, I feel very awkward...." Do not worry if people's fantasies are both widely divergent and contradictory; the similarity of themes will emerge in due course. Be sure to use "I," in order to give each person space to describe her experience in her own words. Generalizing from individual experience can cause unnecessary friction if done prematurely. The exercise introduces in a concrete way the concepts outlined in the book. Inevitably, you will discover huge differences in your self-image fat and thin. You may find, for instance, that in the fat fantasy you are sitting chatting with another person while in your thin fantasy you are a sparkling wit and very much the center of attention; or you may be on your own while fat and dancing with everybody when thin. In particular, the thin images may correspond to the popular conception of thinness discussed before, or your own experiences of being thin. In discussing your fantasies, bear in mind the kind of person you feel that you must/will become when thin. After you have sat with the image for a while see how it corresponds to your personality. Is the thin you a foreigner or, as some women comment, so decidedly different from your habitual self-image that you feel

that you have two distinct personalities—fat and thin.

In our group, we raise the following questions both in the initial meeting and in subsequent meetings because it goes to the very heart of the issue of how to find other means of protecting yourself which work as well as weight:

1. What of myself that emerged in my fat fantasy must I promise to take with me thin?
2. What did I find scary in my fat fantasy so I can promise myself I do not have to do it when I get thin?

In the fantasy, one group member, Maureen, was sitting with another person when fat, and had become a sparkling wit thin. As she explored the qualities associated with these two different states she remarked on the safety and ease she felt chatting with her friend as compared to the driven and insecure quality associated with the sparkling wit. By recognizing the negatives associated with thinness and the benefits of fatness, Maureen saw that, in order for her to lose weight permanently, she must allow herself the possibility that a thin her would not necessarily want to sparkle incessantly. She saw that her view of thinness, while superficially pleasurable and rewarding, was at great variance with her concept of her fat self, and that losing weight did not mean a complete personality change. Neither was the latter possible or desirable. Sparkling all the time for someone who enjoys relaxed conversation is unrealistic. *It is precisely this changed concept of self that puts the weight*

back on because it is enormously stressful trying to be someone entirely different when thin. So Maureen had to promise herself that if she were to lose the weight she would not also have to lose the part of her that enjoyed relaxed chatting. She had to consider the possibility that her desire to chat, for example, was not an attribute of her fat but an aspect of her personality. Similarly, she had to consider that the part of her that wanted to be a sparkling wit did not have to wait to emerge until she were thin. Being overweight does not preclude one from being "the star." It does not mean one always has to be backstage waiting for thinness to bring you forth.

I have used Maureen's example for two reasons; not only because of the frequency with which it comes up, but also to delineate the line of questioning to pursue. Obviously not everybody will find such a clear-cut discrepancy between a fat self-image and a thin self-image at an initial meeting. The fantasy exercise provides a way for the compulsive eater to enrich her view of what fat and thin mean to her. Then we can go on to ask what kinds of unreal expectations are attached to thinness, and what we imagine we shall be giving up in getting there. These questions are ones that need to be continually raised in the group and help to develop a self-image that does not vary with body size.

After everyone has shared their fantasies and, perhaps, seen common threads, we move on to consider the technical work of the group on ways to approach food and hunger. We do another fifteen-minute fantasy trip which aims to highlight current feelings toward food at the same time as

suggesting new possibilities. Tape this or delegate one person to read it while the group gets as comfortable as possible:

Close your eyes.... Now I should like you to imagine you are in your kitchen.... Look around the room and make a note of all the food that is in it... in the refrigerator... closets... cookie tin... freezer.... It probably is not too hard for you to form a complete picture because undoubtedly you know where everything is or is not, including any goodies or dietetic foods.... Look around the room and see how it is affecting you.... Is it painful to see how pathetic the foods are that you generally keep there or allow yourself to eat?... See what your kitchen says about you.... Now go to your favorite supermarket or shopping mall or a place where there is a wide variety of stores under one roof—greengrocer, butcher, delicatessen, dairy, bakery, take-out food store—and I should like you to imagine that you have an unlimited amount of money to spend.... Take a couple of supermarket carts and fill them up with all your favorite foods.... Go up and down the aisles or from counter to counter and carefully select the most appetizing foods.... Be sure not to skimp... if you like cheesecake, take several, take enough so you feel that there is no way you could possibly eat it all in one sitting... be sure to get the specific ones you really like.... There is no hurry, you have plenty of time to get whatever you want.... Cast your eyes over the wonderful array of foods and fill up your cart.... Make sure you have everything you need and then get into a cab with your boxes of food and go to your home.... There is nobody in the house

*and nobody will be around for the rest of the day,
the house—especially the kitchen—is all yours for
you to enjoy. . . . Bring the food into the kitchen and
fill up the room with it. . . . How do you feel
surrounded by all of this food just for you? . . . Does
it feel sinful, or is it a very joyful feeling? . . . Do you
feel reassured or scared by the abundance of food
just for you? . . . Just stay with the food and go
through the various moods that come up . . .
remember nobody will disturb you, the food is there
just for you, enjoy it in whatever way you want
to. . . . See if you can relax in the knowledge that you
will never again be deprived. . . . And now I should
like you to go down the road to mail a
letter. . . . How do you feel about leaving the house
and all the food? . . . Does it give you a warm feeling
to know that when you go back it will still be there
for you undisturbed? Or is it a relief to get away
from it? . . . You have now mailed the letter and are
on your way back to the house. . . . Remember as
you open the door that the food is all there just for
you and no one will interrupt you. . . . How does it
feel to be back with the food? . . . If you found it
reassuring before does it continue to be so? If you
found it scary can you find anything comforting in
being in the kitchen with all this food? . . . Slowly
come back to this room here with the knowledge
that your kitchen is full of beautiful foods to eat that
nobody is going to take away from you . . . and,
when you are ready, open your eyes. . . .*

Responses to this fantasy trip vary enormously
but, as you will find, it rarely generates anything but
dramatic reactions. These range from huge feelings
of relief at having so much food available and the

permission to enjoy it, to horror, fright and worries
about one's ability actually to be in a room with all
that food, from urges to throw it away or throw it
around the room, to even lying in it. For many
women, the trip to the mailbox provides much-
needed relief from the claustrophobic feeling of
being surrounded by "tempting" foods; for others, it
is a serene break from a kitchen that has been
transformed into a beautiful nurturing environment. The fantasy pinpoints our deeply held worries
about food and provides a good starting point for a
discussion about just how much compulsive eaters
deprive themselves of the enjoyment of food and
just how much food has been converted into an
enemy. In conveying a permissive idea toward food
we are attempting to make inroads into the
conception that because one is a compulsive eater or
overweight, one must deprive oneself of food. The
central idea to be conveyed is, in fact, precisely the
opposite and it rests on a challenge to the premise
that a compulsive eater never really allows herself to
eat. She is always acting out of a model that says,
"I'm too fat, I must deny myself certain foods." This
sets up a paradigm in which she is either dieting or
eating a lot of food in preparation for tomorrow's
diet, when she must be "good." The diet is invariably
broken by a binge hardly enjoyed because of its
driven and stolen quality. Then follows a period of
"chaotic eating" and eventually a new diet plan as
the chart below illustrates. None of this kind of
eating contains within it a positive attitude toward
food but rests on a frenetic struggle to control one's
food intake.

This continual struggle to control one's food
intake is a propelling factor in compulsive eating.

The aim of our method is to redefine, for the
compulsive eater, both the function of food and her
entitlement to it. *People need food in order to live.
Food is a life-giving source and not something to be
avoided.* As long as there is plenty, food can be

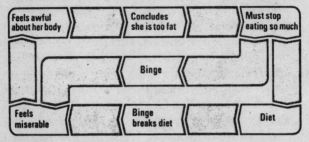

enjoyed. This idea, while hardly revolutionary,
sounds staggering for someone who has been using
food for other purposes. In due course I will discuss
ways to implement this method but what is
important in the first meeting is that group members
share their daily experiences and fears about food.

This then, is the outline for the first meeting.
Subsequent sessions will benefit from continuing
work on the two levels—people's experiences with
food that week and themes in relation to fat and thin
although the time for doing this need not be
structured so rigidly. The self-help groups that we
have started take away a homework assignment for
the first week—to keep a food chart. The purpose of
this chart is to sort out some of the themes that
continually reappear for you when you find yourself
going toward food when you know you are not
physically hungry.

Keep a record along these lines for the first week.
The point of the chart is to *observe* how you eat and
not to judge it. Through the entries on the chart you

can begin to get a sense of what kind of eating
patterns emerge for you. Do you experience
yourself eating chaotically or with some consistency? Did any foods taste particularly satisfying?
How does it feel to realize that your food intake is so
circumscribed by "shoulds?" Wasn't the chocolate
cake and ice cream at three o'clock in the morning
much tastier than the spinach and fish at regulation
suppertime? Come on, wasn't it really a drag to eat
that hamburger and salad in order to get to the
ice-cream sundae you really wanted?

TIME & DAY	WHAT I ATE	WAS I HUNGRY BEFORE EATING?	DID FOOD SATISFY ME OR NOT?	FEELINGS PRIOR TO EATING

In addition to discovering what the chart reveals
about actual food intake, it is also helpful to look at
the circumstances in which you habitually eat. Do
you eat alone? in hiding? never making dates to see
people around traditional mealtimes? or do you eat
with "eating friends" in restaurants? or at home at a
table? or at home walking around your house or
apartment, half in the refrigerator? or in bed? or
watching television? Observe when, how and what
you eat, and when, how and what you enjoy the
most. It may be that you will find that eating alone
so absorbs you that it is nicest to sit yourself down at
a beautifully set table, or you may find that you like

a multi-media show with book open, music playing and the food in the middle.

Notice too the entries under "Feelings prior to eating." Is there any consistency in what triggers the eating when you are not particularly hungry? Can you pinpoint specific emotions which you find hard to cope with that drive you toward the refrigerator? In our groups many women mention boredom, anger, feelings of emptiness, disappointment, and loneliness as triggers. For others, the eating is like a punctuation point between various activities with the food marking the beginning and end of different phases of the day. Other women notice that they eat to give themselves a treat. The food provides— albeit fleetingly—an oasis of pleasure in an otherwise difficult day. As Isabel put it, "If I didn't know I was going to have a few cream donuts during the day I couldn't see how I'd get access to pleasure." In exploring this remark of hers, she dealt with several issues. Why was her life structured in such a way as to preclude other "accesses to pleasure?" What does pleasure mean to her? Is she entitled to it? If she waits for others to give to her is she risking not getting? Must she therefore control it to ensure that she gets it? What other things would she enjoy as much? Does she always want cream donuts when she is hungry for pleasure or are there other pleasure-giving activities as well? These questions are raised in the service of examination. Isabel is not encouraged to give up her cream donuts. Quite the contrary, the aim of the group is to help her to enjoy her food more consistently so that every time she eats she is having a treat—it is a waste of an eating experience not to eat something really tasty. Isabel is encouraged by the group to think about her

concept of pleasure and the immutability of her belief that no one but herself could possibly please her. This behavior, while essential to her, was also a protection against her fear that others would inevitably disappoint her—let her down. Providing her own treats made her less vulnerable while she imagined that her fat kept the world away. This difficulty over pleasure is a familiar one for many women and speaks poignantly to the pain with receiving that they experience.

It is on this level that questions need to be raised. In the first few sessions, as you are getting to know each other, gentle inquiries will help elicit useful information both about group members' behavior and the motivations behind it. Apart from discussing the food chart at the second meeting (and incidentally the chart can be used from time to time to help you check in with what you have been eating and how), you might start to go around the room and share your weight histories with each other. What is important here is not how many pounds you were at a particular point but the circumstances of your life through various weight changes. Notice any particular periods when your weight increased, using a family photo album to jog your memory if you find that helpful. Most likely, your group will include people with a range of stages in weight gain, including childhood, adolescence, leaving home, marriage, divorce, pregnancy or when the kids leave home. Leave yourself plenty of time to go through these histories, extending them over several sessions if necessary, so that you capture both the details and the quality of your own past relationship to your body and food. Make sure that you discuss your family's involvement with your food intake. Did/

does anybody else in the family have an eating problem? What were the unspoken rules and regulations about food? What was the significance of mealtimes in your family? Were meals a harmonious time or very strained? Was there enough food in the house or were certain foods banned and only eaten away from home? Did your mother help you to diet or did she discourage your attempts? Did your husband egg you on to reduce or "tempt" you with forbidden foods whenever you were actually dieting? Were there confusing messages from those close to you about how thin or fat you should be? Did you feel you had to be thin for someone else?

As the group continues and you become involved in trying to determine your own food intake, notice how the significant people in your life continue to play a role in relation to you and food. You may notice that your preoccupation with food has extended to hooking them into your eating behavior so that they either actually are judges or you imagine them to be so. It will be very important for you to be the only one in charge of your eating from now on. This will mean:

1. Disentangling yourself from when and what others wish to eat.
2. Daring to believe that you can begin to take care of your own eating.
3. Getting rid of the person to whom you designated the role of judge.

If your lover has been roped into helping you not to eat "bad foods" in the past and when you have sat down for supper together, his or her presence has

stopped you gorging, reclaim that power for yourself but this time not in order to keep you away from the dangerous activity of eating but in the interest of helping you discriminate and select the foods you really enjoy.

Many people I have worked with have realized that their husbands have encouraged them to eat a lot while at the same time proclaiming their interest in slim, trim bodies. This was not dissimilar to their mothers' attitudes—an insistent "Eat, eat, child," or "A spoonful for Auntie Jane," or "Just one more bite for the poor starving kids in Europe!" These phrases were uttered with such pity and urgency that rejection was almost impossible even though the children were ready to gag. Rejection of the food felt like the rejection of mother. At other times, the same mothers beseeched their daughters to watch what they were eating lest their figures be ruined, or attempted to limit the food when they were larger than the "acceptable" size.

Pull out as much information as possible about past eating patterns and how they relate to your present experiences with food. For those women who were *schtupped* (over-fed) by their mothers, consider what goes through your mind when you feel too full to have another mouthful but still cram in extra food. What would it mean to you to stop at the point of fullness? As you meander back and forth between your own past and present experiences with food, bear in mind that we are trying to challenge the idea that the compulsive eater is not entitled to food. Our view is that compulsive eaters are terrified of food (once having invested it with magical properties—for instance, comfort against loneliness, boredom, anger or depression—it is hard

to see it as just food, a source of nourishment) and are constantly eating or avoiding eating in response to this terror. Just because you feel out of control when near food does not mean you are not entitled to eat.

Many women say that being in charge of their own food strikes them as particularly difficult because although they have been responsible for feeding others they feel that in the one area in which they could take responsibility for themselves they have abdicated it. They are worried that they will not dare or even know how to be that self-concerned. It is important to remember that while compulsive eating feels like an abdication it is, nevertheless, a definite act for which one has been responsible. The meanings behind the compulsive eating may be unclear so that you are left with feelings of being out of control or at the mercy of the food, but this is the conscious experience and at the unconscious level the activity has a purpose. If you can think of converting that responsibility for your food into a concerted effort to notice when you are hungry and what kinds of foods you are wanting, you will be able to approach many social situations which involve food with more confidence. Some common fears that come up in the groups involve practical issues, for instance, how to ensure your own food supply when living with others. In the group, it will be useful to explore the actual situation. Is it a family group, a commune, or roommates? Is food bought and eaten together, is suppertime the only time the household congregates? From this kind of information, alternatives will come. These may include keeping a shelf in the

refrigerator of foods just for yourself and asking
other household members to replace immediately
any foods they take; withdrawing from the com-
munal shop or allowing yourself a certain amount
of money each week for food over the household
budget so that you ensure you are getting what *you*
want; explaining to household members that you
have had a painful time around food and are trying
to learn your body's real needs. Consequently, you
may eat in a rather unorthodox way and would they
please refrain from comments and cajoling. Another situation which frequently crops up is going to
someone's house for supper. Group members often
express alarm at this situation. We suggest several
possible strategies: not to make social engagements
at mealtimes for a while where you cannot choose
what food is available; if it is a close friend the odds
are that she or he has lived through several diets
with you and been subjected to your instructions
about permissible foods before. If this is the case
you will benefit by telling your friend that your new
interest in food may lead you to not eat everything
on your plate and you hope they will understand. If
you get hungry an hour or so before it is time to go,
eat just a little to respond to it. That way the hunger
will still be available to you an hour later. Above all,
remember that you are entitled to eat, however
awful you feel about yourself and your body. Just
because you have used food for other than
physiological reasons in the past, it does not mean
you are to deprive yourself from here on.

As the group progresses you will want to
incorporate the various exercises that are sewn
through the body of this book.

1. Mirror work—in which you are trying to build a center that includes the fat, pages 87–88.
2. Dressing for now—not waiting until you are thin to express yourself, pages 89–91.
3. Leaving food on your plate, pages 122–123.
4. Make your kitchen a supermarket, pages 145–146.

The above exercises will heighten your awareness of your body and help toward a self-acceptance. As I have stressed before, ownership of your whole body, including the fat, is a crucial factor in preparing you for a life at a lower weight. It will be very important for you to feel that your body has power at whatever size and that you can communicate through how you use it. An issue raised frequently throughout this book is how women imagine that their fat keeps people away. It is almost as though their fat is walking in front of them announcing their self-loathing to the world. We are aiming to build confidence to keep people away (if that is what is wanted) which rests on a self-acceptance rather than a self-disgust. The more you are your body, the more you can say "no" with the whole of you. The fat then loses one of its functions as the ability to fend people off gets attributed to *you* and not solely to the fat. To help increase your acceptance and knowledge of your body you might begin to think of it as not simply a stomach or a mouth but an organic whole.

Try to experience the continuity in your body; feel it as one whole. You might try drawing unsigned pictures of yourselves within the group which can then be passed around for people to guess who is who. Since most group members will tend to

represent themselves inaccurately, particularly in
the early stages of the group, other members can
provide help in correcting these perceptions by
giving feedback about the poses, proportions and
stances illustrated in the drawings. Polaroid photos
can also be used to provide insight into how one
projects oneself. As you become more and more
familiar with your body you will be able to throw
out your scales. The scales are yet another of those
external measures of how well you are doing.
Compulsive eaters are frequently hooked on scales.
Every morning or night there is the ritual of
evaluation; one finds out whether one has been
"good" or "bad." The pounds of wisdom have in the
past given one the right either to binge or to starve.
In general, for the compulsive eater, the scales are
the real judge. If you have done well (lost weight)
then the scales allow you to eat. If you have done
badly (gained weight) the scales throw you into a
depression only relieved by a binge or a plan to lose
the weight yet again. So, instead of this twice-daily
torture with its concomitant anxieties, we try to
develop a familiarity with our bodies so that the
feelings can come from the inside rather than the
outside. The scales have become another outside
evaluator which women can afford to do without.

The mirror exercise can help us move toward
self-validation (a hard struggle indeed against the
messages in women's magazines about how we
should look, feel and weigh) and begin to rely on our
own senses of self. For particular parts of your body
that give you trouble try doing the fat/thin fantasy
exercise focused on that specific area. For example,
if you feel tremendous hatred toward your thighs,
imagine yourself with fat thighs and then with ideal

thighs and examine the meanings of the two different body states. One woman I worked with who longed for thinner thighs discovered in her fantasy that the fat around her thighs was like a house around her vagina. The concave thighs she yearned for actually made her feel vulnerable as though there was no protection against her sexuality. Through the fantasy work she was able to accept the "hated thigh fat" and see it as one way she had coped with her sexuality. As she lost weight she began to find other ways to express her interest or lack of interest in sexual contact. For other women, full breasts or stomachs have symbolized one thing in conscious life but quite other meanings have been revealed by doing the fantasy exercises. The insights gained have empowered the women to review the limited ways in which they have communicated with their bodies. In the groups, or alone in front of a mirror, you can experiment with projecting different aspects of your personality through your stance. Try a variety of sexual expressions—project yourself as forceful, timid, retiring or active.

In preparing yourself for being thin without the thin meaning "I must be wonderful, competent, beautiful, clever," spend a few minutes during every day on mundane tasks, imagining yourself thin while doing them. This could be the ride to work, social contact at work or home, going shopping or waking up feeling thin. Particularly watch for anything difficult about being thin in those daily routines. If you find things scary try and investigate just exactly what it is that is frightening and then discuss these experiences within the group. Then try feeling thin without associated elations and fears. Notice how you would walk, stand or sit when thin

and try to incorporate those different poses into your body as you are now. If it is too long a jump, imagine yourself ten pounds lighter rather than dramatically thinner. This image may be more accessible and you may find less discrepencies in feeling the ten-pound difference. As this emerges it will mean that you are ready to lose some weight. Most likely, your body will indicate this by requiring less food. At these points, in particular, you will want to tighten up the process—being sure to eat exactly what you want and stopping precisely when you are full. Many compulsive eaters are unfamiliar with a full feeling that is not a bursting feeling. As an introduction to that bodily experience, eat several mouthfuls of whatever food you are wanting when you are hungry, being sure to taste them as they go down. Now leave the food for fifteen minutes and involve yourself with some other activity. After a quarter of an hour see how your body feels. If it feels hungry and empty, continue to eat whatever food you think will fit that hunger. If it feels comfortable it means you are quite full and you can wait until the next hunger signals to eat again. If you are sure that you will allow yourself to eat whenever you feel hungry, and that you will give yourself whatever kind of food it is that you are wanting, you will find that it is less necessary to stuff yourself. When your body then indicates that it is not wanting much food, it means it is time for you to lose a little weight.

People vary enormously but it has been my observation that in the early stages of the group, members tend to stabilize or gain slightly. For those who do gain weight, this should not be a signal for alarm but an opportunity to experience what the fat

is all about. It is a chance to embrace all the fat before a final goodbye. As you lose weight you will notice you may be inclined to lose a bit and then sit there for a while. It is as though your body is holding still while you do the next level of emotional work exploring fantasies such as "Who will I be?" "Who won't like it if I'm slimmer?" "How will I protect myself if I am ten pounds lighter?"

In the previous chapters I have suggested that fat has a lot to do with conflict about self-definition and assertion and that a worry associated with being thin is that one will be meek and mild and could be blown over. Body work as described above will, of course, help one live within one's body and thus use it more instrumentally in day-to-day living but additional homework exercises which strike at a woman's often-felt unentitlement will also prove helpful. These exercises are loosely grouped under an assertion heading and flow from attempts to define one's food intake.

Attempt to say "yes" to something you want every single day. This could be something that only involves you, for example, taking a bubble bath, reading a book, going for a walk or writing a letter. As you learn to say "yes" you will be fulfilling many things. Primary among these is saying that you are entitled to decide things for yourself. This in turn produces a certain amount of self-confidence and provides a chink in a self-image full of denial. As you are able to say "yes" to a bath, so you will be able to say "yes" to a snack when you want it. As you learn to say "yes" you have the possibility of saying "no." Think of an incident in which you said "yes" but really wanted to say "no." Replay that incident slowly in your mind's eye, only substituting "no"

and expressing the real feeling. Notice how that feels. What are you risking by saying "no?" Now be conscious of the many times you are in this situation. Begin to say "no" to things—even on what may seem like a minuscule level—as you begin to say "yes" to others. Develop the sense of feeling more in charge. This will flow over to the food—being able to say "yes" and to say "no" and, perhaps more centrally, will provide you with a new way to use your mouth in expressing yourself.

The fat/thin fantasy on pages 140–142 can be useful for discovering what different body sizes mean to individual group members in different circumstances. Topics you might find helpful to discuss are: What being fat and thin express for you living in this culture; what fat and thin have to do with sexuality, with anger, with competition, with your mother, with your father, or with your children. Add a specific person or situation to the one in the standard fantasy and draw out the issues as they occur for each person. For example, *"Get as comfortable as you can... imagine you are with your mother/father/husband... you are quite fat...."*

Now it may happen that in some groups only certain people talk or you may discover that the "fat" is working in the group in some of the same ways in which it operates outside the group. If a particular member has experienced a week of bingeing, then she might feel she has more of a right to group time: "If I am fatter, then I'm worse off than everyone else and I've a right to a lot of attention," or if a group member was consistently losing weight she might feel she does not have the right to group time: "If I am thin, then I'm supposed

to be perfect and not have any needs." The woman losing weight might start to overeat in order to ensure her place in the group. If this situation crops up where those who have most difficulty that week get most time and those who have a relatively easy time with food are quiet, you might consider instituting a "twelve-minute rule," which means that each member is assured of twelve minutes of work time to discuss whatever she wishes in relation to food, fat or thin. This way you will be reinforcing neither fantasy—that thin, one has no needs and fat, one is insatiable.

In a self-help group, some people will play a more active role than others. However, it is the group as a whole that has responsibility for working together, selecting exercises, meeting places and times. You may find it helpful to rotate on a weekly basis so that a different person is in charge each time, preparing the exercises, keeping time and starting off the meetings. This is not essential, however, and every group develops its own patterns.

Self-help is an exciting concept in action. The potential to learn what is truly useful to you is enormous and, unhampered by preconceptions of what must or should happen, it opens the way for creative experimentation, evaluation and growth.

The guidelines above are to help you get going on the lines that our experience has shown to be useful, but they are in no sense intended to stifle the energy and imagination that you or your group feels to explore aspects of compulsive eating and self-image that are not addressed in detail here.

Self-starvation—
Anorexia nervosa

There is an elaborate and complicated eating condition closely related to compulsive eating called anorexia nervosa. It too, is characterized by self-imposed restrictions on food intake, a fear and terror of food and an obsessive—although secretive—interest in food. Unlike compulsive eaters, however, those who suffer from anorexia nervosa express their preoccupation with food by becoming very thin indeed—to the point of emaciation and sometimes even to the point of death through starvation. This extreme form of self-starvation is distinguished by a struggle to transcend hunger signals.

It often takes off from an exaggerated application of a diet, started because the potential anorectic
feels fat. Like the compulsive eater, many anorectics
engage in large-scale eating binges. The shame and
self-disgust that follow propel an anorectic to fast,
vomit or take laxatives—to purge her body of the
food that has been taken in. When food is eaten
again, feelings of bloatedness occur very quickly so
food intake continues to be very minimal until
another explosion of seemingly uncontrolled gorging occurs. Weight loss can be very dramatic and, in
turn, creates a wide range of physical symptoms.
Anorectics do not menstruate, often suffer from
insomnia and constipation, hypersensitivity to hot
and cold, excess hair growth on the body, changes in
the color and texture of existing hair, nails and skin,
slow pulse rate and perspiration. These physical
discomforts are endured in an attempt to reach the
overriding aim—to become thin.

While the idea of an interest in becoming fat is
difficult to grasp, few people would have difficulty
in understanding this interest in becoming thin
because it conforms to social expectations for
women. It is also quite easy to understand that 90
percent of clinically diagnosed anorectics are
women and that one of the workers in the field[1]
argues that the definition of anorexia nervosa
should be reserved for a special clinical syndrome
occurring in pre-pubescent and pubescent girls.

It is the fact that anorexia nervosa is almost
exclusively a woman's condition that ties it so
closely to compulsive eating and obesity. For if men
were to suffer from the same problem to a similar
degree we should seek a different explanation. But
the fear of obesity, the obsession with food, the

hidden and furtive eating and the interest in feeding others, leads us to identify the behavior as having origins in the social conditions of women in our society. *Anorexia nervosa is the other side of the coin of compulsive eating. In her rigorous avoidance of food, the anorectic is responding to the same oppressive conditions as compulsive eaters.*

It is important to note that while I have had little direct experience with anorectics, many women who suffer with this problem have sought me out because in reading of the Munter-Orbach view of compulsive eating they have found much with which to identify. Thus, what I have to say will be based on my reading of the works[2] on anorexia nervosa and discussions with women who have had anorexia, rather than on long-term clinical experience. My interest in touching on anorexia in this book is insofar as it sheds light on compulsive eating which is at the other end of the continuum. A feminist interpretation of anorexia confirms the approach used in compulsive eating.

Both anorectics and compulsive eaters binge and starve themselves. However, the anorectic starves for long periods subsisting on as little as an egg and a cookie a day and only occasionally bursting out into a binge which is then purified by even more rigorous fasting or cleansing by laxatives, vomiting or enemas. This bird-like eating is a reflection of a culture that praises thinness and fragility in women. Many women pinpoint the onset of their anorexia as an exaggerated response to dieting and teenage ideals of femininity. As with compulsive eaters, sensing something amiss at adolescence, they sought the answer in their individual biology. Their bodies were changing, becoming curvy and fuller,

taking on the shape of a woman. They were changing in a way over which they had no control—they did not know whether they would be small breasted and large hipped or whether their bodies would eventually end up as the teenagers in *Seventeen*.

These upheavals rendered in these young women feelings of confusion, fear and powerlessness. Their changing bodies were associated with a changing position in their worlds at home, at school and with their friends. A curvy body meant the adoption of a teenage girl's sexual identity. This is the time for intense interest in appearance, the time when girls learn the tortuous lesson about not revealing their true selves to boys whether on the tennis court or in school, or in discussing affairs of the heart. These new rules and regulations governing behavior, and the explosive changes taking place are quite out of tune with what has previously been learned and the feelings they generate are enormously complicated. Several women have said on looking back on this time in their lives—a time when they were growing and yet effectively stopped eating— that they felt so out of phase with all that was going on that withdrawal from food was an immensely satisfying way to be in control of the situation. In transcending hunger pangs they were winning in one area of the struggle with their apparently independently developing bodies. They were attempting to gain control over their shapes and their physical needs. They felt their power in their ability to ignore their hunger.

But this power to overcome hunger results in a contradiction because in her very attempt to be strong, the anorectic becomes so weak that she

becomes less independent, more dependent. She needs more care and concern from others because of her weakened physical state. This adaptation poses yet another dilemma. As Rosie Parker and Sarah Mauger write, "For a great many women manipulation of their own bodies is too often their only means of gaining a sense of accomplishment. The link between social status and slimness is both real and imagined. It is real because fat people are discriminated against; it is imaginary because the thin, delicate ideal image of femininity only increases a person's sense of ineffectualness."[3]

This latter point is, perhaps, the crux of the matter. Anorexia reflects an ambivalence about femininity, a rebellion against feminization that in its particular form expresses both a rejection and an exaggeration of the image. The refusal of food which makes her extremely thin straightens out the girl's curves in a denial of her essential femaleness. At the same time, this thinness parodies feminine petiteness. It is as though the anorectic has a foot in both camps—the pre-adolescent boy-girl and the young attractive woman. This has its echoes too in compulsive eating. For some women who eat compulsively the excess weight is also an attempt to defeat the curviness of the female body which brings in its wake dreaded social consequences. Mary, who had a compulsive-eating problem, started to overeat when she became a teenager and explained with hindsight that she was trying to smooth out her curves. The "puppy fat" she acquired put her less in the girls' camp with the concomitant dating and beautifying rituals. She was able to see herself as one of the kids—rather than one of the potential dating partners. Pre-adolescence suggested a kind of

equality to her, where kids were just kids and could do more or less the same things. Her fat was an unconscious attempt to hide her curves just as the starving anorectic attempts to disguise her form by ridding it of substance. In the ultra-feminine image of the petite woman that anorectics frequently project there is yet another parallel in the compulsive eater.

Some women's largeness conforms to another stereotype of woman, in this case the all-giving, nurturing, reliable, loving, caring, earth mother who excels in feminine skills of caretaking, food preparation and sensual hugs. This aspect of fat is for some women a relatively positive image to hold on to because it is at least an accepted image and smacks less of freakiness, but it is an image that in itself is problematic because it is the extension of the woman's reproductive capacity into the role of being mother to the world. Mothers of the world are forever feeding others and consequently get exceedingly hungry. Petite young ladies are admired and showered on—so goes the myth—and they do not need to take as much in, perhaps because they do not have to give so much out. Their success in womanhood lies in their being cared for and pampered by others and not in caring for and pampering others.

This attempt to balance both fronts, the ultra-femininity and rejection of femininity, is related to another aspect of the syndrome that has been given wide attention. This is the anorectic's intense energy and activity. This activity expresses itself in a compulsion to do well in school, excel at sports, and keep on the go at all costs. Many people will be familiar with the feeling of a second wind in the

midst of an exhausting late night and the kind of tense energy this unleashes. It is a similar feeling to the hyperactivity that anorectics frequently feel for months and months on end. This rushing about is partly motivated by an overpowering desire to lose yet more weight by burning up as many calories as possible. A feminist viewpoint suggests an additional root cause. The young woman's attempt to be involved in as many activities as possible is a protection against the exclusion she anticipates on entering womanhood because, in projecting into her future, she sees that the world is made up of men who are rewarded for being out in the world and women who are either excluded from activity in the world or, even more devious, included but not rewarded. In her frantic activities and involvements it would appear that she is trying to give herself a broader definition than her social role allows. She is striving to make an impact in a world hostile to her sex. This intense activity is painfully mirrored in the response of some anorectics whose fragile sense of self leads them to withdraw from the public world into their rooms, thereby highlighting women's invisibility. For the compulsive eater the reflection is reversed. The outwardly super-efficient, confident fixer and doer who can handle anything and carries the world on her shoulders is the exaggeration of woman as breast to the world. At the same time it underscores a woman's invisibility. The immovable blob—a common fantasy that compulsive eaters talk of—is analogous to the anorectic's intense activity and her experience of her self as ineffectual.

These converging images speak forcefully to a reconsideration of the origins of anorexia and as we

have already seen, compulsive eating. Previous
writers have emphasized some of the social factors.
Mara Selvini Palazzoli[4] suggests that the change
from an agrarian to an industrial society in Europe
has had a profound effect on the stability of the
patriarchal family and that the anorectic young
woman is a challenge to its continuing conserva-
tism. Hilde Bruch[5] addresses current social attitudes
toward body size and considers the extent to which
"the concept of beauty in our society, and our
preoccupation with appearance enter into the
picture. The obsession of the Western world with
slimness, the condemnation of any degree of
overweight as undesirable and ugly, may well be
considered a distorting of the body concept, but it
dominates present day living." Other social factors
such as Peter Dally's[6] observation that the mothers
of many anorectics were frustrated and hence
ambitious for their daughters are described but their
connection to the social situation of women in
society is not explored.

The pinpointing of these factors is extremely
helpful. However, there are still questions to be
answered. That is, why does this happen? Why is it
that some mothers are domineering? Why is
Western society preoccupied with slimness? Why
does the patriarchal family attempt to resist change?
What are the basic assumptions about our society
that women with eating disorders are challenging?
What in their abuse of the hunger mechanism and
their body distortions are these women gagging to
articulate how they feel? If this is a psychological
state that affects women, what is an appropriate
social response? Must not treatment include a
recognition of the social factors that lead women to

compulsive eating and anorexia nervosa?

As we have seen, modern Western societies place definite expectations and prohibitions on women's activities. Women are expected to be petite, demure, giving, passive, receptive in the home and, above all, attractive. Women are discouraged from being active, assertive, competitive, large and, above all, unattractive. To be unattractive is not to be a woman. In the case of compulsive eating, some women's strategy for dealing with these straitjacketed stereotypes is to become large to have bulk in the world; to become large to compensate for always giving out; to become large to avoid packaged sexuality. For the compulsive eater, food carries enormous symbolic meanings that reflect the problems women face in dealing with an oppressive social role. Even though anorectics have adopted the opposite strategy, self-starvation, the similarities to compulsive eating do not leave much doubt that the social position of women is as much reflected in the anorectic's behavior as it is in that of the compulsive eater.

Anorectics share with compulsive eaters a conscious desire not to be noticed. They often feel nervous walking into a room at a party lest all the attention is focused on them. Instead of gaining weight to hide a real self underneath the layers, the anorectic literally becomes paper thin. But this paper thinness attracts more attention than does a "normal"-sized woman. The crucial difference is that for emaciated (and overweight) women the interest they do attract is of a different nature than that which meets the woman of more "normal" size. The quick "once over" evaluation done by both men and women establishes the anorectic (and the obese

woman) as outside the status of a sex object. Broadly, this means that men will dismiss her and other women will relax in her presence. The anorectic will be viewed as pathetic or regarded with sympathy, but in her seemingly narcissistic striving for ultra-femininity she curiously succeeds in desexualizing herself. In addition, two related ways to understand this worry about being noticed suggest themselves. The first is reflected in the repeated theme of women's invisibility—wafer thinness is perhaps the quintessential expression of women's absence/presence. This forced invisibility leads in turn to a desire to be accepted and noticed for just being, rather than for having to look and be perfect and fulfill others' expectations. This desire, strongly felt and rarely satisfied, has little option but to be repressed, to be converted into its very opposite—a fear of being noticed which in its particular form makes the anorectic stand out.

This wish for acceptance stems, for many women, from a feeling of unwantedness and hence unworthiness. This may be either explicit: "We really wanted a boy," or from a sensed disappointment the mother has in bringing a daughter into the world. Whether explicit or implicit, the fact is that many compulsive eaters and anorectics report feeling their mothers expressed enormous ambivalence about their very existence. To say we were hoping for a boy is to say to a daughter that she has let you down. It is a short step from feeling that one has fallen short of one's family's hope to feeling like a failure. In its turn, failure can bring feelings of non-entitlement. At puberty where it becomes obvious that a girl is a girl, the feelings between mother and daughter may become so acute that two

actions collide for the girl. She refuses food in an attempt to wither away, to not exist, to please her mother by disappearing. At the same time, the rage the daughter feels at not having been wanted for who she is, for not having had a mother with whom to identify—how can one identify with a mother who is self-rejecting without also adopting a rejecting self-image?—is expressed by a refusal to take in the one thing the mother consistently gives—food. In a mixture of rage and demureness, the adolescent girl gags on the first mouthful or is full after a few bites. She is rejecting what her mother gives and hurting her in the most powerful way she knows how while simultaneously carrying out what she imagines to be her mother's wish, which is for her to disappear.

The pressure that leads many parents to desire male babies is itself a consequence of living in a world that accords less social power to women. A tragic repercussion of women's inferior social position is that in the transmitting of culture from one generation to the next, the mother has the dreadful job of preparing her own daughter to accept a life built on second-class citizenship. It is in the learning of our gender identity—that is, what it means to be a girl and then a woman in this world—that we find our place in society. What defines this gender identity will vary widely in relation to class and cultural proscriptions so that what it means to be a woman factory worker in Bulgaria will be quite different than what it means to be a nurse in the United States but both these women will have become adults through conception of self, based on available models of feminine behavior, assimilated first from their mothers. It is

in the teaching of this gender identity that the tensions in the mother-daughter relationship explode and the confusing messages of female adulthood are incorporated by the young girl.

One aspect of this tension that seems especially pertinent to anorectics is the concern with having disappointed one's mother for having been a girl in the first place. The girl feels she is a shaky second best with a precarious right to survive. This worry about the right to exist is also linked to the academic excellence and performance aspects of anorexia. Many women have reported that their need to excel academically was a response to feeling that if they should fail they would disappoint their parents. If they did not disappoint their parents they might be accepted—as one woman who suffered from anorexia put it bitterly, "I had to perform. I wasn't just accepted for who I was whereas my brother who was a delinquent was!" In this woman's life there was nothing explicitly stated about her not being desired or wanted, it was rather a feeling she picked up in relation to how she felt her brother was treated. That they were treated differently just because of their ages did not explain to her the feelings she had about herself and her mother's attitudes toward her. The only way she could understand this vast difference in treatment and her terribly painful feelings of being unaccepted was to see it as part of her parents' disappointment with her sex.

In the last thirty years, one of the most striking differences between the upbringing of girls and boys surfaced around adolescence when girls were supposed to be pure and boys were supposed to acquire sexual experience. Sex was definitely bad

for girls and good for boys. To girls it seemed as though boys could only win at this game: they either succeeded and became experienced or were reassured that there was plenty of time. Indeed, there was even a special category of women who provided boys with this experience. For the girls there was no way to win. If you did "it" you were bad, dirty, impure. Thinking about "it" was not much better either. If you did not do "it" boys would call you names, but if you did, you would get a bad reputation. You were preparing yourself for marriage many years hence and sexual activity up to that time was to be kept within definite limits. Against this background it is hardly surprising that young women are terribly confused about their sexuality, seeing it as evil, dangerous and explosive on the one hand and powerful, glorious and desirable on the other. Their sexuality becomes curiously disembodied from the person. It is an aspect of a young woman that in any event she must watch out for, almost as though it is some independent entity she must keep under control. This alienating view of sexuality from which women are now struggling to break free sheds much light on both the anorectic's and the compulsive eater's ambivalence about sexuality. The distortion of one basic body function gets carried over to another basic one, hunger. In the distortion of body size that follows, the manipulation of hunger feelings, the anorectic and the compulsive eater powerfully indict sexist culture. The young woman takes herself out of the only available sexual arena and worries that should she express her sexual feelings her whole world will crack.

In the retreat from a sexual identity the anorectic

young woman is pointing to the difficulties of the various aspects of womanhood. Sexual identity is an aspect of gender identity so that in rejecting models of sexuality one is simultaneously rejecting models of femininity. This is the dilemma that faces many women and is expressed both through the symbolic meanings of being thin and food refusal for the anorectic.

For the anorectic then, the refusal of food is a way to say "no," a way to reject. It is her way to show strength. Her thinness, on the other hand, also expresses her fragility and frailty, her confusion about sexuality and her interest in disappearing. For the compulsive eater the picture would seem to be reversed with the fat expressing rejection, protection and strength and the incessant consumption of food symbolizing capitulation. In both these responses we see the adaptations to a female role which has quite limited parameters. Both syndromes express the tension about acceptance and rejection of the constraints of femininity.

What is interesting in comparing these two responses is to notice just where they converge and where they differ. One area of striking difference rests on the attitudes of those who suffer at either end of the continuum. For the anorectic, her problem is not a matter for public discussion. It is a very private issue which she does not acknowledge as a problem because she herself sees her refusal to eat as an attempt to control her situation, a control that feels precarious and that might be at risk if she were to discuss it. This is quite different from the experience of compulsive eaters who do not regard their overeating as an active state but rather something that happens only when they are out of

control. They are quite happy to discuss this exterior, invading force and often initiate conversation about their "problem." This can partly be explained by the fact that the social pressure to be thin is so great that compulsive eaters feel they must offer an excuse for their size. The anorectic, however fat she sees herself, is, in fact, conforming to society's demand for women to be thin.

Paradoxically, the general public takes anorexia nervosa quite seriously while viewing compulsive eating as the behavior of an overindulgent, greedy person. As we have seen, however, both activities are extremely painful responses to which women may turn in their attempts to have some impact in their worlds.

Medical issues

It is the thesis of this book that compulsive eating in women is a response to their social position. As such, it will continue to be an issue in women's lives as long as social conditions exist which create and encourage inequality of the sexes. Any treatment for overweight women must address this fact.

When a woman goes to see a general practitioner with a weight problem, the doctor will almost invariably tell her to go on a diet. In the doctor's eyes, it is clear that this patient eats too much and to lose weight she must eat less. This attitude is exactly the same as that implicit in all the diets thrown onto

the market every day. The doctor has neither the time nor the interest to examine why this woman got fat in the first place. No dietary advice can help a woman lose weight permanently for the real reasons are not recognized and tackled.

Medical training today is becoming increasingly technical—high grades in scientific subjects have become essential to qualify for medical school and once there, the emphasis is on the technical approach to medicine. The human element of medicine is often lacking. This means that doctors are trained to make use of complex instruments and keep abreast of basic research. They do not acquire the sensitivity to recognize what is often troubling their patients. Therefore, many women are met with an unsympathetic face when they visit the doctor to lose weight. Doctors are no less susceptible than other people to cultural ideas about beauty and thinness and frequently feel entitled to comment on the size of their patient's body even when their medical problems are not related to it. As one woman put it, "They always make me feel guilty, like a naughty girl for eating too much." Clutching new diet sheets they are sent straight back to their homes and jobs and the problems they face there—the problems that were the main causes of their fatness in the first place.

But women come to know that diets and guilt do not work, whether they come from doctors or magazines. Some women may become desperate to find a physiological reason for their persisting fat. They may go further, to a specialist who deals with obesity and in whose interest it is to propose that there are biological factors which cause it. When a woman goes to a specialist she is seeking some

further understanding; she may think "If there is a medical reason for my fat, then there is little I can do. I shall be fat but people should recognize that it is not my fault."

In recent years there has been considerable medical research into the causes of obesity. While few of these theories have been wholly absorbed into the practice of the medical establishment, the publicity they have received and the hope that they instill in overweight people leads me to discuss the most favored ones here.

Doctors and researchers with a mechanistic view of the human body picture it as an assembly of organs (liver, heart, brain), tissue (muscle, nervous tissue, bone), and cells (nerve cells, muscle cells and blood cells). Organs are composed of various kinds of cells, and the cells themselves are pictured as little biochemical factories that work to maintain the organism in good health. This perspective has allowed the development of a picture of obesity as a biological phenomenon. In the body there is tissue between organs like various muscle groups or bone and muscle, which is called connective tissue. This connective tissue has the capacity to accumulate fat that the body does not use. It is called adipose tissue and consists of cells which are called fat cells. It is in the pattern of accumulation of fat in the fat cells that has drawn the attention of many medical investigators.

THE FAT CELL THEORY Ten years ago Hirsch and Knittle[1] developed a method of counting the number and size of fat cells in a sample of adipose tissue. They suggested that obesity in childhood was accompanied by an increase in the number of fat

cells in the body which are not reduced by dieting later in life. The cells themselves will reduce in size when a person loses weight but it is as though they are sitting waiting to be refilled. An extremely obese person can have as many as five times the normal number of fat cells. This theory is offered as an explanation for why some overweight people have difficulty keeping their weight down after dieting.

BIOCHEMICAL THEORIES The functioning of cells depends on the nature of chemical reactions which occur in them. All chemical reactions in the body—the conversion of food into energy, the expenditure of energy in exercise, indeed all human activity—depend on the presence of enzymes. Enzymes are protein molecules which assist the chemical reaction without being used up. Every chemical reaction in the body has an enzyme associated with it. Studies on bacteria have shown that the enzymes are made with the help of information stored in the genes. It is natural, therefore, from this perspective, to see a genetic explanation for obesity. Obese individuals are pictured as having slightly different genes from non-obese people. The different genes then result in slightly different enzymes. These enzymes are the ones that are involved in the chemical reactions related to the storage of fat in the body. The obese person is pictured as having different enzymes and hence their bodies respond to fat in a different way from the bodies of non-obese people.

GENETIC THEORIES Related to biochemical approaches is the genetic approach. The general genetic approach does not specify necessarily where

the genetic variation occurs but simply hypothesizes that it exists, whether in the enzymes, the nervous system, or the hormonal system of the body. This approach leads to studies showing that "obesity runs in families."[2]

A new genetic theory[3] suggests that fat people do not necessarily eat more than thin people. The argument runs that in subsistence agricultural societies, the pattern of eating is feast and fast and that those with the ability to store excess energy efficiently and release it for physical labor have a better chance of survival. In affluent societies where there is a regular and adequate food supply there is not the same need for the body to store and release energy. Furthermore, since we tend to be more sedentary we burn off less excess energy. Computer simulation runs of the pattern of lean and fat deposition in adults are offered as evidence for a biologically determinist view that whereas until recently it was functional to have an inherent tendency toward fatness, nowadays it is functional to have a predisposition to thinness.

INSULIN-RELATED THEORY When sugar and protein are eaten the islets of Langerhans, which are cell clusters in the pancreas, produce the hormone insulin. Insulin is a vital protein that is necessary for cells to take in and utilize sugar as an energy source. If there is an excess of glucose in the bloodstream it is converted into stored energy or fat. If a body does not produce enough insulin, the sugar and carbohydrates accumulate in the blood and do not provide energy to maintain bodily processes and growth. This is diabetes. Two thirds of diabetics are obese and this has led researchers to question whether

there is a link between the two conditions. The theory of hyperinsulinism conjectures that the body produces too much insulin which may itself induce insensitivity to the hormone.[4] It is this latter view that has been popularized by Dr. Atkins.[5] He calls insulin "the fattening hormone" and suggests that excess presence stimulates a person to eat more to maintain the balance. He sees insulin as the crucial link between overweight, low blood sugar and diabetes.

NEURAL THEORY Simple neural theory looks at the body's system of regulation. A region of the brain, the hypothalamus, has been conjectured to be the location where the body's messages about hunger are processed. A satiation center in the hypothalamus provides information on fullness. If there are lesions in this neural area, it is hypothesized, eating will continue beyond normal stopping point. A recent study on rats with ventromedial hypothalamus lesions which raise the set point, delay the onset of satiation and cause obesity, reported various motivational deficits including rats' failure to hoard. This failure to hoard has led the researchers to see a parallel in human motivation and they suggest that obesity causes poverty.[6]

Other researchers see the hypothalamus as less central to the regulation of hunger. The basic principle, however, remains the same. A defect in the body's regulation of hunger is hypothesized as being the cause of overeating.

The shortcoming of some of these theories is that they do not offer a way to determine whether observed differences in human reactions between obese and non-obese persons cause the obesity or

are due to the obesity. The fat-cell theory has a limited use since a high proportion of fat cells in infancy occurs only with massive obesity. Treatment of adults who were obese as children does not prevent weight loss and stabilization.[7] General genetic theories suffer because observed family similarity fits equally with an environmental model.[8] The evolutionary functional theory is weakened by the authors' underestimation of the allowable rates of genetic change in time.[9] The hypothalamus lesion theory first describes rat behavior in human terms and in doing so falls into the trap of assuming that the observations of animal behavior are analogous to those of human behavior.[10]

What is most critical, however, are the treatment procedures which follow from these hypotheses. They offer the promise, through the understanding of human physiology of the development of a substance (a drug, for example), which can melt away excess fat cells, restore the satiation mechanism in the hypothalamus or permit the person's body to utilize more efficiently its fat and sugar intake. This attitude is to be seen in the treatment of diabetes. The body's inability to produce enough insulin is corrected by daily insulin injections. A similar treatment for compulsive eating or its usual effect—obesity—satisfies an often-expressed wish that the fat can be whisked away by a pill and we will be as thin as we like. The history of conflicting medical research into obesity for the last seventy-five years makes it unlikely that such a substance exists. Treatment that is often sought and used has commonly been focused on three major areas: drug therapy, surgical procedures, and diet therapy.

DRUG THERAPY One approach to deal with obesity has been to prescribe thyroxine, a hormone that is secreted by the thyroid gland. Thyroxine is supposed to "speed up metabolism" and in so doing causes the body to burn up food more rapidly. The long-term effects of this treatment are doubtful for it relies on very high dosages of the hormone. As such, it is potentially dangerous in that it can interfere with the body's normal thyroid functioning which is very delicate. Two other drugs are employed in the treatment of obesity. They are called anorectic agents. One class are appetite suppressants and known popularly as amphetamines or speed. The addictive and stimulative aspect of this drug has been well documented as has the patient's need for increased dosages to maintain a suppressed appetite. The other class are drugs such as Flenfluramine which aim to produce feelings of fullness and inhibit the synthesis of triglycerides.

SURGICAL PROCEDURES More frightening are treatment procedures which attempt to bypass the problem by surgery. A jejuno-ileal bypass is an operation in which part of the small intestine is inactivated so that food cannot be absorbed to the same extent. Normally performed in serious inflammatory diseases and cancer of the bowel, the bypass surgery has been performed for extreme obesity for the last twenty years. Its side effects have been extensively studied. Among the problems reported is psychological adjustment. In one follow-up study[11] thirty-two out of forty people experienced distinct crises associated with weight loss. These include, not surprisingly, problems about self-

assertion, loss of identity and loss of boundaries. Another researcher reports[12] persistent overestimation of body size by female subjects two years after their operations after an average weight loss of 100–112 pounds.

An even more direct mechanical approach is the surgical removal of fat cells. In one experiment,[13] three patients were placed on reducing diets and when "normal" weight was achieved 47–60 percent of "excess fat cells" were removed. One patient suffered a thrombosis, one patient regained 81.4 pounds three years later and one patient keeps "a rigorous diet and regularly pursues a strenuous physical exercise program."

DIET THERAPY The diet remains the major treatment prescribed by doctors. Medical researchers investigate the effect of the relationship of various foods and offer their dieting programs accordingly. In comparison with the other treatments, dieting seems rather mild and harmless but it does not differ in principle from the more extreme drug or surgical therapies. It is as though the human body is the biological parallel of an automobile. Obesity is seen as a symptom of biological malfunction rather like a car's excess gas consumption. The human meanings of fat and thin and the social consequences and causes of compulsive eating have no place in this concept.

Although it is not my purpose to criticize those practititioners who are committed to human welfare, it is important to note that the medical profession as a whole has an unfortunate history of direct involvement with the oppression of women in our society. The work of Barbara Ehrenreich and

Deirdre English[14] has shown that the medical profession was established in the United States in the face of opposition from dedicated and informed lay healers, the majority of whom were women. Recently, women's health groups—most notably the Boston Women's Health Book Collective[15]—have rethought medical issues from a feminist perspective and have been engaged in sharing and disseminating the kind of information women need to know about their bodies. The activities of some women's groups have met with opposition from the authorities. In one case, women involved in a self-help group in California[16] were prosecuted (albeit unsuccessfully) for illegal entry of the vagina.

What is distressing about the current medical perspective is its hegemony in such areas as compulsive eating where the root causes and problems have essential social aspects that must be understood for there to be effective treatment and interventions. Even overweight diabetic women can be compulsive eaters and this problem needs to be addressed in conjunction with medical issues.

In the last decade we have seen a significant and increasing turn toward science and medicine to solve problems that are socially and economically based. Medicine is presented as the healer and science as the truth. A new religion reigns—the ideology of science.[17] This new ideology proposes that science is neutral and value free. White-coated men and women work away in laboratories seeking truth and progress. Medical researchers are not only truth seekers but humane too, since their work directly relates to human health. Few ask who funds the research and sets the priorities. Instead, the

public are asked to embrace new technological fixes for human behavior issues.

A glance through the medical journals reveals this attitude in another area. Typically, you see a picture of a distraught woman in her forties slumped over a table in a messy kitchen. The advertisement reads in bold type, "X drug will help relieve the tension so she can cope better." In smaller print the advertisement mentions the familiar situation of the depressed menopausal woman who feels lifeless, with no energy now that her children have flown the nest. It recommends X psychotropic drug to reduce the anxiety. Doctors, who are frequently male, overworked, untrained to see the social issues that have produced distress in their women patients and unlikely to face this kind of distress themselves, recommend tranquilizers and psycho-active drugs to lift the spirits of these women so that they can function well enough again to clean up their own kitchens and not be a nuisance to anyone. The underlying social cause of distress is not dealt with. Medication is offered, the women are drugged.

Compulsive eating is an individual protest against the inequality of the sexes. As such, medical interventions as detailed here are not part of a solution but are part of the problem. The situation requires a major reorientation of medical and scientific education, organization and practice based on the demands of the women's health movement.

Notes

Preface

1. See chapter on medical issues. Analytic psychotherapy views eating behavior as a symptom that will dissolve when the true trauma has been resolved. It has not had any spectacular success in treating the symptom even in those cases where the person seeking therapy has come wanting to focus on compulsive eating as *the* problem.

2. See, for example:
Science for People 34 (winter 1976-7). A discussion on the relationship between food supplies, the politics of world agriculture and the exploitation of the resources of the Third World. Available from the British Society of Social Responsibility in Science, 9 Poland Street, London W.1, England.
    Science for the People 7 (March 1975).

3. In this case it will be important that therapists be extremely sensitive to their client's eating behavior and provide a place for her to feel accepted while she is self-rejecting because of the compulsive eating. It will also be important to look for transference issues both in group work and individual sessions.

Introduction

1. See, for example:
G. Bychowski, "Neurotic Obesity," *The Psychology of Obesity,* ed. N. Kiell (Springfield, Illinois, 1973).
Ludwig Bingswanger, "The Case of Ellen West," *Existence,* ed. Rollo May (New York, 1958).

2. William Ryan, *Blame the Victim* (New York, 1971). This book shows how we come to blame the victims of oppression rather than its perpetrators.

3. Dorothy Griffiths and Esther Saraga, "Sex Differences in a Sexist Society." Paper read at the International Conference on Sex-role Stereotyping, British Psychological Society, Cardiff, Wales, July 1977.

4. John Berger et al., *Ways of Seeing* (London, 1972), p. 47.

5. Simone de Beauvoir, *The Second Sex* (London, 1968).

6. For discussion on this see:
Juliet Mitchell, *Psychoanalysis and Feminism* (New York, 1974). Phyllis Chesler, *Women and Madness* (New York, 1972).

7. D. Brunet and I. Lezine, "I primi anni del bambino." Cited in Elena Gianini Belotti, *Little Girls* (London, 1975), pp. 32–4. While this study took place in Europe it does not rule out its relevance in the American context. The book in which it is extensively quoted is one of the most thoughtful descriptions of the socialization of young girls and the significance of the early sex-linked feeding relationship.

8. Margaret Atwood, *Lady Oracle* (London, 1977), p. 88.

What Is Thin About for the Compulsive Eater?

1. Sharon Rosenburg and Joan Weiner, *The Illustrated Hassle-Free Make Your Own Clothes Book* (San Francisco, 1971).

2. This is an Eastern European Jewish custom meant to bring color to the cheeks.

The Experience of Hunger for the Compulsive Eater

1. The diet industry is extremely profitable. For financial statistics see:
Natalie Allon, "The Stigma of Overweight in Everyday Life." John E. Fogarty International Center for Advanced Study in the Health Sciences. Vol. II, part II. National Institute of Health, Bethesda, Md. Edited by George A. Bray. DHEW publication. U.S. Govt. printing office. October 1–3, 1973, pp. 83–102.

2. Diet organizations will not release figures on recidivism. However, various sources put it at 95 percent. See Aldebaran, "Fat Liberation—A Luxury," *State and Mind* 5 (June–July 1977): 34.

3. Stanley Schachter, "Obesity and Eating," *Science* 161 (1968): 751.

4. For a discussion of this see:
A. J. Stunkard and H. M. McClaren, "The Results of Treatment for Obesity," *Archives of Internal Medicine* 103 (1959): 79.
Stanley Schachter, "Some Extraordinary Facts About Obese Humans and Rats," *American Psychologist* 23 (1971): 129.
Stanley Schachter, "Obesity and Eating," *Science* 161 (1968): 751.

5. Carol Bloom, "Training Manual for the Treatment of Compulsive Eating and Fat." Master's thesis, State University of New York at Stony Brook (1976).

Self-Starvation—Anorexia Nervosa

1. Mara Selvini Palazzoli, *Self Starvation* (London, 1974), pp. 24–5.

2. For useful discussions on anorexia nervosa see:
Rosie Parker and Sarah Mauger, "Self Starvation," *Spare Rib* 28 (1976).
Marlene Boskind-Lodahl, "Cinderella's Stepsisters: A

Feminist Perspective on Anorexia Nervosa and Bulimia,"
Signs 2 (winter, 1976): 342–56.
Mara Selvini Palazzoli, *Self Starvation* (London, 1974).
Hilde Bruch, *Eating Disorders* (New York, 1973).
Peter Dally, *Anorexia Nervosa* (London, 1969).
Anna Freud, "The Psychoanalytic Study of Infantile
Feeding Disturbances," *The Psychoanalytic Study of the
Child II* (London, 1946).

3. Parker and Mauger, "Self Starvation."

4. Palazzoli, *Self Starvation,* pp. 224–52.

5. Bruch, *Eating Disorders,* p. 88.

6. Dally, *Anorexia Nervosa,* pp. 93–4.

Medical Issues

1. J. L. Hirsch and J. Knittle, "Cellularity of Obese and
Nonobese Adipose Tissue," *Federation Proceedings of
the American Society for Experimental Biology* 29
(1970): 1516.

2. W. B. Kannel and T. Gordon, "Some Determinants of
Obesity and Its Impact as a Cardiovascular Risk Factor,"
in *Recent Advances in Obesity Research,* ed. Alan
Howard (London, 1975), p. 14. (Hereafter cited as *Recent
Advances.*)

3. H. E. Dugdale and P. R. Payne, "The Pattern of
Lean and Fat Deposition in Adults," *Nature* 266 (March,
1977): 349.

4. H. Keen, "The Incomplete Story of Obesity and
Diabetes," in Howard, *Recent Advances.*

5. R. C. Atkins, *Dr. Atkins' Diet Revolution* (New
York, 1972).

6. L. J. Herberg, K. B. J. Franklin and D. N. Stephens,
"The Hypothalamic 'Set Point' in Experimental Obesity,"
in Howard, *Recent Advances.*

7. Hilde Bruch, *Eating Disorders* (New York, 1973), p. 36.

8. Michael Schwartz and Joseph Schwartz, "No Evidence for Heritability of Social Attitudes," *Nature* 255: 429.

9. A. Cooke et al., "The New Synthesis Is an Old Story," *New Scientist* 70 (1976).

10. Ibid.

11. E. Espmark, "Psychological Adjustment Before and After Bypass Surgery for Extreme Obesity, a Preliminary Report," in Howard, *Recent Advances*, p. 242.

12. R. C. Kalucy et al., "Self Reports of Estimated Body Widths in Female Obese Subjects with Major Fat Loss Following Ileo-jejunal Bypass Surgery," in Howard, *Recent Advances*, p. 331.

13. J. G. Kral and L. V. Sjorstrom, "Surgical Reduction of Adipose Tissue Hypercellularity," in Howard, *Recent Advances*, p. 327.

14. Barbara Ehrenreich and Deirdre English, *Witches, Midwives and Nurses* (New York, 1973).

15. The Boston Women's Health Collective, *Our Bodies, Ourselves* (New York, 1973).

16. *People v. Carolyn Aurillia Downer* LAMC 31426942 (1972).

17. R. M. Young, "Science Is Social Relations," *Radical Science Journal* 5 (1977): 65.

Further Reading

Allon, Natalie, "Group Dieting Interaction." Unpublished doctoral dissertation, Brandeis University, Waltham, Mass. (1972).

Belotti, Elena Gianini, *Little Girls* (London, 1975).

Bloom, Carol, "Training Manual for the Treatment of Compulsive Eating and Fat." Master's thesis, State University of New York at Stony Brook (1976).

Boston Women's Health Book Collective, *Our Bodies, Ourselves* (New York, 1971).

Bruch, Hilde, *Eating Disorders* (New York, 1973).

Bernard, Jessie, *The Future of Motherhood* (New York, 1975).

Chesler, Phyllis, *Women and Madness* (New York, 1972).

de Beauvoir, Simone, *The Second Sex* (London, 1968).

Deutch, Helene, *The Psychology of Women,* vols. I & II (New York, 1973).

Donovan, Lynn, *The Anti Diet* (New York, 1971).

Ehrenreich, Barbara and English, Deirdre, *Witches, Midwives and Nurses* (New York, 1973).

Figes, Eva, *Patriarchal Attitudes* (Greenwich, Conn., 1970).

Friday, Nancy, *My Mother, My Self: The Daughter's Search for Identity* (New York, 1977).

Gerrard, Don, *One Bowl* (New York, 1974).

Kneill, N., ed., *The Psychology of Obesity* (Springfield, Ill., 1973).

Maccoby, Eleanor Emmons and Jacklin, Carol Nagy, *The Psychology of Sex Differences* (Stanford, Ca., 1974).

Mahler, Margaret, et al., *The Psychological Birth of the Human Infant* (New York, 1976).

McBride, Angela Barron, *The Growth and Development of Mothers* (New York, 1973).

McBride, Angela Barron, *Living with Contradictions: A Married Feminist* (New York, 1977).

Mitchell, Juliet, *Psychoanalysis and Feminism* (New York, 1974).

Pearson, Leonard and Lillian, *The Psychologist's Eat Anything Diet* (New York, 1973).

Reich, Wilhelm, *The Sexual Revolution* (New York, 1969).

Rosaldo, Michele Zimbalist and Lamphere, Louise, eds. *Women, Culture and Society* (Stanford, Ca., 1974).

Rubin, Theodore Issac, *Forever Thin* (New York, 1970).

Rich, Adrienne, *Of Women Born: Motherhood as Experience and Institution* (New York, 1976).

Sager, Clifford J. and Kaplan, Helen Singer, eds., *Progress in Group and Family Therapy* (New York, 1972).

Strouse, Jean, ed., *Women and Analysis* (New York, 1974).

Thompson, Clara, "Penis Envy in Women," *Psychiatry* 6 (1943).

Williams, Elizabeth Friar, *Notes of a Feminist Therapist* (New York, 1977).

Winnicot, D. W., *Mother and Child: A Primer of First Relationships* (New York, 1957).

Zaretsky, Eli, *Capitalism, the Family and Personal Life* (London, 1976).